Finding Lewis & Clark

Finding

Lewis & Clark

OLD TRAILS, NEW DIRECTIONS

Edited by JAMES P. RONDA & NANCY TYSTAD KOUPAL

South Dakota State Historical Society Press

Pierre, South Dakota

© 2004 by the South Dakota State Historical Society Press

All rights reserved. This book or portions thereof in any form whatsoever may not be reproduced without the expressed written approval of the South Dakota State Historical Society Press, Pierre, S. Dak. 57501.

Funds for this publication were provided, in part, by the National Park Service, Lewis & Clark National Historic Trail.

Library of Congress Cataloging-in-Publication Data
Finding Lewis and Clark: old trails, new directions / edited by James P. Ronda and Nancy Tystad Koupal.
   p. cm.
Contains presentations from the conference held in Pierre, S.D., April 11-12, 2003, sponsored by the South Dakota State Historical Society, in honor of the bicentennial of the Louisiana Purchase and the Lewis and Clark Expedition.
Includes bibliographical references and index.
ISBN 0-9715171-9-3 (pbk.)
1. Lewis and Clark Expedition (1804-1806)—Congresses. 2. West (U.S.)—Discovery and exploration—Congresses. 3. West (U.S.)—Description and travel—Congresses. 4. West (U.S.)—Historiography—Congresses.
5. Explorers—West (U.S.)—Biography—Congresses. I. Ronda, James P., 1943- II. Koupal, Nancy Tystad. III. South Dakota State Historical Society.

F592.7.F55 2004
917.804'2—dc22   2004045242

ISBN 0-9715171-9-3

Printed in the United States of America
01 02 03 04 05 06 07 08 09   9 8 7 6 5 4 3 2 1

On the title page: William Clark (left) and Meriwether Lewis (right), drawn by Charles Willson Peale, 1807-1808, Independence National Historical Park, Philadelphia

CONTENTS

Preface vii

    Nancy Tystad Koupal

Introduction ix

    James P. Ronda

Journeys—The Shaping of America 1

    James P. Ronda

Tribal Relations on the Upper Missouri River before

    Lewis and Clark 10

    W. Raymond Wood

Gateways and Guardians:

    Lewis and Clark and the Louisiana Purchase 25

    Peter J. Kastor

In Search of the Historical William Clark 45

    William E. Foley

"To acquire what knolege you can":

    The Scientific Contributions of Lewis and Clark 58

    Robert McCracken Peck

"I wished for the pencil of Salvator Rosa":

    The Artistic Legacy of Lewis and Clark 80

    Joni L. Kinsey

Telling Lewis and Clark Stories:

   Historical Novelists as Storytellers 114

   Richard W. Etulain

Photographing the Lewis and Clark Route of Discovery 134

   Greg Mac Gregor

Over, Above, and Beyond:

   The Lewis and Clark Expedition as Hyperhistory 152

   Joseph A. Mussulman

Using Inquiry to Engage History Students:

   The Lewis and Clark Rediscovery Project 159

   Robert J. Myers

Finding Lewis and Clark by Stepping Away 174

   Elliott West

Contributors 191

Index 195

PREFACE   NANCY TYSTAD KOUPAL

The Louisiana Purchase (1803) and the Lewis and Clark Expedition (1804–1806) are major landmarks in South Dakota and Great Plains history. In the first, the site of the future states of North and South Dakota were added to the land base of the United States. In the second, the country began the historical narrative of multicultural meetings and conflicts that still define the region today. In 1999 as the bicentennial of these events drew near, the South Dakota State Historical Society began to plan for a major conference in Pierre, South Dakota, that would bring multiple perspectives to a discussion of these seminal events in the region's past and their impact on its present and future. Two partners quickly signed on to the venture. James P. Ronda, an expert on the Lewis and Clark Expedition who holds the H. G. Barnard Chair in Western American History at the University of Tulsa, agreed to help organize the program around the theme of "Finding Lewis and Clark: Old Trails, New Directions." Next, the South Dakota Humanities Council agreed to help fund the research and travel of the many participants who would come to Pierre from all over the United States on 11–12 April 2003.

On a sunny Friday (11 April), a distinguished body of historians, anthropologists, geographers, artists, teachers, literary and art historians, naturalists, tribal educators, National Park Service personnel, and an enthusiastic crowd of over two hundred met on the shores of the Missouri River near the mouth of the Bad River to share a magical two days immersed in a consideration of the events of 1803–1806 and their meaning for our times. Professor Ronda and Elliott West, award-winning author and professor of history at the University of Arkansas, gave the keynote addresses that framed the conference and this book. Historian Peter Kastor of Washington University in Saint Louis, and veteran anthropologist W. Raymond Wood of the University of Missouri-Columbia set the historical stage, discussing the Louisiana Purchase and tribal relations along the Missouri River prior to Lewis and Clark's journey. Gary E. Moulton, editor of the definitive new edition of the Lewis and Clark journals, and John Logan Allen, chair of the Department of Geography and Recreation at the University of Wyoming, shared their expertise on the men and route of the expedition. William Foley, professor emeritus from Central Missouri State University, then focused more closely on William Clark.

Robert Peck of the Academy of Natural Sciences of Philadelphia explored the scientific legacy of the explorers, while art historian Joni L. Kinsey looked at the artistic legacy. Paul Hutton of the University of New Mexico discussed the Corps of Discovery as it manifests in popular culture and introduced a special showing of *The Far Horizons*, the only full-length motion picture portrayal of the Lewis and Clark Expedition. An exhibit of Greg Mac Gregor's photographs, displayed at the Cultural Heritage Center and entitled *Lewis and Clark Revisited*, added another visual dimension to the event. Richard W. Etulain, professor emeritus of history at the University of New Mexico, followed the explorers into the realm of fiction, examining a century's worth of novels about the expedition.

Gerard Baker, superintendent of the Lewis and Clark National Historic Trail and Corps of Discovery II, chaired a panel discussion entitled "Lewis and Clark Today in Park and Museum." The panel featured the voices of Roberta Conner, a member of the Confederated Tribes of the Umatilla Indian Reservation and director of the Tamastslikt Cultural Institute; Clarence Mortenson, member of the Cheyenne River Sioux Tribe and chairman of the Wakpa Sica Reconciliation Place; and Paul Hedren, superintendent of the Niobrara/Missouri National Scenic Riverways. Joseph A. Mussulman, producer of the web site *Discovering Lewis and Clark*, and Robert J. Myers, senior designer for the Center of Educational Technologies at Wheeling Jesuit University, wrapped up the two-day event with discussions of Lewis and Clark on the World Wide Web and in the classroom.

Eleven of the nineteen presentations given on 11–12 April appear in the pages of *Finding Lewis and Clark: Old Trails, New Directions*. Not all the voices heard at the conference made it into the pages of the book. In some cases, the speakers only intended the presentations to be an oral sharing of information. In others, busy schedules and prior commitments prevented speakers from participation in the book project. Two final partners in the enterprise made this publication possible. BankWest of Pierre, South Dakota, gave a generous grant just before the conference, and the National Park Service, Lewis and Clark National Historic Trail, through its Challenge Cost Share project, helped to underwrite production and printing costs.

INTRODUCTION JAMES P. RONDA

In his landmark book *Historians' Fallacies*, David Hackett Fischer reminded his readers that "questions are the engines of intellect." Much of the exploration of North America was powered by questions, as well. Fur traders questioned native people about new routes to abundant beaver countries; military cartographers posed queries about topography and potential enemies; and real-estate-company surveyors headed west of Wichita asking after fertile lands for American farmers. Exploration was inquiry set in motion. The Lewis and Clark Expedition—guided by Thomas Jefferson's detailed instructions—is perhaps the best example of exploration as inquiry. Although written as declarative sentences, virtually every line the president prepared for his western travelers can be posed as a question. Where is the fabled northwest passage? What is the "face of the country?" How should native nations be judged and then made part of an expanding American empire?

Just as Jefferson sent his captains questioning their way into the West, now two centuries later we ask new questions about the Lewis and Clark journey and the larger history of the early West. The essays in this collection—and the conference that prompted them—pose four compelling questions about the expedition and the worlds in which it moved and had its being. The first of those questions is the most obvious one, but one with many often contradictory answers. Just what is this expedition journey story all about?

Like the line that Lewis and Clark traced across the continent, the expedition story has a plot, a distinctive narrative. For many years most Americans read Lewis and Clark as an adventure story with a plot shaped by dramatic wilderness exploits and memorable episodes of courage and hardship. Lewis and Clark joined other dime-novel heroes in a triumphant march of conquest across the West. But in Bernard DeVoto's often neglected classic *The Course of Empire* (1952), the story shifted from high adventure and wilderness travel to empire building and international intrigue. DeVoto's Lewis and Clark were Jefferson's chosen agents of empire, busy telling a story about expansion and conquest. Jefferson's own understanding of the expedition's story had changed once it was plain that there was no "direct and practicable water communication across this continent for the purposes of commerce." Within two years of the expedition's return, he was busy rewriting the Lewis and Clark story line. This time he emphasized science, the role of his explorers in expanding the empire of the mind. In the 1960s, that narrative direction was picked up by Paul R. Cutright in his *Lewis and Clark: Pioneering Naturalists* (1969). Now the story seemed more about locating Lewis and Clark within the eighteenth-century Enlightenment and the tradition of natural history. John Logan Allen's seminal *Passage through the Garden: Lewis and Clark and the Image of the American Northwest* (1975) emphasized the explorers as geographers and cartographers.

More recently, the Lewis and Clark narrative has moved yet again. Despite some efforts to return the story to the themes of nationalist triumph and bold adventure, more attention has been paid to the complex cultural interactions between the expedition and American Indians. James P. Ronda's *Lewis and Clark among the Indians* (1984) was representative of that change, and in succeeding years a number of specialized books and essays have advanced what has been called the mutual discovery narrative. Most notable among those are Castle McLaughlin's *Arts of Diplomacy: Lewis and Clark's Indian Collection* (2003) and Carolyn Gilman's *Lewis and Clark—Across the Divide* (2003). From Jefferson to the most recent scholarship, what has emerged is a series of answers to the question about the nature of the Lewis and Clark story. Perhaps now—well into the expedition's bicentennial—we can read not one story but many. Meeting the challenge of telling multiple stories using the most recent technologies is the subject of two important essays in this collection. Joseph A. Mussulman's pioneer work placing Lewis and Clark in cyberspace is matched with Robert J. Myers's experiences using innovative technologies in the classroom. Without denying or diminishing the drama and adventure of the great trek, we can now recognize and appreciate other plot lines, lines that take us into the worlds of empire, science, commerce, and cultural encounter.

Questions about the nature of the expedition story plot have often become bound up in a second query. Who were the characters in the story, the actors in the drama? As William Foley's thoughtful "In Search of the Historical William Clark" makes clear, there is much to learn as we reassess the expedition leaders themselves. For many Americans, the exploring party had just four living beings—Lewis, Clark, Sacagawea, and the Newfoundland dog Seamen. And, of course, an unseen Jefferson hovered nearby guiding the whole enterprise as if by remote control from Monticello. That grade-school wisdom was effectively challenged in 1962 when Donald Jackson published his *Letters of the Lewis and Clark Expedition with Related Documents, 1783–1854*. In his Foreword to that magisterial book, Jackson wrote that "it is no longer useful to think of the Lewis and Clark Expedition as the personal story of two men. Their journey to the Pacific and return in 1804–06 was an enterprise of many aims and a product of many minds" (p. v). With letters and papers from diplomats, bureaucrats, soldiers, and scientists, Jackson's work expanded and enriched the cast of characters. That cast not only included public figures like Jefferson, Secretary of the Treasury Albert Gallatin, and Dr. Benjamin Rush but little-known business owners and craftspeople like seamstress Matilda Chapman and tobacconist Thomas Leiper, Jr. To that list, art historian Joni Kinsey has added a whole roster of artists and illustrators. It has become commonplace to say that Lewis and Clark gave us a western text without pictures. But as Kinsey shows, the expedition prompted a memorable visual record in the work of Charles Willson Peale, John James Barralet, and Charles de Saint-Mémin. These men and women did not make the journey, but they made it possible.

In the past twenty years, the expedition cast of characters has expanded yet again, this time well beyond the Corps of Discovery, its patrons, and suppliers. With increased interest in cultural encounters and mutual discovery, the story now embraces a large number of native people from many nations and tribes. W. Raymond Wood's "Tribal Relations on the Upper Missouri before Lewis and Clark" provides a comprehensive look at an important part of Indian country on the eve of the expedition. The Lewis and Clark journals, now authoritatively edited by Gary E. Moulton, give readers an unparalleled view of native life in the West and Pacific Northwest. For all their cultural biases and blind spots, expedition journal keepers named the names, described the villages, and sought as best they could to comprehend what seemed so often new and strange. Adding native voices to the drama brings meaning and balance to an emblematic American story.

Questions about the Lewis and Clark story (or stories) and the cast of characters invariably lead to interest in the journey itself and key moments on the trail. As the keynote essay "Journeys—The Shaping of America" notes, we are a nation on the road, and the Lewis and Clark Expedition is our first national road story. Little wonder that the events on that journey should capture our attention and imagination. The list is a long one, bright with moments of expectation and fulfillment, tension and anxiety, confusion and violence: the confrontation with the Brulé Teton Sioux near present-day Pierre, South Dakota, in September 1804; the meeting with Cameahwait's Lemhi Shoshones and crossing the Continental Divide at Lemhi Pass in August 1805; the heartbreaking odyssey over the Bitterroots on the Lolo Trail in September 1805; the first views of the Pacific Ocean in November 1805; and the fatal encounter with the Piegan Blackfeet on the Two Medicine River in July 1806. These are some of the "stand out" moments in the life of the expedition. But in many ways, they do not reflect what life was like for this infantry company on the move. What can bring us closer to that company was its daily ordinary, the everyday routines of marching, hauling, paddling, cooking, cleaning, making camp, and living together often in very close quarters. Looking to the high points should never blind us to the common chores that bound each day to itself and the next. The expedition was a human community moving through the lands and lives of other human communities. To see and appreciate each community—whether native or newcomer—in its daily ways is to grasp some of the American fundamentals of life together.

But no question has sparked more interest and generated more controversy than the one about the consequences of the expedition. Despite the assertion by some that the Lewis and Clark journey was of relatively little importance in the history of the American West, most Americans (whether scholars or laypersons) remain persuaded that the expedition's march across the continent was a turning-point moment for the West and the nation. In "Gateways and Guardians: Lewis and Clark and the Louisiana Purchase," Peter Kastor places the purchase at the center of the imperial story, making it fundamental for understanding American history in general and Lewis and Clark in particular. But beyond that there is much disagreement. Some writers have made the connection between the expedition and the development of the Rocky Mountain fur trade, while others have emphasized the growth of geographic and scientific knowledge. Robert M. Peck's detailed survey of the scientific contributions of Lewis and Clark not only describes those contributions but locates them within the context of early nineteenth-century scientific knowledge and practice. Lewis and Clark have been portrayed as agents of an expanding American empire, as imperialists spreading a national political and economic program bound to dispossess native people. Jefferson's captains have appeared as heroic trailblazers, hard-eyed empire builders, Enlightenment-inspired scientists, and even as dutiful army officers bound west on nothing more than an extended tour of duty.

In so many ways, each generation has rediscovered and reshaped the expedition based on its own preoccupations and aspirations. For many who have traveled the Lewis and Clark route in recent times, the expedition has become a yardstick, a way to judge two centuries of environmental change. Greg Mac Gregor's powerful black-and-white photographs of the trail today are compelling testimony to how much has changed and how much yet endures. Perhaps this is the fate of all national foundation myths. William Clark's last journal entry, dated 26 September 1806, contains these words, "We commenced wrighting." Richard Etulain's engaging survey of novelists drawn to the Lewis and Clark story is evidence that the writing about the journey has continued, as has the fascination. The collection concludes with Elliott West's graceful "yah-but" essay, a gentle reminder that the Lewis and Clark story is not the only one worthy of our attention. It is context and balance that West is after, something that has characterized all his brilliant work. Taken together, the essays in this collection are a kind of map marking out what we know about the early West and what remains yet to be discovered and charted. William Clark was right; the writing and the discovering continues.

Journeys — The Shaping of America

JAMES P. RONDA

Consider with me two scenes from the American theatre of memory. North of here, on the Missouri River in mid-August 1806, young John Colter of the Corps of Discovery decided he had not yet seen enough of the West. Pondering an offer made by two trappers—Joseph Dickson and Forest Handcock—an offer William Clark described as "very advantageous"—Colter packed his gear and heeded the siren song of the open road. More than a century later, the Carter Family (The First Family of Country Music) would sing "where's my wandering boy tonight," and John Colter would have answered, "out on the road in search of wealth and adventure." A hundred and thirty-some years after Colter said goodbye to Lewis and Clark, a young black man named McKinley Morganfield studied his future in the cotton fields around Clarksdale, Mississippi. Like so many other African Americans, he calculated his chances in the rural South and headed to the industrial North, to the promised land of Chicago. In May 1943, the man who became Muddy Waters took the Illinois Central Railroad north to the Windy City, setting in motion a musical-cultural revolution whose sounds are with us still.

These are stories about America and roads, about us and the journeys we have made, and about the ways those journeys have made us. These are stories about the power of the journey and the lure of the road. But they are also about home, the promise of home, and what the home place continues to mean for all of us. Lewis and Clark have a place in those stories, but so do Black Cat and Yellow Corn, Woody Guthrie, Willie Nelson, and Jack Kerouac. We are all, in some way or other, Charlie Chaplin's Little Tramp, wobbling alone down a lonely road. We all live and find meaning at the crossroads and in the crossfire between the home and the road.

In some fundamental way, Americans are a people on the road. Whether we have been here ten thousand years or we came yesterday, our common experience has been going someplace, some other place, some great St. Elsewhere. Paradise is always just down the road, around the bend, over the next hill, and across the mountains. Dorothy marches the yellow brick road to Oz, and the rest of us head to Zion, the New Jerusalem, Oleanna, the Land of Enchantment, the Golden State of Bliss, and the Big Rock Candy Mountain. How do we get to these places? because it is what lies at the end of the long, lonesome road that seems so compelling. How do we get *there*, so that the *there* of our dreams will become the *here* of our realities? It is part of the American gospel that salvation is found in mobility. "Hit the road, Jack" is not a kiss-off but a challenge to find a better place somewhere westbound on Route 66. So our past and our present is a web, a tangle of traces and trails, railways and highways. Our national soundscape is the creak of wagons, the throaty call of steamboat whistles, the whine of Peterbilt diesels on I-90 through Mitchell, South Dakota, and the heartbeat clack of the flanged wheel on countless miles of long steel rail. For some of us, the locomotive whistle in the night will always be the most evocative sound of our childhood, conjuring up the promise of what Thomas Wolfe called "starlight on the rails." Perhaps Jack Kerouac put it best in *On the Road*. "The road," he said, "is life."

Because we are now well into the Lewis and Clark bicentennial, it is easy to fix our attention on that American journey. It looms so large that other road stories are almost crowded off the stage. But if Lewis and Clark have become—at least for now—the emblematic voyage of national discovery, then all the other journeys we have made deserve our thoughtful attention. And there have been so many. The cultural landscape of North America is mapped by the names of the roads we have taken. Like ancient monuments they mark, bound, and chart our various histories. Somehow the roads have become our sacred places; to touch them is to touch us. Saying the names is like hearing the voices of now-lost relatives or repeating the litany of some sacred incantation: the Warrior's Path, the Natchez Trace, the Loving-Goodnight Trail, the Mormon Trail, and the Trail of Tears. These join at our historical crossroads with the Mullen Road, the Cumberland Road, the Wilderness Road, and countless (now nameless) lanes, byways, and turnpikes. These are the main-traveled roads, sometimes the roads not taken, the trunk lines of commerce, and the side tracks, the short lines of imagination and fantasy. These are the plain paths to paradise and the rough roads to Perdition by way of Purgatory. Paying attention to the names of the roads can teach us four fundamentals of journey history.

Journeys—The Shaping of America 3

The lure of the open road has enticed Americans in all eras. Across South Dakota, United States Highway 14 beckoned travelers to journey west to the Black Hills and Yellowstone National Park, earning it the nickname of the Black and Yellow Trail. (State Archives Collection, South Dakota State Historical Society, Pierre)

First, the names point us to purpose. Trails and roads were never the result of aimless wanderings across an unpathed countryside. Whatever band of travelers we choose to follow—whether first-comers scouting buffalo tracks or railroad workers blasting through mountains or my Dutch great-grandparents thinking to find "the Venice of America" in southern Colorado—all was done with intention and purpose. Names like the Warrior's Path, the Great Trading Path, and the National Road speak directly to matters of war, commerce, and national ambition. Trail names point us to the daily realities of hard labor and sweaty energy, the stretch of muscles in a world of work.

Second, the names are a portrait gallery, a roster of those characters who found themselves tangled up one way or another, with the twisty lives of the trails. So we are reminded—just by repeating the names—of Jesse Chisholm, Charles M. Goodnight, John Mullen, William Clark, and the redoubtable John Butterfield of overland stagecoach fame. Trail names—and the people behind the names—are a kind of roll call, a memory device to keep before us some actors who might otherwise miss history's curtain call. What this list excludes—because all naming is somehow a process of transformation and exclusion—are those who daily traveled the trails or protested their very existence. So it is the "Lewis and Clark Trail," with barely a nod to those who marched it and mapped it long before Jefferson's captains made their way up the Missouri and across those tremendous mountains. Somehow those famous, ever-present Lewis and Clark highway signs never quite point us to Grey Eyes or Black Cat, White Coyote or Yellow Corn.

Third, the journey names point us toward destinations, and the dreams those places conjured up for so many travelers. This is Wallace Stegner's "geography of hope," what Jack Kerouac's Sal Paradise (so aptly named!) meant when he said, "the East of my youth and the West of my future." There is an echo in Kerouac's line of the more famous one from Henry David Thoreau, "Eastward I go by force but westward I go free." Santa Fe and Oregon, Natchez and California, Colorado's gold and Dakota's golden wheat—these names are reminders of expectations and desires. For Josiah Gregg, Santa Fe promised enterprise and profit; for countless overlanders, Oregon and Dakota offered a farmer's Garden of Eden; and California shouted for gold and instant prosperity. These destination names can be read as a traveler's guide book, a directory to American dreams over the mountains, along the ridge lines, and down the long valleys.

Fourth, the journey names offer us reminders of the road as real-life experience. So we have the Whoop-Up Trail, the Wilderness Road, and the Long Walk. Each of those names represents expectation and reality, of things hoped for and things as they were. And much of that real-life experience got translated into words on the page. Our national literature is filled with journey writing: explorers' journals, overland trail diaries, newspaper accounts of transcontinental railroad adventures, and one of my favorites—Mark Twain's *Roughing It*, surely the wildest stagecoach ride in American literature. And because someone might accuse me of Oklahoma vanity, I will not mention all of Woody Guthrie's songs about hard traveling and blowing down this old dusty road.

Road names are a convenient gazetteer, the historian's map to places where folks on the move met the geography of a sometimes unforgiving country. But the names are also camouflage, ground cover, suggesting the shapes and shadows of our journeys but mysteriously concealing the insides, the tensions and struggles, the conflicts and controversies just beneath the surface. Like great rivers, roads are both emblems and revelations. An emblem is a visible sign of an invisible reality; a revelation is that moment when the sign opens up for us the many meanings of that emblem. My sense is that our journey stories, our collective lives on the road, can reveal some fundamental parts of the American past.

It is one of these elements that I would like to talk about for just a moment. Our collective past—however we decide to define it—seems filled with polar opposites. American history presents us with an on-going play of people, places, and ideas in tension. So there is the city and the country, North and South, master and slave, owner and worker, to say nothing of the obvious polarities of race, class, and gender. The list is obvious, long, and perhaps tediously misleading. Our lives are never so neatly divided one pole or position from another. But as we consider roads and journeys, we might acknowledge the powerful tension in our history between the lure of the road and the promise of home. These two—the home and the road—are everywhere in our national life and literature.

First, the road. The poet Walt Whitman (who made his own western journey to Colorado in 1879) wrote in his "Song of the Open Road" that all the universe is a road. Perhaps that is an overly grand claim, but the road metaphor is everywhere we look. Jack Kerouac writes *On the Road*, and Willie Nelson sings "on the road again." We get our kicks on Route 66, and, along with Delta blues singer Mississippi Fred McDowell, we take 61 Highway north to "Sweet Home Chicago." And all those automobile commercials with their sleek cars sweep us through endless miles of perfect highway. Those ads echo the old song, "Come away with me Lucile, in my merry Oldsmobile." The road spells freedom, adventure, fresh starts, and clean slates. Truck songs, train songs, movin' on songs—they all represent what Whitman called "the irresistible urge to depart."

Then, the home. Standing against the temptations of the road is the promise of home. Home as in "Home Sweet Home," "Home on the Range," and "Home is where the Heart is." Like the ever-changing road, the idea of home has never been fixed, somehow constant and stable. Both as an idea and something we build, the human experience of home has shifted not only with the winds of change but with the availability of materials like wood, stone, hide, and adobe. In seventeenth-century New England, settlers talked about home as "the little commonwealth," a space where work, prayer, education, and good order all came together for the greater glory of the Puritan god. Two centuries later, when Julia McNair wrote her classic advice book *The Complete Family*, the home was defined as a refuge, a place apart from the great world of man's work and public affairs. Many of our current notions of home and family values are still laden with nineteenth-century sentiment and a Victorian idealization of the family. But whatever the definition and the construction, there was one central assumption. The moral home stood in stark contrast to the temptations of the road.

The lure of the road. What did the road represent? What was its perhaps fatal attraction? What did the road offer to the restless, the dissatisfied, the ambitious? It seems to me that all these tracks and trails offered (or seemed to offer) four distinct rewards. Or to put a sharper edge on it, one might say that the open road held out four enticements to the foolish and the unwary.

First, profit. Whether in gold or land, fur, cattle, or oil, the road was—or at least seemed to be—the plain path to prosperity. Travelers on the road might be bound for the diggings on California's American River or land in Oregon's Willamette Valley; trail's end might be Virginia City or Dodge City, or perhaps an oil boom town in Oklahoma appropriately named Slick. But wherever it was going, the road promised money in the pocket and the freedom to spend it. Of course, the unspoken reality was that the song the next morning might be the "Empty Pocket's Blues," and we might all join Woody Guthrie "blowin' down that long, lonesome road feelin' bad."

Second, escape. American travel narratives are filled with stories of escape, and the road is always the means for and the symbol of that escape. Those Americans caught up in what historical geographer Don Meinig calls "The Outward Movement" believed they had much to escape from. The face of poverty peered through every window in a roller-coaster economy whose one sure promise was uncertainty. The poorest of America's poor stayed at home; it was the middling sort who feared a fall from social and economic grace and hoped for prosperity west of Wichita—somewhere out where the states were square and life was bright with promise. Perhaps the road could lead to a place from which escape was no longer a necessity. For those who faced religious, social, or racial prejudice, taking to the road was an escape imposed on them by the hatreds of others. For many on the road to somewhere else, the trail meant release from smothering families or troublesome spouses. And finally, the road promised flight from all sorts of personal and business failures. Ruined merchants, outlaws on the lam, heart-broken lovers, unfaithful husbands, restless wives, and the perpetually disenchanted all found the road an irresistible highway from yesterday's sorrows to tomorrow's land of milk and honey.

Third, adventure. It is fashionable now to soft pedal the part adventure played in pulling women and men on to the western road. Somehow it seems more intellectually satisfying to believe it was economic dislocation or social discontent that set adventuresome faces toward countless high plains boom towns with names like Optima or New Chicago. Pondering the Taos Trail or Route 66, we talk knowingly about abstract social or economic "forces" that drew travelers to the trail. But we should never underestimate the passion so many felt for the unexpected and the new. In doing so, we miss the compelling power of promised adventure. Earlier generations less accustomed to spectator sports and other couch potato diversions idealized adventure and eagerly sought it as a test of personal character and courage. What mattered was not just the destination but the road experience itself. The going was the goal. The journey itself offered the prize of adventure. My sense is that on the road the calculus of motivation was often more emotional than rational, more a matter of feeling than thought.

Finally, mobility. Somehow—perhaps thanks to cars and airplanes—we think that our time has some kind of monopoly on mobility. But many nineteenth-century Americans were far more mobile than we imagine. This mobility was fueled by everything from war to mineral rushes, from regional weather to events on the other side of the Atlantic and the Pacific. And it was made possible by the emergence at mid-century of a vast and quite remarkable transportation system. The road—the wagon road, the canal road, and railroad—all made moving from one place to another an event both imaginable and possible. The road, of whatever shape or construction, represented that possibility.

Every road made promises—some kept, others broken early or late. The journeys did more than simply embody temptation. In some way or other, the roads and the journeys represented a challenge to home. What did the home promise to those who rejected the call of the wild road? Let me suggest four home offerings, four rewards granted to those who did not pack the wagon, sell the place, and head west to paradise.

First, the home promised security. If the lure of the road was flashy profit at trail's end, the home symbolized a good, reliable living from the land. These were the yeoman-farmer virtues, the ones propounded and praised from Hesiod to Jefferson. Home and honest labor stood against the road and quick riches from little work.

Second, the home represented connectedness, a deeply embedded sense of place and being placed. The road was all about adventure, the changes and chances of an unexpected, dis-placed life. That tension was real in the era of the western trails, and it remains so today. Is the best life the venturesome one, the risk-taking, on-the-move life, or is real value to be found at home, in the parlor, with the garden gate securely locked?

Third, the home carried the torch for the reliable, the certain, and the sure. At home were the routine chores, the daily ordinary, the comforts that made life understandable and bearable. These were the familiar faces in all the right places. But on the road anything could happen. Lives could be changed, old ways forgotten, cherished traditions cast aside.

Finally, home promised community. Historian Dale Morgan once described wagon train companies as "communities on the move." And surely there were plenty of opportunities to savor the pleasures of society on the road. But the long, lonesome road also offered the chance to be anonymous, nearly invisible, and hence powerfully free. The home folks would have said, along with Janis Joplin, that freedom can be just another word for nothing left to lose.

Now it may be that I am asking roads and journeys to carry too great a burden. What I am suggesting here is that the stories and lives connected to all these passages can help us appreciate something deep in our past and much alive in our present: the quirky, perhaps inescapable tension between the home and the road. The trails and the travelers help us frame one set of American stories—stories about home, leaving home, being on the road, and perhaps making new homes. The struggle between the home and the road is the plot in a drama of newcomers fresh off the road creating new homes while dispossessing the first-comers from theirs. The war between the home and the road is really all about possession and dispossession, seduction and betrayal, faithfulness and disappointment. Those who ventured to the gold fields and the wheat fields—and those who watched and worried—knew all about that war. They knew that journeys could mean wealth for some and poverty for others; they knew—or soon learned—that homes once made could be suddenly unmade. And above all, they knew that road-trip fantasies and homestead dreams would always dance uneasily in the American imagination. For where else could you find a highway described as "the mother road." That phrase—now often used to describe Route 66—captures both the war between the home and the road and that enduring American impulse to call the road "the mother of us all."

Tribal Relations on the Upper Missouri River before Lewis and Clark

W. RAYMOND WOOD

Tuesday, 25 September 1804. The scene: a sandbar in the Missouri River at the mouth of the Bad River, about one mile downstream from the bridge spanning the river at present-day Pierre, South Dakota. William Clark drew his sword as he faced a group of threatening Brulé Sioux, their bows and arrows at ready. Meriwether Lewis had the Corps of Discovery take up arms and ordered that the swivel gun on the keelboat be leveled at the warriors. It was a tense moment in the annals of the Lewis and Clark Expedition.[1] Fortunately, the moment passed without bloodshed, but it could have been otherwise. The expedition moved on upriver without further such confrontations.

Their instructions from President Jefferson had specified that Lewis and Clark were to act with the Indians "in the most friendly & conciliatory manner which their own conduct will admit."[2] The Sioux facing the Americans on the Missouri River were determined to maintain their grip on trade goods entering their sphere of dominance, and the captains were equally determined to proceed upstream despite Sioux objections. Certainly one of the most dramatic events of the expedition, the scene underscored the world of intertribal politics that Lewis and Clark had entered. The Sioux at that time were, and for many years continued to be, the dominant power along the upper Missouri River.[3]

The Missouri has cut a narrow trench through North and South Dakota from the northwest to the southeast in the millennia since the last ice age, and its fertile floodplain provided the only region in the western portions of those states that had land suitable for cultivation by American Indians (Figure 1). Consequently, it was a magnet for farming peoples, as well as for the nomads that both traded with and raided the gardening tribes. The

FIGURE 1. *Typical terrain along the Missouri River before its inundation in 1963 by the Big Bend Dam and its impoundment, Lake Sharpe. (National Anthropological Archives, Washington, D.C., MRBS Negative 3900-79)*

river was also an artery for trade, especially for the Euro-American traders who had been infiltrating the region for decades before the arrival of Lewis and Clark. This great ribbon of muddy water, lined by bottomland forests, bisected an endless rolling sea of grass interspersed with badlands of tortured beauty and crowded with millions of bison, pronghorn antelope, and prairie dogs. It was a land of striking splendor, desolation, and intrigue.

The Indian world along the Missouri into which the expedition intruded in 1804 was a dynamic one of ever-shifting intertribal rivalries and expansion. What preconceptions did Lewis and Clark have of the Indian nations they would meet as they passed the mouth of the Niobrara River and headed deeper into what would become the Dakotas? It is safe to say those concepts were simplistic. The captains surely had an accurate notion of some of the regional tribal politics obtained from their knowledgeable informants in Saint Louis before they left that city, augmented by the traders they met as they ascended the Missouri and by the French voyageurs that accompanied them as members of the expedition. The scenario they gained from these sources would nevertheless have been woefully incomplete, filtered as it was through the biases of their own eastern aristocratic culture and by their lack of first-hand knowledge of regional Indian customs.

Lewis and Clark were instructed to announce formally the notion of American power to the American Indians they met along their route. The captains were to gain their allegiance—especially that of the Teton Sioux—to the new American government and to bring intertribal peace and stability to the area so that white commercial trade with the tribes was feasible. Lewis and Clark did not realize, or they certainly underestimated, three principles that governed Indian activities and diplomacy. First, there was deep-seated hostility between some tribes that American diplomacy could not possibly overcome. Second, there was no central figure, that is to say, a leader with coercive powers, among either the village or nomadic tribes that could dictate policies to the group. Third, the way to prestige and power among the men of all tribes was to gain honors in warfare.

Many complex and interlocking relations fostered intertribal hostility. One important factor was the desire to maintain status in the intertribal trading network that existed among the tribes of the Northern Great Plains. Intertribal trade, especially between the village tribes and the nomadic tribes in the region, had a long history and was an important factor in native life.[4] The status of this trade was threatened by the arrival of newcomers, especially tribes from farther east who had been displaced by the growing unrest brought about, in part, by the introduction of guns. These weapons upset previous balances of power and led to forced removal and unpredictable relations with new neighbors. The continued and accelerating appearance of white traders exacerbated the growing tensions in the region.

The second principle governing Indian relationships concerned structure. Because it is customary to speak of Indian "tribes," one may gain the impression that some form of overall political organization united their individual villages or bands. No such thing existed. For all practical purposes, each village or band was an autonomous entity—politically, economically, and socially—although its members were bound to fellow tribesmen by a common language, by customs, and by interlocking clans and other social devices. Sometimes, too, villages would collaborate in defensive measures, especially against the oncoming Sioux. In any event, obtaining consent from a tribe for any decision meant obtaining the collective assent of different villages, a process that the captains experienced at the Arikara villages at the Grand River in October 1804.[5]

Decisions were so hard to reach because each village had its own political hierarchy. Chiefs held honorific positions, a status that was obtained by charisma, great generosity, prowess in public speaking, and other qualities respected by the community. Their word was subject to community councils, and each individual was followed only by those whose respect he commanded. If a chief lost that respect, another leader would succeed him. Lewis and Clark persisted in naming "head chiefs" in the groups they visited, men they expected to provide leadership over others—but whose word, in practice, was no better than that of his rival. Chiefs could not control the actions of others, especially those of young men.

Finally, among the Plains Indians, the road to power and prestige for men was through war honors obtained in hand-to-hand clashes with their enemies. It was not possible for a man to become either a peace chief or a war chief, nor attain any real status in the community, without proving his mettle in combat. If all tribes were at peace, there would be no replacements of chiefs by upwardly-mobile young warriors. The road to leadership would be blocked, a situation that was unacceptable to ambitious young men—men who continued the pursuit of hostilities despite the objections of their leaders.[6] Ignorance on the part of the captains regarding this situation and the other principles governing tribal life, therefore, led to wholly unrealistic expectations concerning their peacemaking abilities.

The state of intertribal rivalries and expansionism at the time of the expedition would also play a role in the captains' peace efforts. By the early 1700s, the Northern Great Plains was emerging from the shadows of prehistory into an era that was to set the stage for the dynamic tribal movements that characterized its historical period. French traders were moving up the Missouri River from its mouth, and some had even reached as far north as the Arikaras. Etienne Véniard de Bourgmont had explored the Missouri as far upstream as the Platte River, but as early as 1714, he mentioned that the Arikaras "have seen the French and know them."[7] One such early trader died at the Swan Creek site in northern South Dakota sometime about 1700; his Arikara hosts buried him in their own manner in their cemetery among his former customers. Traders also were reaching out from posts in the Great Lakes area toward the upper Mississippi valley and westward, and European trade goods from the rivers of southern

FIGURE 2. *The Sully site, a pre-1781 Arikara village in Sully County, central South Dakota, contained more than two hundred earthlodges, implying a population of more than two thousand individuals. It now lies beneath the waters of the Oahe Reservoir. (National Anthropological Archives, Washington, D.C., MRBS Negative 39SL-11)*

Canada were trickling into the middle reaches of the Missouri valley. The Sieur de la Vérendrye and his sons had reached the Mandans from the north in 1738, and they mention a French trader plying his trade somewhere near the Grand Detour in 1743.[8]

Three sedentary, horticultural village tribes—the Mandans, Hidatsas, and Arikaras—were then living along the Missouri River. They inhabited permanent villages of earth-covered lodges, usually surrounded by defensive ditches and post palisades and built on high banks facing the river. Their towns overlooked the gardens of corn, beans, and squash that supplemented a diet that depended heavily on bison.[9] Their villages were large and commodious, and many contained one hundred and more homes; indeed, they were far larger than contemporary Saint Louis (Figure 2).

These village gardeners were surrounded on all sides by nomadic hunters and gatherers. These tipi-dwelling people had no fixed place of residence but followed bison herds within a usually predictable region. North and

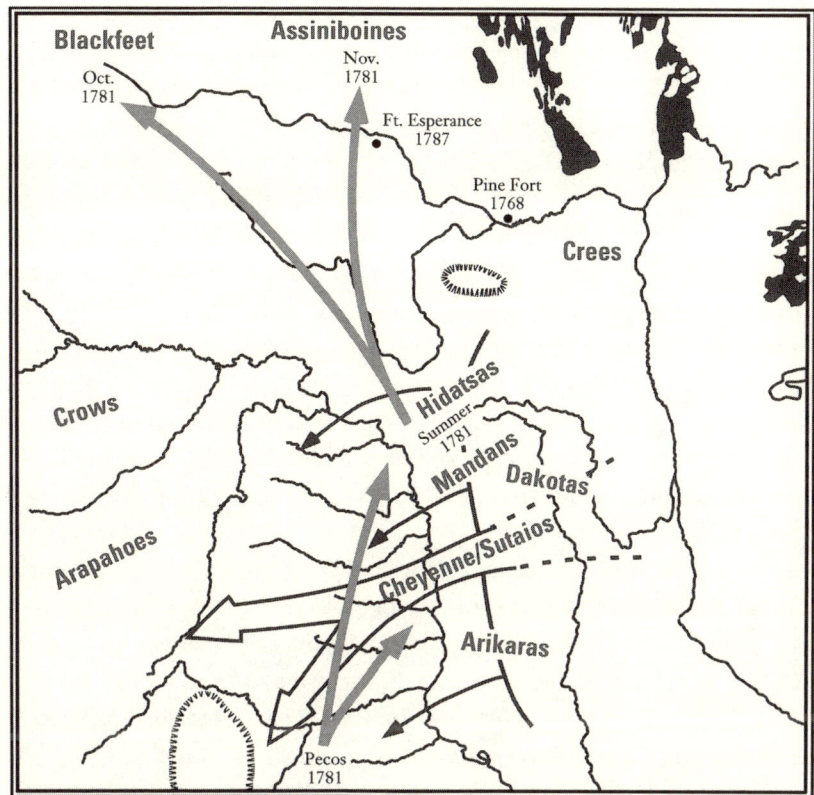

FIGURE 3. *Conjectural map of the Mandan and Hidatsa world as the 1781 smallpox epidemic engulfed the Northern Great Plains. Light arrows show the westward movement of the Sioux and Cheyenne-Sutaios; heavy arrows depict the spread of the disease from the Spanish Southwest. (W. Raymond Wood Collection)*

east of the Missouri River lived the Assiniboines and Plains Crees. To the east were the Cheyennes, Sutaios, Arapahos, and Tetons, all of whom were to expand westward and cross the Missouri. The picture is less clear to the south and west, for only vague stories were told of these groups to the expanding Europeans, but the Crows were living west of the Mandans and Hidatsas in present-day Montana, and to the south were other foot nomads on the high plains of western North and South Dakota and southern Montana (Figure 3).[10]

Three major interlocking problems dominated the intertribal scene at the time of Lewis and Clark: (1) depopulation by disease, (2) westward migration, and (3) trade wars. Smallpox was the most virulent of a series of diseases introduced from the Old World, but diphtheria, measles, typhus, and others also wrought havoc. The effects of these diseases were devastating in every aspect of native life because the people had never been exposed to Old World diseases. Epidemics led to horrific population losses, with consequent changes in social and political institutions, kinship and marriage, and technology.[11] Because so many people died, some specialists in each society were eliminated, leading to the loss of traditions and manufacturing skills. Few people today know how awful smallpox really was. People did not simply die from it; they died in a massively disfigured manner, though usually quickly. The effects of this pathogen on the survivors passed beyond horror: the psychological effects of observing the ravages of this disease on one's loved ones are incalculable. Parents abandoned children; old people were left to die as those well enough to do so fled; and still others took their own lives.[12]

A rough outline of the smallpox epidemic that raced across the Northern Great Plains in the next-to-last decade of the 1700s is reasonably well known. The disease apparently arrived from the American Southwest. Scholars have "traced the source of this scourge to the Valley of Mexico, where between September and December 1779, estimated deaths from smallpox ranged between 18,000 and 22,000." Smallpox reached the pueblos of New Mexico in 1780, and by 1781, the disease had killed about five thousand Indians, with the highest death rates at Pecos Pueblo and among the Hopis.[13] An ideal road existed for smallpox to reach the Northern Great Plains—the active intertribal exchange between New Mexico and the Missouri River villagers. Every fall, nomads from the south and west arrived at the villages of the Mandans, Hidatsas, and Arikaras. They brought horses and other goods to exchange for the products of the villagers' gardens and for the guns the villagers had obtained from traders along the Assiniboine River in southern Canada.[14]

Historical documents offer no figures for the population of the village Indians at the time of the 1781 epidemic, but proxy numbers may be obtained from archaeological data. Donald J. Lehmer calculated a set of such figures based on his estimates of the age of archaeological sites, with village populations based on an historically-derived figure of ten individuals living in each earthlodge. On this basis, he estimated that in 1780 the Mandans numbered six thousand; the Hidatsas, fifty-five hundred; and the

Arikaras, seventy-five hundred—a total of about nineteen thousand individuals. Twenty-four years later, Lewis and Clark reported that the population for the three tribes was a little less than six thousand individuals. This figure, of course, includes population growth in the intervening generation, but even so, it denotes the death of no less than thirteen thousand individuals—a mortality rate of 68 percent.[15]

This catastrophic decline in population made the village Indians vulnerable to attack, and the Tetons increasingly mounted raids on their towns. The Arikaras were forced up the Missouri River from their homes in central South Dakota as the Tetons tightened their grip on the river. Mandan accounts given to Lewis and Clark mention that at least two of the Mandan villages near the mouth of the Heart River were "destroyed" or "killed" by the Teton Sioux, one of them by the Sioux and smallpox combined, and Clark mapped another six nearby Mandan villages as being abandoned.[16] As the Tetons continued westward, they found desperately weak village Indians in their area of dominance, and they remained on the scene to plague the villagers until reservation days.

Migration also played its role in the dynamics of plains cultures. While no boundaries can be specified, there is no doubt that the Tetons were living in and exploiting the grasslands well to the west and southwest of the forested regions of present-day Minnesota by the late 1600s. In other words, they may have been living in the northeastern Great Plains in late prehistoric times and were leading a plains lifeway well before their acquisition of horses.[17] The expansion of the Tetons to the west, across the modern Dakotas, is poorly recorded, but surely they had reached the Missouri River by the early 1700s and had crossed it by 1750. Traditional evidence supports an early Sioux presence on the Missouri River. The winter count of Battiste Good, a Brulé, records that the Sioux killed their first bison on horseback in the winter of 1700–1701, had killed fifteen Arikaras in 1704–1705, and killed some Hidatsas in 1707–1708. Other symbols record that they contacted the Arikaras in 1707–1708, and between 1712 and 1762, they continued to raid the Arikaras, Hidatsas, Omahas, and Assiniboines.[18] Thus, the western Tetons were engaged in widespread warfare against most of their neighbors along and north of the Missouri throughout its course through the Dakotas. By 1781, the Tetons had been living west of the Missouri for many years and were attacking and destroying the disease-decimated Mandan villages at the mouth of the Heart River in the vicinity of modern Bismarck.

FIGURE 4. *The Biesterfeldt site comprises a late-eighteenth-century Cheyenne earthlodge village site on the Sheyenne River in southeastern North Dakota. Half of the site has been obscured by cultivation. (Wood,* Biersterfeldt, Smithsonian Contributions to Anthropology, *no. 15 [Washington, D.C., 1971], pl. 2b)*

In the late eighteenth century, many of the Cheyennes were living in what is now eastern North Dakota, some of them in an earthlodge village on the great southern bend of the Sheyenne River (Figure 4). Their life there closely resembled that of the Arikaras living on the Missouri River: they gardened and made pottery.[19] It is not known when the Cheyennes from this site and others first arrived on the Missouri River and settled near the present boundary between North and South Dakota, but most of their villages were occupied in the second half of the 1700s. Despite statements to the contrary, no Cheyenne earthlodge village in the Missouri region is known archaeologically, a fact that intimates that most of these communities were tipi encampments whose inhabitants had abandoned pottery-making. These villages nevertheless are well attested in historical documents, including those of Lewis and Clark, and in the traditions of the tribe itself and in those of its Dakota neighbors.[20]

As the Cheyennes migrated west across the plains of present southern North Dakota, they funneled into a reach of the Missouri River Valley that was not then occupied by village gardeners. They were constrained in their choice of location to the north by the Mandans, who occupied villages near the mouth of the Heart River, and to the south by the Arikaras, who lived at and below the mouth of the Cheyenne and, later, near the Grand River. After a residence of about half a century on the Missouri, the Cheyennes moved deeper into the trans-Missouri plains. Among their earliest adversaries there were the Shoshones and other nomads, now mounted on horses. The Sutaios, who spoke a dialect closely related to that of the Cheyennes, either preceded them to the Missouri River or joined them there. The Sutaios were soon absorbed by the Cheyennes, becoming one of their bands.[21] At the time of Lewis and Clark, the combined group was living around the northern, eastern, and southern margins of the Black Hills.

Before 1781, the Mandans and Hidatsas were strong and numerous, numbering nearly twelve thousand people, and capable of defending themselves in their strongly fortified villages between the mouths of the Heart and Knife Rivers. Sometime after the epidemic of 1781, the Mandans abandoned their villages near the Heart and moved upriver to live near the Hidatsas. Prior to the epidemic, these two tribes had been the most powerful groups on the Northern Great Plains, though they were surrounded by two expanding and hostile groups. The Tetons were expanding westward and had crossed the Missouri, bypassing them, and the Assiniboines were pressuring them from the north.

The Tetons were also tightening their grip on the Missouri River in central South Dakota, placing increasing pressure on the many Arikara villages there. Responding to this pressure, the Arikaras—decimated by disease—moved up the Missouri and abandoned their old communities near and to the south of the Cheyenne River. By the time of Lewis and Clark, the Arikaras were living in three villages at the mouth of the Grand River north of present-day Mobridge. One was an easily-defensible community built on what came to be known as Ashley Island, and the other two were strongly fortified by palisades on the west bank of the river where they were visited by the Corps of Discovery.[22]

As they paddled up the Missouri in 1804, Lewis and Clark were entering an area where tribal distributions had changed dramatically in only a few decades and were still in flux. Only the Hidatsas were living in their traditional territory in three villages at the mouth of the Knife River. The village tribes, once the power brokers on the Northern Great Plains, had been replaced by the Sioux and were beginning to suffer grievously at their hands: their world had been turned upside down. The east bank of the Missouri was flanked and, in many areas, overrun by a solid wall of Sioux. In southeastern South Dakota were the Yanktons; in the middle reaches were the Brulés; and still other Lakota groups were in the vicinity of the Mandans.

The Sioux now dominated commerce in the region, trading with the Canadian North West Company based on the Des Moines and Minnesota Rivers and with British traders based at Prairie du Chien on the Mississippi River. In turn, they traded with the Arikaras and their other village neighbors on the Missouri River. For the captains, it would be a major coup to wean the Sioux away from the British traders and replace them with American traders downstream. But the Sioux did not want their monopoly disrupted by newcomers. To preserve their trade advantage, they prohibited merchants from downriver from trading with the Arikaras and others on the river above them, or exacted heavy tribute from those wishing to do so. This strategy led to the Teton confrontation with Lewis and Clark at the mouth of the Bad River.[23]

Even though the relationship between the Sioux and their Arikara neighbors was uneasy and the two groups often fought, they also collaborated at times, especially in raids against the Mandans. The captains were unable to convince the Arikaras to abandon their ties with the Sioux. As James P. Ronda has said, "With a naive optimism typical of so much Euro-American frontier diplomacy, Lewis and Clark believed they could easily reshape Upper Missouri realities to fit their expectations." But they failed in bringing peace to the upper Missouri River tribes. It was not to the Indians' advantage: the Arikaras were not going to abandon their Sioux connection for an elusive one in Saint Louis.[24] Nor were the Mandans really serious about making peace with the Arikaras, though they no doubt hoped Saint Louis would be a better source of goods than their Assiniboine neighbors.

The Missouri was a busy highway even as Lewis and Clark began their journey. Traders had been active on the river for most of the preceding century, and no less than five trading posts had been established along its banks in the Dakotas in the decade before the expedition's departure from Wood River. Jusseaume's Post, built by René Jusseaume for the Canadian North West Company, had been erected in 1794 between the Mandan and Hidatsa villages in North Dakota. Later that year, Jean Baptiste Truteau established Ponca House for the Spanish Missouri Company and traded during the winter with the Omahas, Poncas, and Sioux.[25] The post was in what is now Charles Mix County, southeastern South Dakota, a few miles downstream from today's Fort Randall Dam. Loisel's Post (or Fort aux

Cédres) was built about 1800 by Régis Loisel in southeastern South Dakota; it was on Cedar Island (so named for its dense stand of junipers) in the Missouri River just upstream from the Grand Detour. The post was meant to last. Sergeant Patrick Gass described it as "about 65 or 70 feet square, with centry boxes in two of the angles. The pickets are 13 ½ feet above ground. In this square he built a house 45 ½ by 32 ½ feet."[26] It was, nonetheless, short-lived, and Loisel was soon back in Saint Louis. His employees also established two other more modest satellite posts. Hugh Heney founded for him an unnamed post for the Sioux near the mouth of the Cheyenne River, and Pierre-Antoine Tabeau founded one among the Arikaras at the Grand River. These posts were transient affairs. Tabeau occupied part of the lodge of Kakawita, an Arikara chief, in the village on Ashley Island. The trader partitioned his part of the lodge off with upright stakes.[27]

Jacques D'Eglise is the first man known to have visited the Mandans from Saint Louis, reaching them in 1792, but other Frenchmen had been on the upper Missouri for decades. It is little wonder that virtually every stream the Corps of Discovery passed in the first full year of the expedition had already been named by their French trader and voyageur predecessors—names that most of them retain to this day, though often in translation.[28] The captains also recorded no less than nine parties of traders as they descended the river returning to Saint Louis in 1806, men that were going to trade with the Osages, Otos, Pawnees, Omahas, Sioux, and still other tribes. The traffic was intense: they met nearly one hundred fifty men bound for the upper Missouri.

The great western migration had begun. The early traders did not always find it easy; for them, hostility did not end with Lewis and Clark's encounter at the mouth of Bad River. The Arikaras defeated William H. Ashley at the mouth of the Grand River in 1823, an engagement in which about 10 percent of his nearly one hundred men lost their lives.[29] But the way was now open. Less than a half-century later, traders would be replaced by settlers.

Since its "discovery" by Marquette and Jolliet in 1673, the upper Missouri River had been visited by uncounted fur traders, voyageurs, and explorers, but in the decades following Lewis and Clark, the goal of westward moving Americans became the promised lands of Oregon and California, not the arid prairies of the Northern Great Plains. The upper Missouri remained the haunt of American Indians and transient fur traders, as well as a military frontier, throughout most of the nineteenth century. Gradually, however, clusters of Euro-American homes along the river began developing into towns surrounded by farms, and by the end of the century, the frontier vanished as Indian reservations were founded for the now-displaced residents of village and plain.

NOTES

1. Gary E. Moulton, ed., *The Journals of the Lewis & Clark Expedition*, 13 vols. (Lincoln: University of Nebraska Press, 1983–2001), 3:112–13.

2. Donald Jackson, *Letters of the Lewis and Clark Expedition with Related Documents, 1783–1854* (Urbana: University of Illinois Press, 1962), p. 64.

3. Guy Gibbon, *The Sioux: The Dakota and Lakota Nations* (Malden, Mass.: Blackwell, 2003); Raymond J. DeMallie, "Sioux until 1850," in *Handbook of North American Indians*, vol. 13, pt. 2: *Plains*, ed. Raymond J. DeMallie (Washington, D.C.: Smithsonian Press, 2001), pp. 718–60.

4. W. Raymond Wood, "Plains Trade in Prehistoric and Protohistoric Intertribal Relations," in *Anthropology on the Great Plains*, ed. Wood and Margot Liberty (Lincoln: University of Nebraska Press, 1980), pp. 98–109.

5. Moulton, *Journals of the Lewis & Clark Expedition*, 3:150–66.

6. Harold E. Driver, *Indians of North America* (Chicago: University of Chicago Press, 1961), pp. 370–74; Clayton A. Robarchek, "Plains Warfare and the Anthropology of War," in *Skeletal Biology in the Great Plains: Migration, Warfare, Health, and Subsistence*, ed. Douglas W. Owsley and Richard L. Jantz (Washington, D.C.: Smithsonian Institution Press, 1994), pp. 307–16.

7. Frank Norall, *Bourgmont, Explorer of the Missouri, 1698–1725* (Lincoln: University of Nebraska Press, 1988), p. 110.

8. Richard L. Jantz and Douglas W. Owsley, "White Traders in the Upper Missouri: Evidence from the Swan Creek Site," in *Skeletal Biology in the Great Plains*, ed. Owsley and Jantz, pp. 189–201; G. Hubert Smith, *The Explorations of the La Vérendryes in the Northern Plains, 1738–43*, ed. W. Raymond Wood (Lincoln: University of Nebraska Press, 1980), p. 112.

9. Roy W. Meyer, *The Village Indians of the Upper Missouri: The Mandans, Hidatsas, and Arikaras* (Lincoln: University of Nebraska Press, 1977); Douglas R. Parks, "Arikara," and W. Raymond Wood and Lee Irwin, "Mandan," both in *Handbook of North American Indians*, Vol. 13, pt. 1: *Plains*, ed. Raymond J. DeMallie (Washington, D.C.: Smithsonian Institution Press, 2001), pp. 349–90.

10. The relations between the villagers and the nomads are brilliantly outlined in Preston Holder, *The Hoe and the Horse on the Plains: A Study of Cultural Development among North American Indians* (Lincoln: University of Nebraska Press, 1970).

11. *See*, for instance, its impact on Arikara tribal politics in Pierre-Antoine Ta-

beau, *Tabeau's Narrative of Loisel's Expedition to the Upper Missouri*, ed. Annie Heloise Abel (Norman: University of Oklahoma Press, 1939), pp. 123–24n.74.

12. Francis A. Chardon, *Chardon's Journal at Fort Clark, 1834–1839*, ed. Annie H. Abel (Pierre: South Dakota Department of History, 1932), pp. 121–45, 181, 394–96; Elizabeth A. Fenn, *Pox Americana: The Great Smallpox Epidemic of 1775–82* (New York: Hill & Wang, 2001); R. G. Robertson, *Rotting Face: Smallpox and the American Indian* (Caldwell, Idaho: Caxton Press, 2001).

13. Ann F. Ramenofsky, *Vectors of Death: The Archaeology of European Contact* (Albuquerque: University of New Mexico Press, 1987), p. 130. Elizabeth Fenn's recent work, *Pox Americana*, also supports an ultimate Mexican and Southwestern origin for the epidemic.

14. W. Raymond Wood and Thomas D. Thiessen, eds., *Early Fur Trade on the Northern Plains: Canadian Traders among the Mandan and Hidatsa Indians, 1738–1818*, American Exploration and Travel Series, no. 68 (Norman: University of Oklahoma Press, 1985).

15. Donald J. Lehmer, "Epidemics among the Indians of the Upper Missouri," in *Selected Writings of Donald J. Lehmer*, ed. W. Raymond Wood (Lincoln, Nebr.: J&L Reprint Co., 1977), p. 107; Moulton, *Journals of the Lewis & Clark Expedition*, 3:400–405.

16. Moulton, *Journals of the Lewis & Clark Expedition*, 1:maps, pp. 27–28.

17. W. Raymond Wood, "The Plains-Lakes Connection: Reflections from a Western Perspective," in *Archaeology, Ecology and Ethnohistory of the Prairie-Forest Border Zone of Minnesota and Manitoba*, ed. Janet Spector and Elden Johnson (Lincoln, Nebr.: J&L Reprint Co., 1985), p. 4.

18. Garrick Mallery, "Picture-Writing of the American Indians," in *Tenth Annual Report of the Bureau of Ethnology to the Secretary of the Smithsonian Institution, 1888–1889* (Washington, D.C.: Government Printing Office, 1893), pp. 293–325.

19. W. Raymond Wood, *Biesterfeldt: A Post-Contact Coalescent Site on the Northeastern Plains*, Smithsonian Contributions to Anthropology, no. 15 (Washington, D.C., 1971), p. 49.

20. See George Bird Grinnell, *The Cheyenne Indians: Their History and Ways of Life*, 2 vols. (New York: Yale Cooper Square Publishers, 1962). Grinnell's evidence is summarized in Wood, *Biesterfeldt*, pp. 60–68, fig. 16.

21. Grinnell, *Cheyenne Indians*, 1:2; John Moore, *The Cheyenne Nation: A Social and Demographic Study* (Lincoln: University of Nebraska Press, 1987), p. 68, map 1.

22. Richard A. Krause, *The Leavenworth Site: Archaeology of an Historic Arikara Community*, University of Kansas Publications in Anthropology, no. 3 (Lawrence, 1972).

23. Ronda, *Lewis and Clark among the Indians* (Lincoln: University of Nebraska Press, 1984), pp. 28–31.

24. Ibid., p. 55; see also p. 60.

25. Abraham P. Nasatir, *Before Lewis and Clark: Documents Illustrating the History of the Missouri River, 1785–1804*, 2 vols. (Saint Louis, Mo.: Saint Louis Historical Documents Foundation, 1952), 1:280, 331.

26. Moulton, *Journals of the Lewis & Clark Expedition*, 10:42. See also G. Hubert Smith, *Big Bend Historic Sites*, Smithsonian Institution River Basin Surveys, Publications in Salvage Archeology, no. 9 (Lincoln, Nebr., 1968), pp. 47–50.

27. Tabeau, *Tabeau's Narrative*, pp. 136, 145.

28. W. Raymond Wood, *Prologue to Lewis and Clark: The Mackay and Evans Expedition* (Norman: University of Oklahoma Press, 2003), pp. 197–203; Nasatir, *Before Lewis and Clark*, 1:82.

29. Dale L. Morgan, ed., *The West of William H. Ashley: The International Struggle for the Fur Trade of the Missouri, the Rocky Mountains, and the Columbia, . . . in the Diaries and Letters of William H. Ashley and his Contemporaries, 1822–1838* (Denver, Colo.: Old West Publishing Co., 1964), book 1, pp. 1–87.

Gateways and Guardians
Lewis and Clark and the Louisiana Purchase

PETER J. KASTOR

We are now in the midst of two competing bicentennials: the Lewis and Clark Expedition and the Louisiana Purchase. The winner is obvious. The Lewis and Clark Expedition has been the subject of best-selling books, numerous documentaries, major national events, and local commemorations spanning the considerable length of the Lewis and Clark Trail; all this more than a year before 2004 marked the actual bicentennial of the expedition's departure from Saint Louis. Meanwhile, the Louisiana Purchase commemoration continued to plod away in relative obscurity. The thirtieth of April 2003 (the bicentennial of the day when French and American negotiators completed work on the purchase) came and went, and few people seemed to notice. I cannot help but lament this state of affairs. Of course, anybody interested in the Lewis and Clark Expedition cannot ignore the Louisiana Purchase. The problem is usually how they look at it. We frequently misunderstand the relationship between these two events. Too often, any study of Lewis and Clark establishes the Louisiana Purchase as a dramatic precursor. Worse still, taken together these two events often lead to erroneous conclusions about the nature of the American Union and the trajectory of American expansion. With that in mind, I would like to suggest a different way of understanding the relationship between the expedition and the purchase.

The Louisiana Purchase is the crucial first step toward understanding Lewis and Clark, whether the Lewis and Clark Expedition itself or the subsequent lives of Meriwether Lewis and William Clark. First and foremost, it was the purchase that not only enabled the Voyage of Discovery to proceed but also redefined its purpose; indeed, it *gave* the expedition a purpose of national import. Second, it was the Louisiana Purchase and the challenges that came from it that shaped the public careers and personal destinies of Meriwether Lewis and William Clark. Looking at the purchase from these perspectives helps to create a different portrait of the expedition. Lewis and Clark are often seen as the physical embodiment of America's expansionist impulse, which was expressed in diplomatic form in the purchase. I would argue the opposite. The expedition and the purchase both reflect the tremendous concerns and problems that came with expansion. More than anything else, Lewis and Clark served as gatekeepers and guardians, attempting to control what people and forces came from the West.

The Louisiana Purchase defined the context of continental and transatlantic affairs in which the expedition of 1804–1806 took place. Even if Lewis and Clark lost touch with that reality while they traversed the North American West, officials in Washington certainly did not. It was the purchase, and not the expedition, that dominated concerns in the nation's capital. And once Lewis and Clark returned, they would understand why.

The starting point for understanding the role of the purchase is Thomas Jefferson's various instructions to Meriwether Lewis. On 20 June 1803, Jefferson's instructions captured the president's reasons for organizing the Corps of Discovery, and they framed the way Lewis and Clark approached their planning and organized the materials they gathered along the way. Jefferson's June instructions are a masterful combination of orders given and latitude granted. He established the expedition's primary goal by ordering Lewis "to explore the Missouri river, & such principal stream of it, as, by it's course and communication with the waters of the Pacific ocean, whether the Columbia, Oregan, Colorado or any other river may offer the most direct & practicable water communication across this continent for the purposes of commerce." Jefferson also instructed Lewis to study the American Indians, to gather botanical samples, and to survey the landscape.[1] In other words, Jefferson constructed the mission as people often understand it today: as a quintessential expression of the Enlightenment that called on Lewis to serve as ethnographer, botanist, and surveyor.

But let us look at another set of instructions. I refer to the communication Jefferson wrote on 16 November 1803. The president began on a familiar subject, reminding Lewis, "The object of your mission is single, the direct water communication from sea to sea formed by the bed of the Missouri & perhaps the Oregon." But then Jefferson added: "As the boundaries of interior Louisiana are the high lands inclosing all the waters which run into the

Thomas Jefferson, by Thomas Sully, 1856 copy after Sully's 1821 original. (Monticello/Thomas Jefferson Foundation, Inc., Charlottesville, Virginia)

Missisipi or Missouri directly or indirectly, with a greater breadth on the gulph of Mexico, it becomes interesting to fix with precision by celestial observations the longitude & latitude of the sources of these rivers, and furnishing points in the contour of our new limits."[2]

Much had happened in the months between these two messages. When Jefferson wrote to Lewis in June 1803, the expedition was going nowhere. The Spanish had made it clear that they would not offer passports, and with the Spanish in command of the lower Missouri River, the expedition could hardly proceed on its route without being immediately intercepted. Yet, by November, circumstances had changed sufficiently to remove those Spanish impediments. This change becomes clear through an understanding of the complex and often confusing status of the place called "Louisiana."

Explaining the impact of the purchase — as well as the contested definition of Louisiana — requires a review of events that occurred long before the purchase itself. In 1763, France had ceded its colony of Louisiana to Spain. The boundaries of this vaguely defined colony stretched from the Gulf of Mexico to the Canadian border and from the Mississippi River to the Rockies. Within this massive land mass, the Missouri River became the primary thoroughfare. It was the Missouri River Valley of Spanish Louisiana that Jefferson had long hoped to understand and exploit by dispatching an expedition of exploration. No sooner did Jefferson become president in 1801, and appoint Lewis his personal secretary, than he received news that Spain had returned Louisiana to France the year before in a secret agreement that became known as the retrocession. Further complicating this situation was an arrangement by which Spain would continue to govern Louisiana even though France actually "owned" the colony.

The retrocession dominated the agenda of the newly installed Jefferson Administration. American policymakers worried that the Treaty of San Ildefonso (the instrument of the retrocession) would implicitly nullify agreements with Spain that guaranteed the right of American merchants to trade down the length of the Mississippi River. These fears proved accurate, and by the end of 1802, Spanish restrictions on American trade led to a "Mississippi Crisis" that threatened nothing less than national survival. Planning for the Lewis and Clark Expedition actually made things worse. The Spanish had made clear to the United States that they would not permit the expedition to proceed, and who can blame them? Regardless of Jefferson's assurances to the contrary, the Spanish could reasonably assume that an

American expedition under the leadership of two army officers who hoped to seek commercial opportunities and build alliances with Indians was only the first step in an American effort to undermine the Spanish hold on its North American colonies. Jefferson described the expedition as "pacific," but the Spanish concluded that Jefferson's real goals were to extend American influence to the Pacific at the cost of Spain.[3]

The Spanish conclusion was reasonable, but it was, in fact, inaccurate. Jefferson often discussed the potential of the "West," a wonderfully vague term that people would subsequently assume referred to the whole of North America. Throughout much of his life, however, the West that mattered most to Jefferson extended from the Appalachian Mountains to the Mississippi River, not only because he saw a future for Americans in that region, but also because he feared that for all its potential this West was the most likely site of disunion. And he was hardly alone in this viewpoint. Regardless of their political affiliations, American policymakers worried about how best to govern the West in ways that would preserve both liberty and union.[4]

By 1803, the greatest concern was consolidation of the United States east of the Mississippi rather than expansion anywhere to the west of that region. Of course, Jefferson had written occasionally about a United States that reached to the Pacific, but he saw that in the distant future. By 1803, he certainly had taken no steps toward acquiring land west of the Mississippi River. Jefferson's directions to Meriwether Lewis—whether from June or November 1803—referred to *exploring* the West, not *settling* it. Consider as well another set of instructions, this one from Secretary of State James Madison to Robert R. Livingston and James Monroe, the American diplomats in Paris who were negotiating to settle the Mississippi Crisis. Madison informed the diplomats, "The object in view is to procure by just and satisfactory arrangements, a Cession to the United States, of New Orleans, and of West and East Florida, or as much thereof as the actual proprietor can be prevailed on to part with."[5] This cession was the Louisiana Purchase the United States sought in 1803, a parcel of land that did not even include the area that Lewis and Clark were supposed to explore.

Thus by the time Jefferson sent his June 1803 instructions to Lewis, he was anticipating a breakthrough in American international relations with France and Spain that would enable the United States to acquire a small area of land in the South and allow the Lewis and Clark Expedition to proceed through a Louisiana that remained under foreign ownership and management. Up to that point, however, all the news from Paris and Madrid had been bad. Still Jefferson remained confident that eventually something would change. What he did not know was that such a breakthrough had already occurred for reasons that had little to do with the United States. France had reacquired Louisiana from Spain as a means of supplying and defending its more profitable colonies in the Caribbean. First among these colonies was Saint-Domingue, the site of a revolt by slaves and free people of color. By 1803, the success of that revolt had led Napoleon Bonaparte to conclude that Saint-Domingue was not worth the cost, especially when he was planning for a war in Europe. As Napoleon made plans to abandon the Caribbean colony, he decided to dispense with Louisiana as well. In 1804, the successful revolutionaries in Saint-Domingue declared the independent Republic of Haiti. Meanwhile, Louisiana had changed hands one last time.[6]

In April 1803, the French informed the American delegation of their intention to sell everything they owned in North America. On 30 April, American and French negotiators completed work on a Louisiana Purchase that could not have been more different from the acquisition the administration sought. The most obvious change was what had been added: a vast domain north and west of New Orleans. Equally troubling was what it did not include: any guarantees of American possession of the Gulf Coast. News of the treaty took weeks to cross the Atlantic. In the meantime, Jefferson sent his 20 June instructions to Lewis before receiving the report. The first public announcements of the purchase came in the days surrounding 4 July 1803, and in the months that followed, Americans celebrated the purchase primarily because it ended the Mississippi Crisis, not because it extended the national domain.[7]

With the Spanish removed from the picture and a new American government taking charge of the lower Missouri, the Corps of Discovery could proceed west. Not only had the purchase enabled the expedition to go forward, but Jefferson's 16 November 1803 letter suggested just how important the expedition had become. After all, Jefferson had informed Lewis that "it becomes interesting to fix with precision by celestial observations" the rivers that formed the boundaries of Louisiana. The understatement here was considerable because establishing boundaries had become a vital matter of public policy. While a price of less than three cents per acre suggested that the Louisiana Purchase was a great bargain, it was nonetheless a poorly executed real estate deal. Nowhere in the detailed documents approved by France and the United States did it say exactly what constituted "Louisiana." In the second half of 1803, Jefferson and Madison ransacked their libraries, only to conclude that the vagueness of the treaty reflected the absence of a clear definition of Louisiana.[8]

As a result, the purchase had done more than facilitate the expedition; it had redefined it. The Louisiana Purchase unleashed a host of questions that could only be answered through expeditions like the Corps of Discovery. After 1803, the corps would have to do everything it had been created to do, but it would also have to help map the boundaries of the United States, establish who lived within its vastly expanded domain, and attempt to extend federal sovereignty over a landscape of powerful Indians, independent-minded frontiersman, and residual representatives of European empires. In the simplest terms, the Lewis and Clark Expedition mattered.

Nowhere did these new goals for the expedition become more clear than in a set of queries that Jefferson dispatched in July 1803 to a host of recipients throughout North America. The queries were similar to Jefferson's June instructions to Lewis, but they more directly applied to the particular concerns of the Louisiana Purchase. His first question was blunt: "What are the boundaries of Louisiana, and on what authority does each portion of them rest?" When it became clear that any boundary would be the subject of dispute, Jefferson made his understated comment to Lewis in November that it "becomes interesting to fix with precision by celestial observations" those boundaries. The rest of Jefferson's queries were a far stretch from his instructions to Lewis. His second query concerned "the distance from New Orleans to the nearest point of the Western boundary," and those that followed further reflected Jefferson's continued concern about the lower Mississippi valley. He asked about military fortifications, legal systems, and land claims. He sought details on the population, but mostly the white and black populations who dominated lower Louisiana rather than the Indians who dominated the north. Like his instructions to Lewis, these queries made no direct reference to settlement. They did not even concern exploration. Instead, they sought information that would be vital for the practical task of governing Louisiana.[9]

When the Corps of Discovery began its ascent of the Missouri River in the summer of 1804, Congress had already approved the Louisiana Purchase; American officials had taken charge in New Orleans and Saint Louis;

and Congress had just completed a contentious debate over creating a permanent territorial structure west of the Mississippi.[10] During the two years that followed, the Corps of Discovery was not only out of sight but truly out of mind within the administration. While Jefferson was, no doubt, personally concerned about the fate of his friend Lewis and his compatriots, other matters that seemed far more important to American policymakers overshadowed the fate of the expedition. Members of Congress and the administration were struggling to come to terms with the purchase in ways that hardly reflected the sort of confidence that the expedition might suggest. These challenges emerged in two arenas: the foreign pursuit of settling boundary disputes with Spain and the domestic pursuit of establishing a government for Louisiana.

While Lewis and Clark considered themselves successful in their diplomatic negotiations with American Indians, there was no such confidence concerning foreign relations in Washington. To the contrary, the years after the Louisiana Purchase would be among the most disastrous in American diplomatic history. Throughout the rest of his first term, Jefferson tried without success to secure a Spanish cession of the Floridas, which, it had become clear, were not part of the purchase. Meanwhile, relations with Great Britain became so strained that, by 1807, the administration had secured congressional approval to suspend all United States foreign trade, convinced the policy would coerce a change in London. The Embargo of 1807–1809 proved to be the most colossal failure of Jefferson's two terms, shattering the domestic economy, undermining the political base of the Jeffersonian Republicans, and fostering resistance throughout the republic.[11] James Monroe, the administration's point man in Europe, captured the sentiment of American policymakers in 1807 when he admitted that it was "painful to touch on" his experiences in Europe. "I [should] feel myself deficient in candour," he continued, "if I did not observe that at no period of my life was I ever subjected to more inquietude."[12]

The reasons for these failures were simple. The United States lacked the means to force change in Europe. Perhaps more important, the warfare unleashed by the French Revolution and the Napoleonic regime continued to dominate European affairs, and no European power would make strategic concessions to what looked like a weak and irrelevant republic in North America. The easy resolution of the Mississippi Crisis through the Louisiana Purchase had led the Jefferson Administration to an unrealistic sense of its own ability to influence world affairs. Before Lewis and Clark returned, however, the administration had received a dose of reality.

If American efforts to settle the diplomatic residue of the Louisiana Purchase had failed, things were not much better on the domestic front. Once again, the direct comparison to Lewis and Clark's experiences serves as a useful indicator. By the Mandan winter of 1804–1805, the time in which Lewis and Clark were learning how to live amicably with the Indians, a moment that suggested possibilities for interracial harmony, every other indication was that the Louisiana Purchase would bring disputes that could be costly, violent, or even disastrous. No sooner did the United States establish itself in Louisiana, than local residents began to resist the federal government. Much of the trouble came in lower Louisiana, an area redefined as the Territory of Orleans and corresponding roughly to the current state of Louisiana. Similar problems developed in the north, especially in the area that now constitutes Missouri, where the very weakness of the American hold prevented a more confrontational atmosphere.

When Congress extended the territorial system to envelop Louisiana, white Louisianians immediately protested the absence of elected offices, restrictions on the slave trade, and the activities of federal officials who showed little respect for local customs. While the federal government promised that Louisiana's residents would be incorporated into the United States, Louisianians claimed that the territorial government "does not 'incorporate us in the Union,' that it vests us with none of the 'rights,' gives us no advantages, and deprives us of all the 'immunities' of American citizens." Reminding Congress of the Declaration of Independence, the citizens of Louisiana asked: "Are truths, then, so well founded, so universally acknowledged, inapplicable only to us? Do political axioms on the Atlantic become problems when transferred to the shores of the Mississippi?"[13] While few Louisianians resisted the federal government, and statements like these actually suggested the benefit they saw from membership in the national community, policymakers in Washington nonetheless concluded that white Louisianians might yet join with Europeans to restore foreign control of the Mississippi.

Of even greater concern were signs of an imminent slave revolt modeled after the successful revolution in Saint-Domingue. In November 1804, for example, residents of Pointe Coupée, a plantation district outside New Orleans, rushed a petition with 105 signatures to William C. C. Claiborne, the territorial governor. "The revolution of St Domingo and other Places," the creatively spelled petition reported, "has become common amongs our Blacks.... A Sprit of Revolt and Mutyny has Crept in amongt Them."[14] Claiborne did not need much convincing. He also saw a "Spirit of Insurrection among the Negroes at Point Coupee."[15]

Last but not least, the Indians of the Mississippi River Valley and the eastern prairies were far more threatening to the administration than the Indians who welcomed Lewis and Clark, in large part because these Indian villagers were close at hand and because they refused to acknowledge American sovereignty on the administration's terms. In 1805, for example, Indian agent John Sibley informed the administration that the Spanish had told the Choctaw that "the Americans holding this country were all wind; that, if they were wise, they would abandon us and attach themselves to them, (the Spaniards,) for their old friends would not forsake them." Worse still, the Choctaw reported that the Spanish claimed they would "soon build a fort in Opelousas, and another at Attakapas, and one at or near Natchitoches, and proceed on towards New Orleans."[16] In September 1807, Indian agent Henry Bry put things more simply. He described the Choctaws as "very numerous & troublesome neighbours," a sentiment common to American officials regardless of the Indian villages they faced.[17]

In response to these challenges, the administration was forced to devote unprecedented resources to extending its territorial system. Dozens of public officials attempted to create a civil government in Louisiana. More than half the United States Army went west, settling in to stay as a safeguard against foreign powers or unruly residents. Not only did managing this system consume the time of federal leaders, but it proved tremendously expensive. It was only through the most elaborate financing that the United States had been able to afford the $15 million pricetag for the Louisiana Purchase. Managing Louisiana now rivaled the cost of buying it in the first place. If anything, this state of affairs seemed to affirm the administration's original intent *not* to seek the purchase of upper Louisiana, but rather to pursue commercial opportunities through ventures like the Lewis and Clark Expedition.

Lewis and Clark's return in 1806 corresponded with the moment at which the consequences of the Louisiana Purchase seemed most likely to cause domestic and foreign crises that might rip the nation apart. The ongoing boundary dispute with Spain and disagreements with Indians on the

Texas-Louisiana borderlands had exacerbated international tensions to the point that many observers predicted war, either between the United States and Spain or between the United States and southwestern Indians. Meanwhile, Jefferson had received reports that his own former vice-president, Aaron Burr, was organizing a separatist scheme designed to carve an independent republic in the Southwest. In the end, both crises defused themselves. American, Spanish, and Indian negotiators settled the boundary crisis by creating the Neutral Ground, a strip of land between Texas and Louisiana that would be off-limits to both nations. Federal troops arrested Burr and hauled him back to the East Coast for trial on various charges. Although eventually acquitted, Burr soon left the United States. Yet these victories hardly reduced the administration's fears. To the contrary, they seemed to prove that the United States had only the most precarious hold on the Louisiana Purchase.[18]

In the months after their return, Lewis and Clark would also be reminded of just how much could go wrong when Americans attempted to explore Spanish territory. Jefferson had dispatched two other major expeditions. The first, under Thomas Freeman and Peter Custis, ascended the Red River along the contested Louisiana-Texas borderlands in the summer of 1806. In the second, Zebulon M. Pike ventured out to explore the headwaters of the Arkansas River that same summer. Both expeditions endured the fate that could have awaited Lewis and Clark before 1803. The Spanish intercepted Freeman and Custis, forcing a premature end to their expedition. Meanwhile, Pike got lost in the Rockies, eventually descending the Rio Grande before he and his men were arrested by the Spanish. They traveled to Mexico City and endured imprisonment in a Spanish jail before they eventually returned to the United States.[19]

In contrast, by the fall of 1806, Lewis and Clark had returned safe and sound from a transcontinental journey, in no small part because the purchase had cleared the way. That anybody other than a small community of scientists and cartographers cared about the expedition was also a result of the purchase. Lewis and Clark could describe in detail a land that had suddenly become "American." Even so, governing the West—not exploring it— was now the dominant concern of the Jeffersonian Republicans. The fact that purchasing Louisiana had been simpler than governing it also helps explain the fate of Lewis and Clark after the expedition. In the context of the Corps of Discovery, the logical focus is the relationship between Lewis,

Clark, and Jefferson, but in understanding Lewis and Clark's broader professional careers—especially as they relate to the Louisiana Purchase—the focus shifts away from Jefferson toward James Madison.

As an author of the United States Constitution and a member of Congress from Virginia, Madison wielded a profound impact on federal policymaking. That he was also Jefferson's closest confidante only increased his influence once Jefferson became president in 1801. At the same time, Madison also became secretary of state in an age when that office possessed unprecedented powers. In addition to supervising foreign affairs, the State Department was the nexus for domestic policymaking. The secretary served as the president's liaison with Congress and with state governors. During this time, too, the attorney general served primarily as legal counsel to the president, and the State Department coordinated many of the activities that would later become the purview of the Justice Department. Most importantly, however, the State Department had direct responsibility for civil government in the far-flung federal territories.[20] In 1803, the acquisition of Louisiana made James Madison the chief official for a series of territories that almost outnumbered the existing states and certainly exceeded them in geographic area. When Madison became president in 1809, he was unwilling to surrender much real power to his own secretary of state, Robert Smith, whom he distrusted. Only when James Monroe succeeded Smith in 1811 did Madison begin to loosen his grip on domestic policymaking.

By the fall of 1806, under Madison's supervision, the Louisiana Purchase had become two American jurisdictions. Congress initially divided the purchase in 1804 into the Territory of Orleans (including much of what now constitutes the State of Louisiana) and the District of Louisiana (including everything else). The District of Louisiana actually came under the jurisdiction of the Indiana Territory, a fact that generated the unrest that, together with agitation throughout the purchase territories, so worried the Jefferson Administration. In 1805, Congress revised the governments of both territories, creating a distinct Territory of Louisiana, which would have its own governor and civil apparatus separate from Indiana.

Jefferson and Madison struggled to find acceptable men to take on the considerable challenges of governing the new Louisiana Territory. In 1806, Lewis and Clark seemed to be the logical selections, and they certainly fit the profile for territorial officials. Western men of proven talents, unquestioned loyalty to the Jeffersonian Republicans, and frontier experience,

Lewis and Clark had the same resumés as a host of officials who took charge of federal territories during the first quarter of the nineteenth century. Born in the 1770s, trained either in the military or in civil appointment, these men reflected a cohesive Jeffersonian vision of how government in an extended republic would work.[21] As governor of the Louisiana Territory, Lewis was responsible not only for civil government but also for promoting commercial prosperity, preserving a system of racial supremacy over slaves and Indians, and safeguarding the national borders against Spanish America to the south and British Canada to the north. Clark would be a crucial player in this policy, serving as a general in the territorial militia and as director of Indian affairs, which were related appointments, for the territorial militia's primary task was to serve as a force against Indians.

Lewis's failure as governor of Louisiana has been linked to causes ranging from alcoholism, to mental illness, to undue personal attacks by his subordinates, to a lack of support from his superiors in Washington. His relationship with Madison certainly seems to suggest the importance of these personal matters. Lewis and Madison were never close. The two men had certainly met, if not before 1801, then certainly after Madison became Jefferson's secretary of state and Lewis his personal secretary. Neither man ever complained about the other, and both probably respected one another. Yet neither man *wrote* to the other, a stunning fact in a time when public officials were regular correspondents. The fact that they could easily meet in the federal capital does not explain the absence of correspondence. Jefferson and Madison maintained a voluminous correspondence, even when their offices were in neighboring buildings. The extent of conversation between Lewis and Madison is epitomized by a rare 1807 letter from Lewis. Short and formal, it focuses entirely on matters related to his recompense as governor. "You will find herewith inclosed an Account with a receipt annexed for my salary as governor of the Territory of Louisiana," Lewis wrote from Philadelphia on 28 June 1807.[22] This businesslike relationship between the two men only deteriorated in the years that followed.

But an emphasis on personal or emotional factors has profound limitations, in large part because it ignores other factors related to the particular challenges emerging from the Louisiana Purchase. By the time that Lewis left Saint Louis for Washington, D.C., in the fall of 1809, it was abundantly clear that the governor had failed to achieve the objectives of territorial policy. He was supposed to promote a stable political system; his own shrill response to his opponents showed his failure to do so. He was supposed to establish a vigorous system of regional trade; his debts showed his failure there, too. He was supposed to establish federal sovereignty over Indians; by 1809, most tribes remained independent polities. All these goals—political development, commercial prosperity, and racial supremacy—were supposed to secure the Union in the West. On all fronts, Lewis failed, a failure so great because the stakes were so high. Many Americans were convinced of the need to consolidate control over the purchase territories in order to avoid regional chaos that might eventually consume the whole Union.[23]

If the story of Meriwether Lewis's suicide in October 1809 now seems a tragic tale, in the early 1800s, it was more cautionary than anything else. It suggested the dangers of dissipation and the high cost of failure. Within only a few years, William Clark would provide an equally compelling story, but in his case, the tale would illustrate the ways in which the frontiers of North America created opportunities for men of talent to realize their capacities while also making important contributions to the nation. At the most basic level, Lewis died a single man in great debt with his public career in shambles, while Clark left a small fortune to his children after acquiring a reputation as one of the West's leading citizens. But I would also suggest that if Lewis exemplified the administration's fears about how the governance of the Louisiana Purchase could spin out of control, Clark exemplified the sort of western man who could preserve the Union as it expanded.

Like Lewis, William Clark was faithful to the administration. Unlike Lewis, he also seemed reliable, especially to James Madison. Clark remained in his post of militia commander and Indian agent as a series of men served as governor of the Louisiana Territory. Finally, in 1813, Madison selected him to serve as governor, just as the region was renamed the Missouri Territory to avoid confusion with the State of Louisiana, created the year before. Clark governed under extremely trying circumstances. He coordinated Missouri's defenses during the War of 1812 against the possibility of a British invasion from the north or (more likely) an Indian assault from the west.

Clark also oversaw the rapid growth in white settlement, which led to increasingly common conflicts with Indians and growing demands for statehood. As early as 1812, residents of the Territory of Louisiana argued that the "sister territories of Orleans, Mississippi and Indiana, are fast approaching to political manhood."[24] By 1819, Congress was ready to debate Missouri statehood. The results of that debate transformed American politics. Members of Congress opposed to the expansion of slavery began to argue that Congress should alter Missouri's proposed constitution in ways that would lead to the elimination of slavery. The explosive debate within Congress spread to the nation at large, establishing slavery at the center of American politics in the decades that followed and defining the antebellum era in ways different from the early republic.[25] As Missouri stood poised to enter the Union, Clark's role changed once again, as he failed in his bid to become the first elected governor of the State of Missouri. The loss reflected the broader changes signaled by the debate on slavery. The increasingly democratic politics of the West left no room for Jefferson's western men, who, like Lewis and Clark, had spent their lives securing appointment from above rather than election from below.

As we have seen, Lewis and Clark's personal fates were inextricably tied to events surrounding the Louisiana Purchase, just as their mission in 1804–1806 had been redefined by that event. In addition, the context of Jefferson's instructions before and after the purchase agreement allows for a reconsideration of their diplomacy among the American Indians. Scholars, popular writers, and general commentators have tended to describe the Corps of Discovery in two ways. One portrait emphasizes the relatively amicable relations between the Corps of Discovery and most of its numerous hosts. Another portrait describes Lewis and Clark as the vanguard of an Anglo-American onslaught that would lead to the betrayal and wholesale destruction of Indians in the North American West on a scale that no European power ever attempted. Both portraits are, in fact, accurate, even if they remain contradictory. Lewis and Clark *were* committed to cultivating friendly relations with Indians. Jefferson had ordered Lewis in June 1803 to "treat them [the Indians] in the most friendly & conciliatory manner." This order had the practical benefit of insuring safety and securing future good will. In June 1803, Jefferson had no intention of extending American sovereignty to encompass those Indians, nor had he learned that American negotiators had in fact signed a treaty that would force him to do so.

Once the United States owned Louisiana, however, Jefferson began to think of western Indians in much the same way that he perceived others throughout the United States. The native peoples had to acknowledge American sovereignty and power. In February 1803, Jefferson had informed

William Henry Harrison, governor of the Indiana Territory, that "our settlements will gradually circumscribe and approach the Indians, and they will in time either incorporate with us as citizens of the United States, or remove beyond the Mississippi. The former is certainly the termination of their history most happy for themselves; but, in the whole course of this, it is essential to cultivate their love. As to their fear, we presume that our strength and their weakness is now so visible that they must see we have only to shut our hand to crush them, and that all our liberalities to them proceed from motives of pure humanity only."[26] After the Louisiana Purchase, Jefferson and subsequent presidents would extend this logic farther west.

Jefferson made those comments in the context of governance rather than exploration. Lewis and Clark's efforts to combine those two worlds, however, led them to pursue strategies that put them at odds with white settlers. Lewis's efforts to reach a just accommodation with Indians proved problematic at best. White settlers resented his efforts on behalf of Indians, while at the same time, "the Osage Indians Appear to be much dissatisfied in Consequence of a treaty that was made by Governor Lewis in 1808," the army reported.[27] Clark's longevity in office eventually led him to become an agent of the principles that Jefferson articulated in his letter to Harrison, although Clark continued to advocate humane and honest relations with Indians. As territorial governor, however, his primary responsibility was to white settlers. In 1815, for example, he reported, "eight parties of the hostile Indians . . . have visited the frontiers of this Territory and killed ten men. One of these parties (a fiew days ago) attacked a small french Village . . . they killed 4 men plundered the houses and burnt down part of the Town." In the same letter, he expressed his own pleasure that the War Department had dispatched a force of five hundred troops to the Missouri Territory "as a Check to the Indians."[28] In time, the administration of Andrew Jackson abandoned the Jeffersonians' schizophrenic approach to Indian policy for the blunter process of forced removal. As superintendent of Indian affairs at Saint Louis, William Clark eventually helped implement that policy in the Missouri region.

During the 1820s, white settlers rushed to acquire land that seemed cheap, fertile, and abundant in the West. In the process, these people began to transform the meaning of expansion. In 1803, the Lewis and Clark Expedition had sought commercial opportunities through the waterways of the

North American interior, and the Louisiana Purchase had sought to preserve security east of the Mississippi. To the American policymakers who orchestrated both events, every piece of evidence indicated that the far West did not lend itself to permanent agricultural settlement. The American Indians who lived in that West, however, had found that the Great Plains were, in fact, the site of magnificent bounty. A generation after Lewis and Clark, white settlers reached the same conclusion. At that point, the Louisiana Purchase and the governors of its territories were hardly guardians against dangers in the West. Rather, they became the gatekeepers to new opportunities.

NOTES

1. "Jefferson's Instructions to Lewis, [20 June 1803]," in *Letters of the Lewis and Clark Expedition with Related Documents, 1783–1854*, ed. Donald Jackson, 2d ed., rev., 2 vols. (Urbana: University of Illinois Press, 1978), 1:61–66.

2. Jefferson to Lewis, 16 Nov. 1803, ibid., p. 137.

3. Alexander DeConde, *This Affair of Louisiana* (Baton Rouge: Louisiana State University Press, 1976), pp. 107–46; James E. Lewis, Jr., *The American Union and the Problem of Neighborhood: The United States and the Collapse of the Spanish Empire, 1783–1829* (Chapel Hill: University of North Carolina Press, 1998), pp. 29–32.

4. Andrew R. L. Cayton, "'Separate Interests' and the Nation-State: The Washington Administration and the Origins of Regionalism in the Trans-Appalachian West," *Journal of American History* 79 (June 1992): 39–67; Lewis, *American Union and the Problem of Neighborhood*, pp. 29–32; Drew R. McCoy, "James Madison and Visions of American Nationality in the Confederation Period: A Regional Perspective," in *Beyond Confederation: Origins of the Constitution and American National Identity*, ed. Richard Beeman, Stephen Botein, and Edward C. Carter II (Chapel Hill: University of North Carolina Press, 1987), pp. 226–58; Peter S. Onuf, "Liberty, Development, and Union: Visions of the West in the 1780s," *William and Mary Quarterly* 3rd. ser., 43 (Apr. 1986): 179–213.

5. Madison to Livingston and Monroe, 2 Mar. 1803, in *The Papers of James Madison: Secretary of State Series*, Vol. 4: *8 October 1802–15 May 1803*, ed. Mary A. Hackett et al. (Charlottesville: University Press of Virginia, 1998), p. 364.

6. Thomas Fiehrer, "Saint-Domingue/Haiti: Louisiana's Caribbean Connection," *Louisiana History* 30 (1989): 419–37; Tim Matthewson, "Jefferson and Haiti," *Journal of Southern History* 61 (May 1995): 209–49.

7. Jerry W. Knudson, "Newspaper Reaction to the Louisiana Purchase, 'This New, Immense, Unbounded World,'" *Missouri Historical Review* 63 (Jan. 1969): 182–213; Betty Houchin Winfield, "Public Perception and Public Events: The Louisiana

Purchase and the American Partisan Press," in *The Louisiana Purchase: Emergence of an American Nation*, ed. Peter J. Kastor (Washington, D.C.: CQ Press, 2002), pp. 38–50. For a general history of the Louisiana Purchase, see Jon Kukla, *A Wilderness So Immense: The Louisiana Purchase and the Destiny of America* (New York: Alfred A. Knopf, 2003).

8. Jefferson, "An Examination into the Boundaries of Louisiana," 7 Sept. 1803, in *Thomas Jefferson Papers* (Washington, D.C.: Library of Congress Microfilm Collection, n.d.), vol. 135, pp. 23267–71; Madison to Monroe, "An inquiry concerning the Northern Boundary of Canada and Louisiana," 1803, in *James Madison Papers* (Washington, D.C.: Library of Congress Microfilm Collection, n.d.), Reel 8.

9. Jefferson, "A series of 17 questions on Boundaries," [July 1803], in *Jefferson Papers*, vol. 137, pp. 23705–8. The quest for a definition of Louisiana that fit the administration's goals also explains Jefferson's reference to "a greater breadth on the gulph of Mexico" in his 16 November letter. Much of his library exploration into the boundaries of Louisiana had been a search for evidence that West Florida might indeed be covered by the new treaty. By the end of the year, however, even Jefferson and Madison had to admit that the purchase did not encompass the Floridas, and the Spanish had made clear they would not relinquish control anyway.

10. James E. Scanlon, "A Sudden Conceit: Jefferson and the Louisiana Government Bill of 1804," *Louisiana History* 9 (1968): 139–62; U.S., *The Public Statutes at Large of the United States of America*, 8 vols. (Boston: Charles C. Little & James Brown, 1845), 2:283–89. The details of congressional debate are scattered throughout U. S., *Annals of Congress: Debates and Proceedings of the Congress of the United States* (Washington, D.C.: Gales & Seaton, 1834–1856).

11. Lewis, *The American Union and the Problem of Neighborhood*, pp. 55–59; Burton Spivak, *Jefferson's English Crisis: Commerce, Embargo, and the Republican Revolution* (Charlottesville: University Press of Virginia, 1979); J. C. A. Stagg, *Mr. Madison's War: Politics, Diplomacy, and Warfare in the Early American Republic, 1783–1830* (Princeton, N.J.: Princeton University Press, 1983), pp. 22–30, 136–39; Reginald C. Stuart, "Special Interests and National Authority in Foreign Policy: American-British Provincial Links during the Embargo and the War of 1812," *Diplomatic History* 8 (1984): 311–28.

12. Monroe to Jefferson, 1 June 1807, in *The Writings of James Monroe*, 7 vols. (New York: G. P. Putnam's Sons, 1898–1903), 5:5n.1.

13. "Remonstrance of the People of Louisiana against the Political System Adopted by Congress for Them," 31 Dec. 1804, in *American State Papers: Documents, Legislative and Executive, of the Congress of the United States*, 38 vols. (Washington, D.C.: Gales & Seaton, 1832–1861), 22:396–97. See also 2:582.

14. "Petition to Governor Claiborne by Inhabitants of Pointe Coupée," 9 Nov.

1804, in *The Territorial Papers of the United States*, ed. Clarence E. Carter, 28 vols. (Washington, D.C.: Government Printing Office, 1934–1975), 9:326. See also Claiborne to District Commandants, 8 Nov. 1804, ibid., pp. 325–26; Marquis de Casa Calvo to Claiborne, 9 Nov. 1804, ibid., pp. 328–29; and John Watkins to the City Council, 14 Mar. 1806, in *Messages from the Mayor to the Conseil de Ville*, 18 vols. (New Orleans: New Orleans Public Library Microfilm Collection, n.d.), 2:29–31.

15. Claiborne to Richard Butler, 8 Nov. 1804, in *The Letter Books of William C. C. Claiborne, 1801–1816*, ed. Dunbar Rowland, 6 vols. (Jackson: Mississippi State Archive, 1917), 3:1.

16. John Sibley to Henry Dearborn, 1 May 1805, in U.S., *Annals of Congress*, 9th Cong., 1st sess., p. 1205. Captain Edward Turner sent a similar report based on identical sources. See Turner to James Wilkinson, 3 May 1805, ibid., p. 1206.

17. Henry Bry to Henry Dearborn, 1 Sept. 1807, Letters Received, Records of the Secretary of War, Record Group 107, National Archives Microfilm Publication M22, Roll 4, B-295.

18. Villasana Haggard, "The Neutral Ground between Louisiana and Texas, 1806-1821," *Louisiana Historical Quarterly* 28 (1945): 1001–1128.

19. Dan Flores, ed., *Jefferson & Southwestern Exploration: The Freeman & Custis Accounts of the Red River Expedition of 1806* (Norman: University of Oklahoma Press, 1984); Donald Jackson, *Thomas Jefferson & the Stony Mountains: Exploring the West from Monticello* (Urbana: University of Illinois Press, 1981), pp. 226–34, 242–63.

20. By comparison, the vice-president wielded limited constitutional powers and even more limited political power. As a result, men aspiring to become president coveted the office of secretary of state. Indeed, every president from 1801 to 1829 served as secretary of state. Jefferson served as both secretary and vice-president, but the latter office was a fluke of the original constitutional structure, which required that the candidate for president with the second most electoral votes become vice-president. Once the Twelfth Amendment established specific candidates for both president and vice-president, the vice-presidency was occupied by a series of aging politicians selected to deliver regional support. Martin Van Buren began his cabinet service as Andrew Jackson's secretary of state, only to switch to the vice-presidency in 1832, which began the process of establishing greater power and influence for subsequent vice-presidents.

21. Marion Nelson Winship, "The Territorial Aspirations of William Charles Cole Claiborne: A Western Success Story from the Jeffersonian Empire," paper presented at the 1998 meeting of the Society for Historians of the Early American Republic, State College, Pa.

22. Lewis to Madison, 28 June 1807, in *Territorial Papers of the United States*, ed. Carter, 14:131.

23. For Lewis's tenure as territorial governor, see Robert A. Rutland et al.,

eds., *The Papers of James Madison: Presidential Series*, 5 vols. (Charlottesville: University Press of Virginia, 1984–2004), 1:381n.2; William E. Foley, *The Genesis of Missouri: From Wilderness Outpost to Statehood* (Columbia: University of Missouri Press, 1989), pp. 190, 213–14.

24. Letter to the editor, 17 Aug. 1811, *Louisiana Gazette* (St. Louis), 3 Oct. 1811. The statement may seem to represent the strangest of mixed metaphors, but it was entirely consistent with the sort of language that people used at the time. Politics was a fundamentally masculine activity, and statehood represented political maturity for Missouri. At the same time, Americans also referred to "sister states" when emphasizing equality and sentimental attachments among the polities that together formed the Union. For documents leading up to statehood, *see* "Petition to Congress from the Inhabitants of the Territory of Louisiana," 9 Sept. 1811, and "Resolutions of a Meeting of the Town and District of St. Louis," 5 Nov. 1811, both in *Territorial Papers of the United States*, ed. Carter, 14:471–72, 484–85.

25. Robert E. Bonner, "Empire of Liberty, Empire of Slavery: The Louisiana Territories and the Fate of American Bondage," in *Louisiana Purchase*, ed. Kastor, pp. 129–38; Glover Moore, *The Missouri Controversy, 1819–1821* (Lexington: University of Kentucky Press, 1953).

26. Jefferson to Harrison, 27 Feb. 1803, in *Thomas Jefferson: Writings*, comp. Merrill D. Peterson (New York: Library of America, 1984), p. 1118.

27. Capt. Eli B. Clemson to Secretary of War William Eustis, 28 Mar. 1810, in *Territorial Papers of the United States*, ed. Carter, 14:399.

28. William Clark to Secretary of War James Monroe, 17 Apr. 1815, ibid., 15:25.

In Search of the Historical William Clark

WILLIAM E. FOLEY

In the grand narrative of American progress and achievement, William Clark stands proud and tall at the side of his friend and partner Meriwether Lewis, almost as if joined at the hip. Their exploits have become a source of national pride, and the bicentennial of their great odyssey promises to further elevate their status as American icons. The journey to the Pacific was as remarkable as it was daunting. It was a team effort, and while circumstances may have relegated Clark to second billing, he was no second fiddle. Almost every schoolchild who has studied the expedition knows the drill. Clark was a superb cartographer, a skilled waterman, and a loyal partner with a knack for Indian diplomacy to boot. With his African-American servant York usually nearby, the stalwart Clark provided a welcome and steadying presence as he and Lewis guided their tiny band through uncharted wilderness territory in search of a practicable passage to the western sea. And it was Clark who befriended the Indian woman Sacagawea, her French husband Charbonneau, and the boy Pomp. All this of course is true, but as compelling as this familiar tale of triumph and success may be, it is in many ways a caricature that obscures the complexities and ambiguities of the historical William Clark.

In truth, William Clark is not an easy person to fathom, and any effort to take his full measure must draw from the totality of experiences in a life that spanned nearly threescore and ten years. His was a long and complicated journey that began in the gentrified world of Revolutionary Virginia during the seedtime of the American republic and ended in the booming western entrepot of Saint Louis during a commercial revolution then transforming the American marketplace. William Clark devoted the greater part of his life to public service as a soldier and as a government bureaucrat. The peripatetic official's assignments frequently placed him at center stage in the national quest to possess and occupy North America's vast western expanses. Important as it was, the Voyage of Discovery represents only a single episode in what was for Clark a lengthy wilderness journey. The celebratory tone of so many of the bicentennial observances intended to honor Clark seems to belie the reality of a lifetime in which disappointment, pain, and adversity all too often crowded out public adulation and private contentment. That should not be taken to mean that his was a life bereft of satisfaction, success, and happiness, for such was not the case. But it does suggest that the totality of William Clark's experiences make him far more interesting and human than some heroic figure on a pedestal.

William Clark was born in Caroline County, Virginia, on 1 August 1770, the ninth of John and Ann Rogers Clark's ten children. The Clarks' modest landholdings and small number of slaves were sufficient to bestow social respectability and more than a nodding acquaintance with some of Virginia's better families, but like so many other members of the lesser gentry, John Clark continued to hope for more. Billy, as the family liked to call him, grew up in a household where dances, parties, and family gatherings were an integral part of life. One can credit that social milieu for nurturing the sociability, good manners, and gentlemanly bearing that William Clark exhibited as an adult. But that genteel Virginia society also rested on a slaveholding system that treated African Americans as human chattel, and Clark bore that mark as well.

During the Revolutionary War, the Clarks were staunch defenders of the American cause, and all five of Billy's older brothers served as officers in Virginia fighting units. Too young to take up arms, Billy was relegated to following the conflict vicariously through the military feats of his siblings. After the war in 1784, John and Ann Clark and their four youngest children yielded to Kentucky fever and joined the growing exodus of Virginians bound for "Cantuck" in search of a new and better life. Billy's brother George Rogers Clark, who had won fame for his exploits in the Revolution's westernmost theater, had long urged them to join him there. Billy, who was fourteen at the time, took to his new surroundings with nary a glance backward in the direction of Old Virginny. Brother George helped him hone the survival skills that were so essential to successful wilderness living—shooting, hunting, and navigating in the woods, and it was not long before the rapidly maturing youngest son felt comfortable in venturing forth into the countryside on his own.

William Clark, *attributed to John Wesley Jarvis, ca. 1810*
(Missouri Historical Society, Saint Louis)

Because the Clarks prized literacy and learning, they did not neglect the more traditional components of Billy's education. There were fewer schools and tutors on the Kentucky frontier than in Virginia, so he had to be mostly home schooled. While he did not have the advantages of a classical education, Billy Clark was an eager learner whose natural inquisitiveness prompted him to pursue knowledge throughout his life. The youthful scholar shared his brother George's fondness for history, geography, and natural history and began developing his skills as a draftsman. He occasionally found time to enjoy an entertaining novel, and in later years when the opportunity presented itself, he seldom passed up a good play. The deficiencies of his education—particularly his creative spelling—have been well documented and more than a little overblown. Spelling variations were commonplace even in the writings of the best-educated Americans, and over the course of time, Clark's spelling improved. His vocabulary bespoke someone who was well read, and while he might spell velocity "verlocity," he knew the word's meaning. Clark seldom used more words than necessary to deliver his message, and his simple and to-the-point style offers an unadorned eloquence that modern readers still find captivating.

By the time that William Clark reached his eighteenth birthday in 1788, the amiable, physically-fit six-footer stood ready to strike out on his own. From his close-knit and high-achieving family, he acquired steady habits, ambition and a desire to succeed, and the personal qualities of honesty and integrity. He had learned other lessons as well. The unhappy consequences of George Rogers Clark's sometimes-volatile temperament and his growing intemperance alerted Billy at a young age to the dangers of inconstancy and excess. As he matured, William became a steadying presence in his much-admired older brother's tempestuous life. It was a role that he would master and frequently put to good use—most notably in his friendship with an equally troubled Meriwether Lewis.

His Anglican parents' belief in a higher power gave him a conviction "that religious duties consist in doing justice, loveing mercy, and endeavouring to make our fellow creatures happy," but such altruistic notions did not dampen his appetite for financial gain.[1] Growing up in eighteenth-century Virginia's planting society, William Clark learned to value land as a measure of status and success and to believe that its ownership helped guarantee personal freedom and independence. He also absorbed the principles of Enlightenment thought and the commitment to republican ideology that Virginia's revolutionary generation embraced so ardently. As he later wrote: "My political character is well known to be republican. It was formed in the school of those who have engaged the confidence of the American people."[2]

William Clark's Kentucky years did not fundamentally alter those basic Virginia precepts. The distinctive conditions of the American frontier simply opened new avenues for realizing his by then well-established ambitions. Kentucky was in the 1780s a dark and bloody ground where land-hungry newcomers battled with the native peoples who for generations had hunted, farmed, and made their homes in the now-contested zone. Given his family's commitment to duty and military service, Billy Clark's decision to enlist in a Kentucky militia company at age nineteen came as no surprise, nor did his 1792 acceptance of a lieutenant's commission in the regular United States Army.

During his four-year army stint, he served under General Anthony Wayne, participated in the historic Battle of Fallen Timbers as a member of the Fourth Sub Legion, and briefly commanded Ensign Meriwether Lewis. After considerable soul searching, Clark determined to leave military service and, as he put it, "seek some more honorable employment for my youthful days." His decision was driven by poor health (a burden he bore most of his life with relatively little complaint), a nagging sense that his army superiors had never properly recognized his efforts, a yearning to try his hand in the world of commerce, and a sense of obligation to his aging parents and his brother George, who increasingly stood in need of his assistance.[3]

After resigning his army commission, he set about to put George's troubled finances in order. In rushing to his brother's aid, William Clark assumed obligations that jeopardized his own financial standing, subjected him to endless suits and litigation, and at times threatened to leave him impoverished. He tried his hand at business and looked after the family farm outside of Louisville, which he inherited from his father in 1799, even though a farmer's life never seemed William Clark's preferred calling. With both of his parents gone, he settled into the boredom of a quiet life at Mulberry Hill in the company of his brother George, whose chronic alcoholism had hastened his decline.

Seeking opportunities that yet might yield that elusive fortune that was always just beyond his grasp, William Clark embarked in 1801 on a grand tour that took him to Philadelphia, Baltimore, Washington, D.C., and the old Virginia neighborhood where brothers Jonathan and Edmund still resided. In the unfinished new federal city, he paid a call on his friend Meriwether Lewis, who recently had accepted a position as President Thomas Jefferson's private secretary and personal aide. While visiting the President's House, Clark had his first opportunity to meet the illustrious Mr. Jefferson, so well known to others in his family.[4]

Upon his return to Louisville, William Clark learned that a fire at Mulberry Hill had destroyed his mill along with many tools and implements. Yet another judgment against George threatened them both with financial ruin and eventually forced William to take drastic measures to stave off bankruptcy. In 1803, he sold the Jefferson County properties he had inherited from his parents to his more prosperous brothers Jonathan and Edmund, now in Kentucky. William and George moved across the river to Clark's Point in Indiana, where they occupied a simple cabin that was a considerable step down from their family home.[5]

On the eve of his thirty-third birthday, William Clark was unmarried and unemployed, with few immediate prospects in either category. His efforts at soldiering, farming, and business had produced only modest gains, but unknown to him at that gloomy moment, destiny was about to call. With his fortunes at low ebb, it was little wonder that Clark jumped at the chance to accept Lewis's invitation to join the president's proposed western tour with its proffer of "honors & rewards."[6] That epic journey rescued him from a humdrum existence at Clarksville and thrust him into the pages of history in the company of Meriwether Lewis. Forever after, Clark would be remembered as Lewis's partner.

In September of 1806, Lewis and Clark returned to a rousing welcome in Saint Louis before setting off on a triumphal parade eastward that ended in the national capital, where a grateful president offered Lewis the governorship of the Louisiana Territory and named Clark to serve as the principal United States Indian agent for tribes west of the Mississippi River and as brigadier general of Louisiana's territorial militia. Clark's acceptance of those positions marked the beginning of a lengthy and productive association with the territory and state of Missouri, which he would come to call "the home of my choice and the country of my permanent residence."[7]

Compensation from the Pacific expedition, along with a promise of the two posts in the Louisiana Territory, emboldened William Clark at long last to seek a proper wife. He was almost giddy as he teasingly hinted to those in his immediate circle that he had marriage on the mind.[8] His intended was a pretty, well-born Virginia lass named Judith Hancock, twenty-one years his junior. In her honor, he christened the scenic Montana stream that he had first seen in May 1805 the Judith River.[9] In January 1807, Clark even passed up attending a gala dinner hosted in his honor in the federal city to tarry a bit longer in Virginia. Julia, as Clark always called her, obviously reciprocated his interest, and before he departed to take up residence in the Louisiana Territory, she had consented to marry him early the next year.

Following his arrival in Saint Louis in May 1807, in Lewis's absence Clark immediately took steps to counter the growing British influence among the Indian tribes in the region and to shore up the territory's inadequate defenses. Among other things, he worked with local officials to improve the state of military readiness by revising territorial militia laws, but he devoted most of his time to Indian matters. Like Jefferson and Lewis, Clark viewed trade as a crucial element in securing tribal acquiescence to the American regime and, more importantly, as a tool for securing land concessions. Late in the year, he hurried back to Virginia to marry Julia in early January. When the happy couple arrived in Saint Louis to set up housekeeping the following June, Governor Lewis, who by then had made it to the Louisiana Territory, welcomed them with open arms.

Not long thereafter, Lewis dispatched Clark on a mission to establish a combined United States trading factory and military fort on the Missouri River and to negotiate land concessions from the powerful Osage Nation. Clark oversaw the construction of the new installation known as Fort Osage, and with the aid of Paw-Hiu-Skah, a compliant tribal leader, he persuaded representatives of the Osage Nation to sign a treaty that ceded their Missouri and Arkansas homelands to the United States. That treaty soon came under fire and had to be renegotiated when angry members of the fragmented Osage tribe rejected Paw-Hui-Skah's claims to leadership and questioned his authority to represent them in negotiations. Nonetheless, this 1808 Osage Treaty was the first of more than thirty such agreements negotiated under William Clark's superintendence.[10]

Although Clark had been willing to do what was necessary to secure tribal acquiescence to the Osage land cession, on more than one occasion in his role as Indian superintendent he came to the defense of beleaguered native people. In 1810, he recommended a presidential pardon for a Sac Indian convicted of murdering a white trader. Later that year, he characterized a band of transplanted Shawnees as "a peaceable and well disposed people . . . of great service to our frontier settlements."[11]

Clark did not allow his public responsibilities to keep him from doing business on the side. With a family to support, he was eager to supplement his modest government salary. In January of 1809, Julia had given birth to their first child, a son whom they proudly named Meriwether Lewis

Clark. He was the first of the couple's five children. Later that year, Clark had joined forces with Manuel Lisa, Pierre Chouteau, and several other prominent local traders and merchants to form the Saint Louis Missouri Fur Company, and for a time he acted as the firm's principal agent in Saint Louis.

Governor Lewis's decision to give the Saint Louis company a lucrative government contract for returning the Mandan chieftain Shehekeshote, or White Coyote, to his village on the upper Missouri River drew fire in Washington and prompted Lewis to undertake a trip to the federal capital to defend his actions. Clark shared Lewis's assessment that the arrangement was justified and defensible, but the official censure was simply one more disappointment for the already despondent governor. His tragic death on the Natchez Trace was a blow to William Clark, but the shocking news had not come as a total surprise, and Clark always believed that his partner had taken his own life. He declined an invitation to replace Lewis as governor but elected to remain in Saint Louis in his current posts. Clark also had to assume the added burden of arranging for the long-delayed publication of the expedition's journals. As the years passed, Lewis and Clark's once celebrated feats faded from the public memory, and William Clark moved ahead with his life.

The outbreak of the War of 1812 presented him with new and more serious challenges, especially after he relented in 1813 and finally agreed to serve as Missouri's territorial governor, a post he occupied until Missouri became a state. With only limited means at his disposal, Governor Clark sought to strike an uneasy balance in his dealings with Indian people. In 1814, he led a controversial military expedition to Prairie du Chien on the upper Mississippi in the heart of British country, a move that his critics would later question. After the war, Clark played a key role in peace negotiations with the numerous western tribes who had taken up arms against the United States.

Although Indian affairs occupied much of Governor Clark's time, he also had to address the problems of governing a frontier territory where personal feuds and animosities frequently exacerbated disagreements over public policy. Despite an inclination to favor influential members of the territorial establishment, Clark proved to be the best by far of Missouri's territorial governors. But his noteworthy record as a public servant proved insufficient to counter a popular perception that he was stiff, reserved, inhospitable, and too friendly with Indians. Missouri voters overwhelmingly rejected his bid to become the new state's first elected governor in 1820.

After statehood, Clark retained his position as United States Indian agent, and in 1822, federal officials gave him the title of superintendent of Indian affairs at Saint Louis, a post he held until his death there in 1838. Notwithstanding his more elevated title, Clark's power and influence slowly declined during the final two decades of his career. Superintending the largest United States Indian agency and looking after his family occupied most of his time. A parade of distinguished writers, artists, and foreign travelers routinely called on him in Saint Louis, and he delighted in conducting them through his little museum filled with Indian artifacts and miscellaneous curiosities.

Such are the barest of facts about William Clark, but they only hint at the complexities of a man who lived a life replete with contradictions. William Clark was a lifelong government official who was never elected to a single office. His only attempt to win popular approval at the polls ended with a humiliating loss. He was a leader who knew how to take charge and whose actions commanded the respect and loyalty of those who served under him, but unlike many of his cohorts, he was reluctant to offend. This ninth-born child in a family of high achievers always seemed eager to please. Consider how the British Nor'Wester Charles McKenzie contrasted Clark with his partner Lewis following a visit to Fort Mandan during the winter of 1804–1805. McKenzie declared that, in spite of Lewis's erudition and civility, he "could not make himself agreeable to us . . . [because of] his inveterate disposition against the British." Clark, on the other hand, while he was clearly no Anglophile, elicited a far more sympathetic reaction from the observant trader. In McKenzie's words, "[Clark's] conversation was always pleasant, for he seemed to dislike giving offence unnecessarily."[12] Whether in personal conversation or in official negotiations, Clark usually sought to occupy the middle ground.

Clark lived most of his life in the rustic and unfinished American backcountry, but he always bore the mark of his gentrified origins. Noah Ludlow, an actor and theatrical entrepreneur who first met Governor Clark in Saint Louis in 1820, remembered him as "the finest specimen of the old Virginia gentleman."[13] Ludlow considered the illustrious westerner's gentlemanly bearing charming, but when he ran for office that same year, Clark's political opponents successfully cast him as an out-of-touch aristocrat. He was neither snobbish nor arrogant, but he shared the class consciousness of his eastern forbears. As a young officer in the United States Army, Lieutenant Clark once confided to his sister Fanny that a fellow officer's wife "was of low burth & less breading. She is not noticed at all."[14] Perhaps that is why he chose not to marry until he could marry well.

Clark did not wed the first time until he was thirty-seven, but he relished the joys of marital bliss and was a doting husband and father. Twice married, he found comfort in his companions and the children they bore him. But along with the familial happiness that had always eluded his friend Lewis, Clark had to endure more than his fair share of sadness and sorrow. Julia died after a lengthy illness in 1820, leaving him with five children all under the age of eleven. His beloved seven-year-old daughter Mary Margaret followed her mother to the grave barely a year later.

With four surviving children to care for, Clark remarried in November 1821. His new spouse, Harriet Kennerly Radford, was a widow with three children of her own. The happy couple had two more sons prior to Harriet's death in 1831. Their second child, Edmund, lived less than a year, and thirteen-year-old John Julius Clark, a child impaired by severe physical disabilities, died a few short months before his stepmother. Clark's remaining four sons would survive him, but they all struggled in different ways, and their welfare was constantly in their father's thoughts. Second-born William Preston Clark was in many ways the most tragic of all. Perhaps the brightest of the boys, he attended the University of Virginia and Harvard but never found his calling. Near the end of his troubled life, the family briefly had him committed to a Kentucky asylum. In his roles as son, brother, husband, and father, the dutiful William Clark never shirked his responsibilities.

For someone who savored the comforts of home, Clark was seldom there. He seems to have been a man constantly on the go. Until the very end of his days, he routinely journeyed to Kentucky, eastward to the Atlantic seaboard, and into Indian Country for both business and pleasure. We know about his travels because he kept detailed journals logging his frequent trips. As a novice militiaman, Clark had initiated his lifelong practice of keeping a journal. It is no happenstance that his systematic writings provide the most complete coverage of the Pacific expedition. He was also a methodical and meticulous record keeper, whose precision and attention to detail helped make him an efficient public servant and a careful businessman. Clark had a remarkable talent for keeping abreast of his voluminous public and private accounts. While he was scrupulous in his oversight of public business, Clark had no qualms about using his position to secure government appointments and contracts for family and friends.

Clark knew how to enjoy himself and have a good time. He delighted in sharing a dram and perhaps a ribald tale with traders in a frontier outpost, but he seems to have been equally adept in carrying on polite conversation in a Washington, D.C., drawing room. Yet, despite his congenial nature and gregarious ways, he seems to have formed few close attachments beyond the confines of family. He seldom chose to reveal his true thoughts on personal matters to anyone outside the family circle.

Indian diplomacy occupied much of Clark's time. The dutiful soldier and bureaucrat never wavered in his commitment to an expansionist national agenda that expected Indians to surrender their lands and abandon their traditional ways, but the consequences of the policies that Clark so vigorously championed frequently moved him to demonstrate genuine concern for the plight of native people. His attempts to intercede on their behalf prompted Indian-hating frontier settlers to brand him an Indian lover. Paradoxically, many of the very people whose dispossession and forced relocation Clark helped engineer chose to view the red-headed chief as their friend.

Like so many of his contemporaries, William Clark succumbed to the evils of slavery. An indulgent parent who found it difficult to deny the whims of his prodigal sons, Clark could be cruel and indifferent to his slaves. His treatment of York following the expedition was particularly reprehensible, but his long-time servant and companion was not alone in receiving his master's wrath. Scipio, another of Clark's slaves, apparently killed himself when he learned that he was about to be sold down the river.[15] Clark did show solicitous concern for his old and infirm slaves, but his insistence on viewing his African-American servants as possessions made it possible for a man who modeled decency and integrity in most facets of his life to treat them shamefully.

Clark seems eventually to have freed York, but for financial reasons, he delayed far too long. In justifying his course of action with York, Clark told his brother that he needed to be mindful of his fortunes or, as he put it, "to beleve that there might be a raney day."[16] For a man with the good fortune to be born into a family with some means, Clark had to struggle to make ends meet on his government salary. Financial reverses, such as the collapse of the Bank of Missouri in which he served as an officer, compounded his problems. Clark possessed extensive land holdings, but until late in his life, many of their titles were still in dispute. At the time of his death, William Clark was able to bequeath princely sums to his heirs, but most of those gains had been long deferred.[17]

Difficult as the challenges he faced might have been, William Clark refused to allow his misfortunes to overwhelm him, and only rarely did he permit himself to dwell on his disappointments and failures. Throughout his life, he exhibited a dogged perseverance and determination that made him, among other things, a successful explorer, soldier, government official, Indian diplomat, family man, and, above all else, a steadying presence and a comfort to those who knew him best.

NOTES

1. William Clark Notebook, 1798–1801, Western Historical Manuscripts Collection (WHMC), State Historical Society of Missouri, Columbia, Mo.

2. "To the People of Missouri" (political circular), 2 July 1820, William Clark Papers, Missouri Historical Society (MHS), St. Louis, Mo.

3. William Clark to Jonathan Clark, 25 Nov. 1794, Draper Mss., 2L37, State Historical Society of Wisconsin, Madison, Wis.

4. William Clark Notebook, 1798–1801, WHMC.

5. William Clark to Samuel Gwathmey, 4 July 1823, with list of payments made by William Clark for George Rogers Clark, William Clark Papers, and James J. Holmberg, ed., *Dear Brother: Letters of William Clark to Jonathan Clark* (New Haven, Conn.: Yale University Press and Filson Historical Society, 2002), pp. 9, 54n.29.

6. William Clark to Meriwether Lewis, 18 July 1803, in *Letters of the Lewis and Clark Expedition with Related Documents, 1783–1854*, ed. Donald Jackson, 2d. ed., rev., 2 vols. (Urbana: University of Illinois Press, 1978), 1:110.

7. "To the People of Missouri," 2 July 1820.

8. William Clark to Meriwether Lewis, [after 15 Mar. 1807], in *Letters of the Lewis and Clark Expedition*, ed. Jackson, 2:388; William Clark to Jonathan Clark, 22 Jan. 1807, in *Dear Brother*, ed. Holmberg, pp. 122, 126n.11.

9. Gary E. Moulton and Thomas W. Dunlay, eds., *Journals of the Lewis & Clark Expedition*, Vol. 4: *April 7–July 27, 1805* (Lincoln: University of Nebraska Press, 1987), pp. 215–16, 220n.1.

10. On Clark's role as Indian agent and superintendent, see Jay H. Buckley, "William Clark: Superintendent of Indian Affairs at St. Louis, 1813–1838" (Ph.D. diss., University of Nebraska-Lincoln, 2001).

11. William Clark to James Madison, 10 Apr. 1810, in *Territorial Papers of the United States*, Vol. 14: *The Territory of Louisiana-Missouri, 1806–1814*, ed. Clarence E. Carter (Washington, D.C.: Government Printing Office, 1949), pp. 445–46.

12. "Charles McKenzie's Narratives," in *Early Fur Trade on the Northern Plains: Canadian Traders among the Mandan and Hidatsa Indians, 1783–1818*, ed. W. Raymond Wood and Thomas D. Thiessen, American Exploration and Travel Series, no. 68 (Norman: University of Oklahoma Press, 1985), p. 238.

13. Noah M. Ludlow, *Dramatic Life as I Found It* (1880; reprint ed., Bronx, N.Y.: Benjamin Blom, 1966), pp. 184–85.

14. William Clark to Fanny Clark, 1 July 1795, in *Dear Brother*, ed. Holmberg, p. 276.

15. Joseph Charless to John B. C. Lucas, 18 Apr. 1819, Lucas Collection, MHS.

16. William Clark to Jonathan Clark, 10 Dec. 1808, in *Dear Brother*, ed. Holmberg, pp. 184, 185–86n.6.

17. Estate of William Clark, 1838, St. Louis Probate Court Records, Missouri State Archives, Jefferson City, Mo.

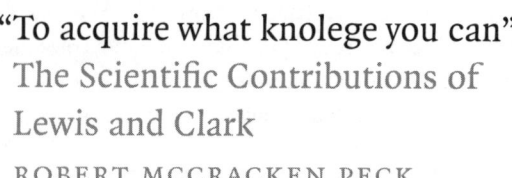

"To acquire what knolege you can"
The Scientific Contributions of Lewis and Clark
ROBERT MCCRACKEN PECK

The two-volume report of the Lewis and Clark Expedition, edited by Nicholas Biddle and published in Philadelphia in 1814, is probably the most famous American expedition narrative ever published. The publication is flawed in a number of ways, however. It lacks any visual documentation and is notably weak in scientific content.[1] While the omission of illustrations may be attributed to budgetary considerations and a lack of interest in visual embellishments by the report's editor, the narrative's dearth of scientific substance was calculated and intentional. Scientific information was omitted from volumes one and two so as not to duplicate the contents of a planned third volume, which was to focus exclusively on the scientific discoveries of the expedition. One of the great tragedies of the Lewis and Clark legacy is that the third volume was never produced.

Under Lewis's direction, the scientific report was to have been organized and written by Benjamin Smith Barton, the talented Philadelphia naturalist who had advised Lewis on techniques for collecting, identifying, and preserving plants prior to his departure for the West. Barton was a professor of botany, natural history, and medicine at the University of Pennsylvania. He was a friend of Thomas Jefferson and an active member of the American Philosophical Society. Lewis met with him repeatedly during his month-long stay in Philadelphia in the spring of 1803. Although a number of other eminent botanists and horticulturists worked in Philadelphia at the time, Barton was the most experienced teacher in the field and, probably for this reason, was identified by Jefferson as the best qualified to instruct Lewis.[2] As an accomplished taxonomist and published authority on a wide range of natural history topics, he was also Lewis's logical choice as the person to help write up the scientific discoveries of the expedition.

Barton's textbook, Elements of Botany (1803), was the first of its kind to be published in America. It is one of the dozen or so books that Lewis carried with him as part of his "traveling library" during the expedition.[3] It is still unclear why Lewis had to buy a copy of Barton's book (records show that he paid six dollars for it),[4] for the botanist was extremely generous in lending him other books, most notably his own copy of Du Pratz's History of Louisiana (1774).[5] Lewis evidently so valued the information that this book contained, as well as the friendship with Barton that its loan represented, that he carried it with him on the trip and returned it with this lengthy inscription four years later:

> Dr. Benjamin Smith Barton was so obliging as to lend me this copy of Monsr. Du Pratz's history of Louisiana in June 1803. it has been since conveyed by me to the Pacific Ocean through the interior of the Continent of North America on my late tour thither and is now returned to it's proprietor by his Friend and Obt. Servt. Meriwether Lewis. Philadelphia, May 9th, 1807.[6]

Barton's copy of Du Pratz's book, later purchased by the Library Company of Philadelphia, is one of the most remarkable relics of the expedition. It says much about Lewis's commitment to scholarship that he would carry it with him across the continent and back, and about his integrity that he would return it to its owner four years after its loan.

Barton's role as an advisor to Lewis covered not only botanical subjects but some medical ones as well. He was one of the country's leading experts in materia medica, the medicinal use of plants.[7] Although there is no written record to prove it, it seems inconceivable that Barton would not have given Lewis a copy of his collected essays on this subject, which he first issued in 1798 as Collections for an Essay towards a Materia Medica of the United States and then republished several times over the next two decades. The pamphlet would have been light and easy to carry and contained a detailed series of instructions for the use of plants for every conceivable illness — just the sort of publication Lewis would have wanted to have in his medical kit.

Barton also may have given Lewis another publication that would have been invaluable to the young explorer on the expedition: a small but useful booklet by the English naturalist Edward Donovan entitled Instructions for Collecting and Preserving Various Subjects of Natural History (1794), which was in wide use among American naturalists at the time Lewis received his training from Barton.[8] Again, there is no specific reference to this document in Lewis's journal, but the skill with which natural history specimens were collected and preserved during the expedition gives abundant circumstantial evidence to suggest that the explorers had ready access to this work, or to a comparable set of instructions, during their time in the field.

Barton's advice to Lewis in the months prior to his departure for Saint Louis did much to sharpen the focus and hone the effectiveness of the explorer-naturalist. The numbers of plants and animals discovered, described, collected, and successfully transported to the East by the Corps of Discovery is a testament to Lewis, who oversaw the scientific activities of the expedition, and to Barton and Lewis's other academic mentors, who directly and indirectly inspired such efforts. Had Lewis's premature death and Barton's declining health not prevented the publication of the projected volume of the expedition's scientific discoveries, we might well remember the Corps of Discovery and its leaders today as scientific trail-blazers, as well as geographical pioneers.

It is, at least in part, a reflection of Barton's influence on Lewis that so many plant specimens were collected during the expedition. Of these, 232 have survived to the present day. All but 10 are preserved in the herbarium of the Academy of Natural Sciences in Philadelphia. They represent about 173 species of which 70 to 75 were new to science at the time of their discovery.[9] Some of the plants that made it back to the East Coast were lost through subsequent mishandling and the predation of insects, but those that have survived are in remarkably good condition. Sadly, many more plants collected by Lewis and Clark were lost in the field when the expedition's cache at Great Falls was destroyed by flood waters during the winter of 1805 and early spring of 1806. It is not surprising, then, that roughly two-thirds of the surviving plant specimens—about 140 species—were discovered by the expedition west of the Continental Divide.

Given the tremendous interest in the plants and seeds that Lewis and Clark did bring back, it is curious that it took another seven years before any of them were officially described and illustrated. Although undoubtedly intended for inclusion in the unpublished third volume of the expedition report, the descriptions ultimately appeared in Frederick Pursh's landmark book *Flora Americae Septentrionalis*, published in London in the winter of 1813–1814.[10] Pursh, a German botanist who worked for Benjamin Smith

Barton in Philadelphia from 1805 to 1808, was asked by Lewis to examine the specimens when it became clear to the explorer that Barton's workload and deteriorating health would prevent him from publishing a monograph on the botanical discoveries of the expedition. When Pursh's descriptions were not included in the official report, he decided to use them, along with descriptions of many other American plant discoveries, in a book of his own.

In Flora Americae Septentrionalis, Pursh described 124 plants collected by Lewis and Clark. Of the 27 hand-colored lithographic illustrations in the book, 13 plates, almost half, were based on the plants from the Lewis and Clark Expedition. Some are so closely copied from the specimens in the herbarium that a side-by-side comparison shows that even the arrangement and imperfections of individual leaves were accurately recorded in the illustrations for Pursh's book.[11] Given Barton's inability to publish the expedition's botanical findings, many feel that Pursh deserves credit—and indeed praise—for putting the findings of the expedition into the scientific literature. More than many of his predecessors, Pursh acknowledged the sources from which he drew the contents of his book. He even named two new genera and three new species in honor of Lewis and Clark.[12] Some historians, however, have portrayed Pursh as an unscrupulous opportunist who took advantage of his privileged access to the newly discovered western species in order to advance his own self-interests. In 1942, Merritt Lyndon characterized him as "one of the most active and apparently unscrupulous early Philadelphia botanists."[13] The controversy that still swirls around Pursh had its origin in the botanist's unauthorized travels with Lewis's plants.

Following Lewis's death in 1809, Pursh, who had been working for three years with the expedition specimens in Philadelphia under the direction of Benjamin Smith Barton and Bernard McMahon, left for New York. After three more years there and a further collecting trip to the West Indies, he departed for London, where he would eventually publish his landmark book on North American plants. Unknown to anyone at the time, and certainly without the permission of any of the principles, Pursh took with him—first to New York and then to London—some fifty-seven Lewis and Clark specimens, or 25 percent of the total surviving botanical specimens from the expedition. While in London, Pursh received the patronage of a wealthy collector-naturalist named Alymer Lambert, the vice-president of the Lin-

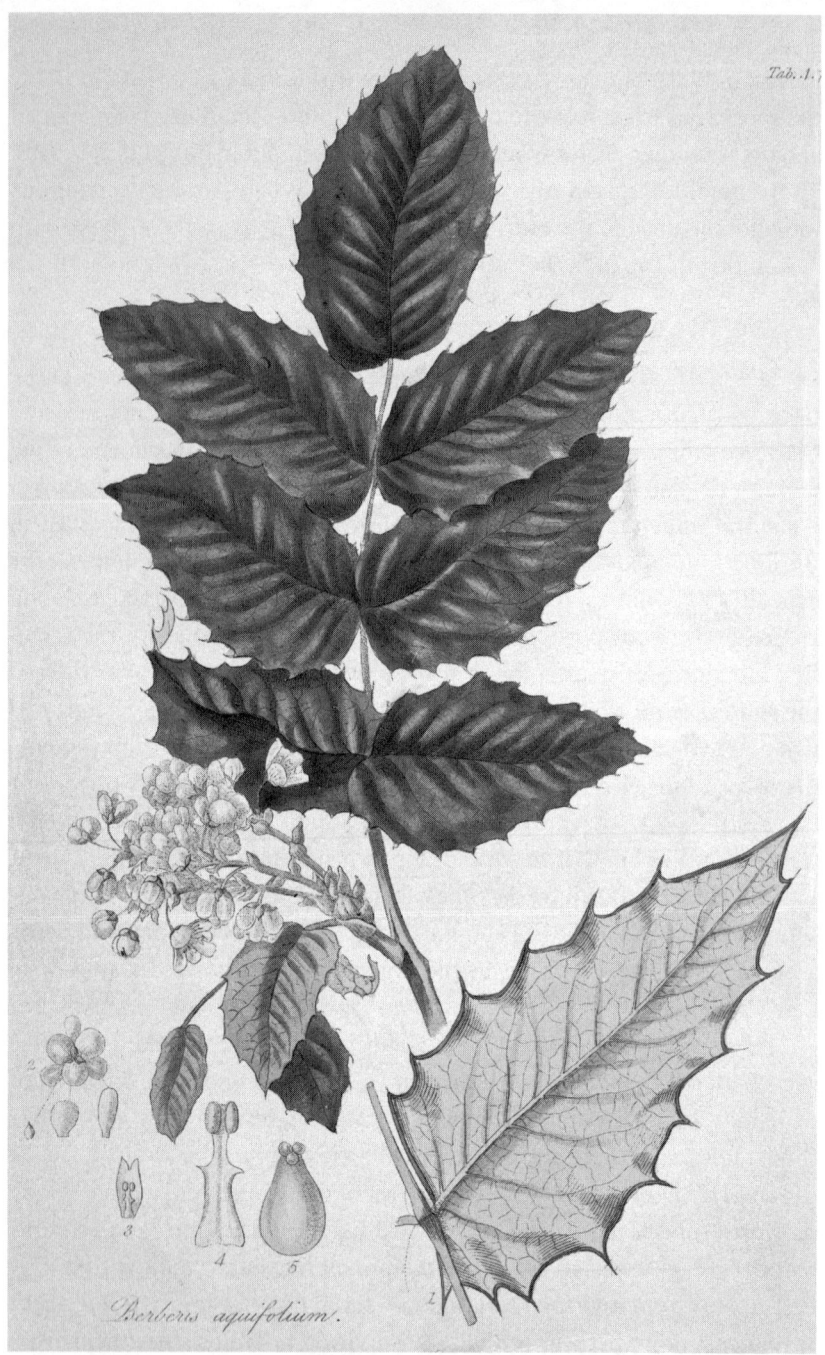

This plate, showing Berberis aquifolium, or "Oregon grape," appeared in Frederick Pursh's Flora Americae Septentrionalis (1814). (Academy of Natural Sciences of Philadelphia, Ewell Sale Stewart Library)

Lewis collected the specimen of Berberis aquifolium on which Pursh's illustration was based on the Great Rapids of the Columbia on 11 April 1806. (Academy of Natural Sciences of Philadelphia, Department of Botany)

naean Society. When Pursh died in 1820, the specimens he had brought with him from Philadelphia went into Lambert's extensive personal herbarium. Although their original labels had been transcribed by Pursh, the Lewis and Clark specimens were buried and their importance forgotten in the overwhelming totality of Lambert's collection.

In 1842, following Lambert's death, his entire collection was put up for auction. As luck would have it, an American botanist named Edward Tuckerman happened to be in London at the time. "At Lambert's sale," he later recalled, "I acquired one half of his old American [herbarium]. This was disposed in 2 cabinets—the first contains all Pursh's plants [those actually collected by Pursh]—and the 2d—all the rest. . . . This last I bought."[14] With this inspired purchase, Tuckerman, who would later go on to chair the Botany Department at Amherst College, acquired the most important historical collection of American plants ever to be sold at auction. The lot contained not just Pursh's purloined Lewis and Clark specimens but also plants collected by Thomas Nuttall, Louis Fraser, and John Bradbury, which Pursh had also acquired during his stay in the United States. Lumped together, these specimens had all been sold under the broad but generic title "American Plants." As a result, they held little interest for the British and European collectors who had gathered for the auction. Tuckerman noted that the amount he paid for his prize was relatively small because he had encountered so little competition.[15] Recognizing them for the treasures they were, he brought the plants back to the United States and, in 1856, presented them to the Academy of Natural Sciences in Philadelphia, where they have been cared for ever since.

Meanwhile, the rest of the Lewis and Clark specimens, which had remained in Philadelphia, were lost and forgotten after their deposit at the American Philosophical Society (APS) by William Clark and Benjamin Smith Barton in 1810. Incredibly, no one seems to have given them further thought until 1896, when Harvard botanist Charles Sprague Sargent suggested to Thomas Meehan, the botanist at the Academy of Natural Sciences, that the "lost" specimens might still exist. Even more incredibly, after searching the APS, Meehan found bundles of plants in their original packages, squirrelled away in the attic of that venerable institution. "With the freedom of three-quarters of a century," Meehan noted, "the museum beetles had made sad work in the bundles. In a few cases the specimens had been wholly reduced to dust, and only fragments were left in other cases.

Generally, however, they were in fair condition." He arranged for a transfer of the collection to the Academy of Natural Sciences, where they have been kept since 1898.[16]

Given this inattention to botanical discoveries following the Lewis and Clark Expedition, it is tempting to wonder how an earlier, aborted expedition might have fared. When Jefferson asked Lewis "to acquire what knolege [sic] you can of . . . the soil & face of the country, it's growth & vegetable productions, . . . the animals of the country generally, & especially those not known in the U.S.,"[17] his instructions were almost identical to those which he and the APS had given to the French botanist and explorer Andre Michaux ten years earlier. Michaux had offered to make a scientific expedition up the Mississippi and Missouri Rivers and on to the Pacific Coast. The original set of instructions given to Michaux and the subscription list for that earlier expedition were discovered at the American Philosophical Society in 1979. Its roster of supporters, whose signatures appear at the bottom, was headed by George Washington (with a generous pledge of one hundred dollars). Other commitments of financial support came from Jefferson and his political rival Alexander Hamilton, as well as Secretary of War Henry Knox and one of the major financiers of the American Revolution, Robert Morris. The document also records the support and financial commitments of John Adams and James Madison, among many others.[18] To Jefferson's dismay and the disappointment of the APS, the expedition was aborted when Michaux became embroiled in international politics.[19]

Because their projected destinations were similar, one has to wonder how different from the Lewis and Clark Expedition Michaux's might have been. Undoubtedly, there would have been a greater emphasis on botanical discovery. Along with his son Francois Andre Michaux, who was slated to accompany him on the western expedition, Andre Michaux was one of the most knowledgeable and accomplished botanists working in North America in the early nineteenth century. Focusing entirely on plants as they traveled to the Pacific coast, the two men might have added hundreds, if not thousands, of new species to the scientific literature. The elder Michaux's book, Flora Boreali-Americana, published in 1803 just as Lewis and Clark were preparing for their trip, was the most complete treatment of North American trees and shrubs prior to the publication of Pursh's Flora Americae Septentrionalis a decade later. One can only imagine what kind of book the Michauxes would have published on their return from the Pacific—assuming, of course, they would have made it all the way to the coast and back with their collections.

As it was, Meriwether Lewis, while not a trained botanist, did a remarkably thorough job in collecting and noting the "vegetable productions" of the territory through which he passed. His journal entries, as well as the detailed collection data he noted with the specimens themselves, have enabled subsequent botanists to identify most, if not all, of the plant species described by Lewis.[20] In some ways, it may have been better that Lewis and Clark were not entirely focused on a single area of natural history. Fortunately, their interests were as broad as the assignments they had been given. Take, for example, their contributions to the field of ornithology.

While bird specimens are far more difficult to collect and preserve than plants, Lewis and Clark did see and record dozens of bird species that were new to science. From their winter camp among the Mandan Indians, the expedition sent a collection of specimens to Jefferson on 7 April 1805. This included a live sharp-tailed grouse, a live prairie dog, and four live magpies. All were species common in the areas of present-day North Dakota where they had been collected but were great rarities in Washington, D.C., where they arrived in August 1805, after a four-month journey of some four thousand miles. On 12 August, Etienne Lemaire, a member of Jefferson's White House staff, wrote the president, then summering at Monticello, "I have just received by [way of] Baltimore a barrel and 4 boxes, and a kind of cage in which there is a little animal very much resembling the squirrel, and in the other a bird resembling the magpie of Europe." In a letter on the twentieth, he advised Jefferson that he had put the single surviving magpie and prairie dog "in the room where Monsieur receives his callers."[21] Jefferson evidently kept these curious specimens as pets for some time before forwarding them on to Charles Willson Peale in Philadelphia, where they were put on public display in Peale's museum.

Many of the bird species that Lewis and Clark saw and described in their journals were not so easily captured as the magpies. In most cases, the explorers were lucky just to get a good look at the birds, let alone catch them alive. Some birds, like the sage grouse, were of more than ornithological interest, for they often doubled as foodstuffs for the hungry explorers. Lewis was the first Anglo-American to describe this species from a specimen seen along the Marias River in present-day Montana in June 1805.[22] Other birds, like the northern fulmar found on the Pacific coast, were of little culinary interest but of considerable scientific interest to the explorers. Lewis gave a detailed description of the bird and made a sketch of its distinctive bill structure in a journal entry dated 7 March 1806.

For all of Lewis and Clark's ornithological discoveries, the three birds that are the most closely associated with their expedition are the western tanager, Clark's nutcracker, and Lewis's woodpecker. This last bird was discovered by Lewis on 20 July 1805 just north of Helena, in what is now Lewis and Clark County, Montana. "I saw a black woodpecker [or crow] today," wrote Lewis. "[It is] about the size of the lark woodpecker [and is] as black as a crow."[23] About a month later, Clark discovered the bird that now bears his name near the present town of Tendoy (on the Lemhi River) in Idaho. Clark described it as a kind of woodpecker, but it is, in fact, a *corvid*, which puts it in the same family as the jays and crows. The species was originally named Clark's crow before receiving its current name, Clark's nutcracker.[24] The western tanager (originally called the Louisiana tanager) was first described by Lewis after a memorable encounter on the Clearwater River in present-day Idaho on 6 June 1806. Lewis called it "a beautiful little bird," which seems an understatement given its dazzling yellow and red plumage.[25]

Specimens of these three species and many others were collected, skinned, and preserved with tobacco dust and ground pepper before being shipped back to Jefferson. The birds were eventually given to Alexander Wilson, a Scottish-born poet, weaver, and school-teacher who was then writing, illustrating, and publishing the first book devoted exclusively to the birds of North America. Wilson's *American Ornithology* would eventually extend to eight volumes, two of which were published after his death in 1813. Pencil-and-ink drawings of Clark's crow, Lewis's woodpecker, and the western tanager were made by Wilson at Lewis's request. They were based on the specimens brought back by the expedition and deposited in Peale's Philadelphia museum. The drawings were subsequently given to the Academy of Natural Sciences by the family of Alexander Lawson, who engraved the illustrations for Wilson's book.[26]

If Nicholas Biddle had not taken out so many of the scientific observations made in the original expedition journals, and if ill health and/or early deaths had not caused Lewis, Wilson, Barton, and others to abandon the projected third volume of the expedition report, the discovery of many more bird species would certainly have been credited to Lewis and Clark.[27]

Alexander Wilson made these pencil-and-ink drawings of Clark's crow and Lewis's woodpecker for publication in his American Ornithology *(1813). (Academy of Natural Sciences of Philadelphia, Ewell Sale Stewart Library)*

As it was, later observers were given the privilege of officially describing and naming many of the birds that Lewis and Clark saw first. The western meadowlark, for example, was discovered by Lewis at Great Falls, Montana, on 22 June 1805, but it was not officially recognized as a new species until John James Audubon published its description in the octavo edition of *The Birds of America* in 1844, almost forty years later. Audubon, who re-

In the plate engraved by Alexander Lawson for Wilson's book, a third western species, the Louisiana tanager, was included with Clark's crow and Lewis's woodpecker. (Academy of Natural Sciences of Philadelphia, Ewell Sale Stewart Library)

traced Lewis and Clark's expedition route up the Missouri River in 1843, named the bird *Sturnella neglecta* because he believed it had been neglected by earlier explorers.[28]

If one traces most of the natural history discoveries made by Lewis and Clark from their first sightings in the field to their eventual publication in the scientific literature, the trail inevitably leads to and through Charles Willson Peale. A fascinating figure in his own right, Peale plays a pivotal role in the Lewis and Clark story, especially after the successful return of the expedition. Not only did he paint the best known and most frequently reproduced portraits of the two explorers, but he was also the person entrusted with most of the natural history specimens sent to Jefferson. At the time of the Lewis and Clark Expedition, Peale was the proprietor of what was unquestionably the finest natural history museum in America, rivaled in the comprehensiveness and originality of its displays only by the Leverian Museum in London.[29] It was in Peale's museum that artist-naturalists like Alexander Wilson had a chance to see the newly discovered western species and describe them for the scientific community. While it never received the federal funding its owner hoped it would, Peale's museum was the defacto national museum of the United States through the first few decades of the nineteenth century. It contained literally tens of thousands of natural history specimens from America and around the world.

The patriotic Peale put such importance in the discoveries of Lewis and Clark that he created a separate room in his museum devoted entirely to display of their collections. In addition to his portraits of Lewis and Clark, Peale created a life-size wax manikin of Lewis for the gallery, using it to display some of the buckskin clothing Lewis wore during the trip, including the "tippit" presented to him by the Shoshone chief Cameahwait. Many of the nonbotanical natural history specimens, as well as a large collection of anthropological artifacts, were displayed in Peale's Lewis and Clark gallery. Jefferson presented the museum director with the skins and skeletons of dozens of the animals collected by the expedition, leaving it to Peale to reconstitute and mount the skins in a lifelike way. Peale's efforts in taxidermy not only honored the expedition and advanced the cause of science, but they also attracted visitors to his popular museum. Many specimens were subsequently lost in fires; those that survived are now in the care of the Peabody Museum at Harvard.[30]

Of the various mammal discoveries of the expedition, the pronghorn was one of the most interesting. While the animal had been seen earlier in the trip, the first specimen was collected near the mouth of Ball Creek in present-day South Dakota in September 1804. The expedition members enjoyed eating its meat before packing its skin and skeleton for shipment back to Jefferson. Clark described the species as follows: "I Killed a Buck Goat of this Countrey, about the hight of the Grown Deer, its body Shorter, the horns which is not very hard and forks 2/3 up one prong Short [and] the other round & Sharp arched, and is imediately above its Eyes the Colour is a light gray with black behind its ears down its neck, and its Jaw white round its neck, its Sides and its rump round its tail which is Short & white verry actively made, . . . his Norstrals large, his eyes like a Sheep— he is more like the Antilope or Gazelle of Africa than any other Species of Goat."[31]

Of course, the descriptions of wildlife that drew the greatest attention were those of the grizzly bear. The many quotable lines about this creature in Patrick Gass's journal and in the official expedition report are well known. Clark's description of 5 May 1805 in present-day Montana is a good example. "I went out with one man Geo. Drewyer & Killed the bear," wrote Clark, "which was verry large and a turrible looking animal, which we found verry hard to kill we Shot ten Balls into him before we killed him. & 5 of those Balls through his lights <before> This animal is the largest of the Carnivorous kind I ever Saw."[32] None of the expedition participants would ever forget this species. Nor would visitors to Peale's museum. The director exhibited the grizzly bear skins that the expedition sent back to Jefferson, but when Peale received two live grizzly cubs sent east by Zebulon Pike in 1808, the museum had an attraction that superseded all others.[33]

Given the extraordinary interest in these and other western species encountered by Lewis and Clark, it is surprising that it took so long for their descriptions to find their way into the scientific literature. George Ord, a Philadelphia zoologist active with both the American Philosophical Society and the newly founded Academy of Natural Sciences, was responsible for publishing the first scientific account of the grizzly bear in 1815. Not surprisingly, he named it *Ursus horribilis*, or the "horrible bear." Ord also published the first accounts of the mountain goat, the pronghorn, the prairie dog, and several other Lewis and Clark discoveries. His friend and fellow academy member Thomas Say, who would follow Lewis and Clark to the West on the Long Expedition a few years after their return, described the coyote, the plains gray wolf, the short-tailed shrew, and the swift, or kit, fox, all of which had been seen and collected by the Corps of Discovery.[34] The descriptions of these important western species by Say, Ord, and others cited Lewis and Clark's specimens, but more often they used the detailed descriptions of other naturalists who had traveled through many of the same areas a few years after the Corps of Discovery. Once again, the fact that most information about the animals that Lewis and Clark had so carefully recorded had been edited out of the official expedition report adversely affected the scientific legacy of the Corps of Discovery.

Another underrated scientific achievement of the Lewis and Clark Expedition is the detailed description of western topography that the captains provided. In addition to finding an easy water route to the Pacific Ocean, Jefferson had asked the explorers to "acquire what knolege you can of . . . the soil & face of the country . . . [including] the mineral productions of every kind."[35] In one of these tasks, recording "the face of the country," Clark seems to have had unusual talent. He may have received training in mapping and navigation as part of his service in the military, or he may have developed his cartographic skills on his own. However he acquired them, his talents as a cartographer were formidable, and the results of his efforts impressive. Lewis was not as inherently talented in this area, but he made up for any deficiencies in his earlier education through the pre-trip training he received in Lancaster and Philadelphia from Andrew Ellicott and Robert Patterson, respectively. In the spring of 1803, Jefferson asked these men, two of the country's most distinguished astronomers and mathematicians, to familiarize Lewis with various navigational and surveying instruments and to coach him on how best to record the lay of the uncharted land. Lewis and Clark's field notes and the final published map of the expedition route reveal how effective their training was. Given all of the logistical and political complexities of the expedition, it is remarkable that its topographic reporting was so thorough and accurate.[36]

In reporting on the soils and minerals of the newly acquired territory, Lewis and Clark were equally, if not always as consistently, diligent. As testament to their seriousness in this regard, they carried with them Richard Kirwan's two-volume work on mineralogy, which, though published a decade earlier, was the most widely accepted work on the subject.[37] Kirwan (and his predecessor Abraham Gottlob Werner) had done for mineralogy what Carl Linnaeus had done for botany; that is, they provided a universal system for classification of ores and minerals. We know from Lewis's

A specimen of Gypsum selenite collected by Lewis and Clark still bears a catalogue number from the Adam Seybert mineral collection. (Academy of Natural Sciences of Philadelphia, Department of Mineralogy)

diary and correspondence, and from the accession records at the American Philosophical Society, that Lewis included mineral specimens in several of his early shipments to Jefferson. Unfortunately, most samples received by the APS have since been lost. A few specimens that can be traced to the expedition were acquired at the time by a mineral collector named Adam Seybert.[38] These survivors were purchased, along with the rest of Seybert's collection, by the Academy of Natural Sciences in 1812. Among the Lewis and Clark specimens contained in Seybert's collection are four specimens of *Gypsum selenite*. Their museum exhibition labels indicate that they were originally from Calumet Bluffs.[39] Fortunately, they still bear Seybert's original catalogue numbers, which enable us to trace them directly to the Corps of Discovery.

Another Lewis and Clark specimen once owned by Seybert is a piece of pumice that expedition members found floating on the Missouri River. It was, they thought, a sure sign of recent volcanic activity in the area. They collected several pieces, but only one survives. Its various catalogue num-

Patrick Gass collected this fossil fish jaw (Saurocephalus lanciformis) on 6 August 1804. (Academy of Natural Sciences of Philadelphia, Department of Vertebrate Paleontology)

bers, including Seybert's, enable us to verify its provenance. A piece of lava-like slag that caught Lewis's attention while he was investigating a strata of burning coal near Fort Mandan was also collected and included among the twenty-five boxes and trunks of specimens and artifacts sent to Washington in April 1805. Jefferson forwarded it to the American Philosophical Society, which, in turn, gave it to Seybert who later sold it to the Academy of Natural Sciences. An early exhibition label that still accompanies the specimen notes its original source as the APS.[40]

One other specimen has survived the ravages of recent history as well as those of the millennia preceding the expedition. It is a fossilized fragment of the upper jaw bone of a fish from the Cretaceous era that Patrick Gass found in a cave near the Missouri River on 6 August 1804. It is the only surviving vertebrate fossil collected during the expedition, and it, too, is preserved at the academy. Richard Harlan described and illustrated it for the *Journal of the Academy of Natural Sciences* in 1824.[41] To Jefferson, whose fascination with prehistoric creatures led him to send Clark to Big Bone Lick, Kentucky, to collect a mastodon tooth just one year after his return from the Pacific Coast, the fossil Gass collected must have been among the most interesting finds of the Corps of Discovery.[42]

Less intriguing than the fish jaw, but probably more eagerly received by others on the East Coast, were the seeds and live plant specimens the expedition sent back for propagation. These plants were put in the care of William Hamilton, a wealthy and well-connected horticulturist whose country estate, called the Woodlands, was perched picturesquely on the banks of the Schuylkill River in West Philadelphia. Hamilton's garden (where Frederick Pursh worked as chief gardener and botanist from 1803 to 1805 before being employed by Benjamin Smith Barton) became the propagation center for dozens of the western plant species discovered by Lewis and Clark. Carefully guarded for years at the Woodlands and at Monticello as part of a sacred trust, the offspring of these plants were eventually distributed to other gardens on the East Coast and in Europe. By 1828, species discovered by Lewis and Clark were offered for sale commercially through Bartram's Garden in Philadelphia. The most popular of these were the Osage orange, Mandan tobacco, flax, gooseberry, and several kinds of ornamental currant.[43] These plants are separate and distinct from those collected as specimens and preserved in the Lewis and Clark herbarium, for these are the living legacies of the expedition. Some, only a step removed from the explorers themselves, are still growing today in Philadelphia.

How, then, do we gauge the scientific contributions of Lewis and Clark? Impressive lists of the many species of plants and animals they discovered or described have been compiled by Elijah Criswell, Donald Jackson, Paul Cutright, James Reveal, H. Wayne Phillips, and others who have painstakingly combed the expedition's journals to find the references to their discoveries, both explicit and implied. A recent bibliography has documented the massive amount of literature, scientific and otherwise, that has been spawned by the Corps of Discovery over the last two hundred years.[44] No doubt the bicentennial of the expedition will stimulate even more. The Lewis and Clark Expedition was the first American expedition to attempt a comprehensive survey and scientific inventory of the new Louisiana Territory. It should be remembered, however, that it was but one of hundreds of exploratory expeditions into North America and around the globe that both satisfied and stimulated the public's wish to know more about the natural world.

The Corps of Discovery accomplished much in the realm of science, more, in fact, than its official report revealed, but its greatest contribution *may be yet to come*. If new generations studying the remarkable achievements of Lewis and Clark can be inspired to adopt some of their intellectual curiosity and can-do spirit and apply these traits to the challenges of future exploration, research, and the wise stewardship of the natural world, then Lewis and Clark's efforts will leave a legacy that goes well beyond the daunting assignments Jefferson set for them two centuries ago.

NOTES

1. Biddle, ed., *History of the Expedition under the Command of Captains Lewis and Clark to the Sources of the Missouri*, 2 vols. (Philadelphia: Bradford & Inskeep, 1814). The Dublin edition of 1817 contains a view of the Great Falls of the Missouri by John James Barralet (ca. 1747–1815), which Lewis commissioned (along with a view of the Falls of the Columbia), but it was inexplicably omitted from the American editions. The original drawings have since been lost. For more on this topic, see Joni L. Kinsey's essay in this volume.

2. William Bartram's botanical garden, begun by his father John Bartram, was one of the best known in the country, making it curious that no evidence survives to confirm that Lewis either visited his garden or met with Bartram during his time in Philadelphia. There is also no evidence to suggest that Lewis met with William Hamilton, in whose garden Lewis's collected seeds and cuttings were propagated after the expedition.

3. For a discussion of the expedition's traveling library, see Donald D. Jackson, "Some Books Carried by Lewis and Clark," *Missouri Historical Society Bulletin* 16 (Oct. 1959): 3–13, and Stephen Dow Beckham et al., *The Literature of the Lewis and Clark Expedition: A Bibliography and Essays* (Portland, Oreg.: Lewis & Clark College, 2003), pp. 23–42.

4. Donald Jackson, ed., *Letters of the Lewis and Clark Expedition with Related Documents, 1783–1854*, 2d ed., rev., 2 vols. (Urbana: University of Illinois Press, 1978), 1:96.

5. The book was originally published in two volumes in 1758. Lewis carried the one-volume second edition of 1774.

6. Quoted in Paul Russell Cutright, "Lewis and Clark and Du Pratz," *Missouri Historical Society Bulletin* 21 (Oct. 1964): 35.

7. This subject was also familiar to Lewis because of his own mother's knowledge in this area. H. Wayne Phillips, *Plants of the Lewis and Clark Expedition* (Missoula, Mont.: Mountain Press Publishing Co., 2003), p. 1.

8. See Robert McCracken Peck, "Preserving Nature for Study and Display" and "Alcohol and Arsenic, Pepper and Pitch: Brief Histories of Preservation Techniques," in *Stuffing Birds, Pressing Plants, Shaping Knowledge: Natural History in North America, 1730–1860*, ed. Sue Ann Prince (Philadelphia: American Philosophical Society, 2003), pp. 11–53.

9. For a complete discussion of the surviving specimens, *see* James L. Reveal, Gary E. Moulton, and Alfred E. Schuyler, "The Lewis and Clark Collections of Vascular Plants: Names, Types, and Comments," *Proceedings of the Academy of Natural Sciences of Philadelphia* 149 (29 Jan. 1999): 1–64.

10. Pursh, *Flora Americae Septentrionalis*, ed. Joseph Ewan, Historiae Naturalis Classica Series (reprint ed., Germany: J. Cramer, 1979). Ewan's excellent Introduction (pp. 7–117) to this edition of Pursh's book provides information about its contents and the history of its publication.

11. The only place where inaccuracies occurred was in the coloring of the plates. The most conspicuous distortion occurs in the specimen of *Clarkia pulchella*, which was painted blue when it should have been pink. For a detailed discussion, *see* Linda Rossi and Alfred E. Schuyler, "The Iconography of Plants Collected on the Lewis and Clark Expedition," *Great Plains Research* 3 (Feb. 1993): 39–60.

12. The two genera were *Clarkia pulchella*, or "ragged robin," and *Lewisia rediviva*, or bitterroot. The new species were: *Linum lewisii*, or Lewis's wild flax; *Mimulus lewisii*, or Lewis's monkey flower; and *Philadelphus lewisii*, or Lewis's syringa.

13. Quoted in *Botanical Exploration of the Trans-Mississippi West, 1790–1850*, by Susan Delano McKelvey (Jamaica Plain, Mass.: Arnold Arboretum, Harvard University, 1955), p. 73.

14. Quoted in Joseph Ewan, "Frederick Pursh, 1774–1820, and His Botanical Associates," *Proceedings of the American Philosophical Society* 96 (Oct. 1952): 625.

15. Tuckerman to John L. LeConte, 3 May 1856, quoted in *Lewis and Clark: Pioneering Naturalists*, by Paul Russell Cutright (Urbana: University of Illinois Press, 1969), pp. 364–65.

16. Meehan, "The Plants of Lewis and Clark's Expedition across the Continent, 1804–1806," *Proceedings of the Academy of Natural Sciences of Philadelphia* (1898): 13–14. The focus of a recent Save America's Treasures grant, the Lewis and Clark specimens from the Lambert Herbarium and the APS are now better documented and in better storage conditions than at any time in the last two hundred years.

17. "Jefferson's Instructions to Lewis [20 June 1803]," in *Letters of the Lewis and Clark Expedition*, ed. Jackson, 1:62–63.

18. This document is the only one known to have been signed by each of the first four presidents of the United States.

19. Michaux became a principle player in "the Genet affair," which involved a conflict between French and Spanish interests in the Louisiana Territory. For more on Michaux, *see* Henry Savage, Jr., and Elizabeth J. Savage, *Andre and Francois Andre Michaux* (Charlottesville: University Press of Virginia, 1986).

20. For a checklist of plants discovered by Lewis and Clark, *see* Cutright, *Lewis and Clark: Pioneering Naturalists*, pp. 399–423.

21. Quoted ibid., pp. 377–78.

22. Lewis, 5 June 1805, *The Journals of the Lewis & Clark Expedition*, Vol. 4: *April 7–July 27, 1805*, ed. Gary E. Moulton and Thomas W. Dunlay (Lincoln: University of Nebraska Press, 1987), pp. 260–61.

23. Lewis, 20 July 1805, ibid., p. 406.

24. Cutright, *Lewis and Clark: Pioneering Naturalists*, p. 435.

25. Lewis, 6 June 1806, *The Journals of the Lewis & Clark Expedition*, Vol. 7: *March 23–June 9, 1806*, ed. Gary E. Moulton (Lincoln: University of Nebraska Press, 1991), pp. 339–40.

26. The tanager drawing, not a part of the Lawson gift, has apparently been lost.

27. For a checklist of all birds seen, described, or collected by Lewis and Clark, *see* Cutright, *Lewis and Clark: Pioneering Naturalists*, pp. 429–38.

28. For a discussion of Audubon's scientific discoveries during his Missouri River expedition, *see* Robert McCracken Peck, "Audubon and Bachman: A Collaboration in Science," in *John James Audubon in the West: The Last Expedition*, ed. Sarah E. Boehme (New York: Harry N. Abrams, 2000), pp. 71–115. Interestingly, when he was in Saint Louis preparing for this journey, Audubon was given Clark's original manuscript field notes from 11 through 31 December 1805, which recorded courses and distances of the route Audubon was about to travel. Clark's diary also contained first drafts of his descriptions of daily activities during the earlier expedition. Fortunately, Audubon considered the volume too precious to risk taking it upriver, and he left it with friends in Saint Louis. It is now owned by the Missouri Historical Society.

29. For a description of the Leverian Museum, *see* Richard D. Altick, *The Shows of London* (Cambridge, Mass.: Harvard University Press, 1978), pp. 28–33.

30. Charles Coleman Sellers, *Mr. Peale's Museum: Charles Willson Peale and the First Popular Museum of Natural Science and Art* (New York: W.W. Norton & Co.,1980), pp. 174–86. The wax figure of Lewis was based on a portrait by Charles Saint-Mémin. For a detailed account of the surviving ethnographic collections, *see* Castle McLaughlin, *Arts of Diplomacy: Lewis and Clark's Indian Collection* (Seattle: University of Washington Press and Peabody Museum, Cambridge, Mass., 2003).

31. Gary E. Moulton and Thomas W. Dunlay, eds., *The Journals of the Lewis & Clark Expedition*, Vol. 3: *August 25, 1804–April 6, 1805* (Lincoln: University of Nebraska Press, 1987), p. 71.

32. Ibid., 4:114–15.

33. Sellers, *Mr. Peale's Museum*, pp. 206–9. One bear eventually escaped, and Peale had to destroy both bears. Being the great showman that he was, he immediately stuffed the grown siblings and put them back on view.

34. Ord, "Zoology of North America," in *A New Geographical, Historical and Commercial Grammar and Present State of the Several Kingdoms of the World*, by William Guthrie

(Philadelphia: Johnson & Warner, 1815), pp. 291, 299–300, 302–3, 308–9. For information on Say, *see* Patricia Tyson Stroud, *Thomas Say, New World Naturalist* (Philadelphia: University of Pennsylvania Press, 1992).

35. "Jefferson's Instructions to Lewis [20 June 1803]," pp. 62–63.

36. Gary E. Moulton and Thomas W. Dunlay, Introduction to *The Journals of the Lewis & Clark Expedition*, Vol. 2: *August 30, 1803–August 24, 1804* (Lincoln: University of Nebraska Press, 1986), pp. 5–6. For an assessment of the expedition's topographic achievements, *see* Guy Meriwether Benson, with William R. Irwin and Heather Moore Riser, *Lewis and Clark: The Maps of Exploration, 1507–1814* (Charlottesville: University of Virginia Library, 2002).

37. The book, *Elements of Mineralogy*, was first published in one volume in 1784. Lewis probably had the two-volume 1794 edition with him on the expedition. Beckham et al., *Literature of the Lewis and Clark Expedition*, pp. 30–31.

38. The American Philosophical Society asked Adam Seybert to examine all minerals collected by Lewis and Clark. It is probably through this contact that he was able to acquire specimens for his own collection.

39. Seybert's records indicate that one of these specimens was collected "on the bank of the Missouri" on 23 August 1804. Adam Seybert Mineral Collection, Academy of Natural Sciences, Philadelphia, Pa.

40. The surviving nineteenth-century labels are not Lewis's or Seybert's, but they were probably transcribed from Lewis's accompanying field notes by curators at the academy shortly after acquisition.

41. Harlan, "On a new fossil genus, of the order *Enalio Sauri* (of Conybeare)," *Journal of the Academy of Natural Sciences of Philadelphia* 3 (1824): 331–37. Unfortunately, neither Lewis, Clark, nor Gass make mention of this discovery in their respective journals. The information regarding its collection comes from an accompanying label in Lewis's hand.

42. Silvio A. Bedini, "Jefferson: A Man of Science," *Frontiers Annual* 3 (1981–1982): 10–23.

43. Peter J. Hatch, "'Public Treasures': Thomas Jefferson and the Garden Plants of Lewis and Clark," *Twinleaf Journal* (Jan. 2003): www.twinleaf.org. *Twinleaf Journal* is published at Monticello, Charlottesville, Va.

44. Beckham et al., *Literature of the Lewis and Clark Expedition*.

"I wished for the pencil of Salvator Rosa"
The Artistic Legacy of Lewis and Clark
JONI L. KINSEY

For all the uniqueness of the Corps of Discovery in American history, the expedition is also remarkable for what it was *not*. It was not illustrated. No artists were included to make pictures, and with the exception of a smattering of relatively amateurish drawings within Lewis and Clark's journals, no images were brought back from the historic journey. In retrospect, this lack is especially surprising since Thomas Jefferson, the overseer of the enterprise, had an extraordinary aesthetic sensibility and a long history of associating with artists and things visual. He had also written in his instructions to Lewis a wish list of virtually everything the expedition would encounter.[1] That he did not think to ask for pictures or provide the means for obtaining them is both astounding and, of course, regrettable, not only for us today as we wish for a more comprehensive view of that path-breaking enterprise, but also for the travelers themselves as they earnestly sought to convey to their president every aspect of the wondrous country that had so recently become their own.

Even without a draftsman, however, the Lewis and Clark Expedition had a significant artistic dimension that found expression in a variety of ways. First are the journals themselves, which, sprinkled with occasional drawings and graced with written visual references, are at once tantalizing in their allusions and frustrating for their brevity. These passages demonstrate the incomparable deficiency that an artist could have alleviated, and, at the same time, they reveal the writers', especially Lewis's, sensitivity to aesthetic conventions that clearly dictated relationships to sights and scenes the party encountered.

Second is the intriguing confluence of visual culture that congregated around the expedition. Specifically, Jefferson's own artistic sensibility and his and Lewis's interactions with artists—men such as Charles Willson

Peale and his sons, the portraitist Charles de Saint-Mémin, and others—fostered a notable aesthetic context for the expedition and its publications. Although these individuals had varying degrees of involvement, they nevertheless participated in the conception, production, and dissemination of the visual record of the Corps of Discovery. Their relationships to the project offer important insights into the aesthetic culture that influenced its success, however subtly.

Third, of course, is the visual record itself—the illustrations that accompanied the published journals and histories, the drawings made from the artifacts the party sent or brought back east, and the several portraits of the expedition leaders. Although made by artists who did not accompany the explorers, these works nevertheless add substantially to art history as they graphically convey experiences, objects, and people from the adventure and contribute to the discourse about its achievements and encounters.

And finally, there is the long-term legacy, the subsequent and varied history of western art that ultimately rested on the shoulders, in one way or another, of the Corps of Discovery. This vast legacy largely lies beyond the scope of this study. Most directly related, as many have noted, are the private artistic excursions of George Catlin (1796–1872) and Karl Bodmer (1809–1893), who almost literally followed in the expedition's footsteps in the 1830s, at least as far as the upper Missouri River. No less important are the many federal surveys of the West after 1806 that did include artistic documentation, a clear acknowledgement by the United States government that visual imagery was a necessary adjunct to the written accounts, scientific data, and material artifacts of exploration that were and are so vital to our conception of the West. The expedition has its progeny in everything from numismatics and popular culture (the recent issuance of the Sacagawea dollar is one example) to high art (including the several public sculptures of Lewis and Clark, Sacagawea, and other members of the party, not to mention the countless painted representations of the expedition and its members). For an event conspicuous for its visual deficiency, the Lewis and Clark Expedition's artistic impact has been broad and remarkably sustained.

Although the journals the men kept during their two-year journey are most often preoccupied with daily events—miles covered, natives encountered, sustenance acquired, and obstacles overcome—they do contain a number of drawings that reveal an awareness of the ability of images to convey an object graphically and immediately. Most of these drawings are quite small and relatively cryptic, depicting everything from birds and plants to American Indian adornments, and they are imbedded in the texts that describe the objects. The fish that Lewis and Clark each included in their 1806 journals from Fort Clatsop (Figure 1) are perhaps the most striking of these images, both for their size and relative accomplishment. The drawings display an effort at shading through delicate cross-hatching and a strong linearity overall.[2] They are also remarkably artful in their diagonal placement within the text, although the placement more likely reflects a frugal use of paper than any conscious aesthetic intent. Most importantly, whether large or small, dramatic or not, the journal drawings make clear that both leaders recognized the value of visual imagery to a distant reader or viewer. Charming as they occasionally are, however, these drawings are limited in number, subject matter, and descriptiveness, and they are hardly a satisfying substitute for the work of a professional draftsman.

The great contribution of the journals, of course, lies not in their images but rather in their copious text. Correspondingly, most of the expedition's references to aesthetics appear in the written commentary, especially in the descriptions of landscape that are scattered throughout. Even prosaic accounts of the party's movements, for example, contain frequent references to "prospects," elevated vantage points from which the leaders surveyed the scenery, took measurements, and developed ideas about the terrain and its potential.[3] As Lewis wrote:

> after going to Several Small Mounds in a leavel plain, I assended a hill on the Lower Side, on this hill Several artificial Mounds were raised, from the top of the highest of those Mounds I had an extensive view of the Serounding Plains, which afforded one of the most pleasing prospect I ever beheld, under me a Butifull River of Clear Water of about 80 yards wide Meandering thro: a leavel and extensive meadow, as far as I could See, the prospect very much enlivened by the fiew Trees & Srubs which is bordering the bank of the river.[4]

The term *prospect* had a long history in art and aesthetics, and the captains' use of it in the journals indicates at least a passing familiarity with its many implications. In the most basic definition, a prospect referred to a position from which a view could be obtained, as well as the scene visible from that spot. It also referred to the depiction of such a scene (a paint-

of small fish which now begin to run and are taken in great quantities in the Columbia R. about 40 miles above us by means of skiming or scooping nets. on this page I have drawn the likeness of them as large as life; it as perfect as I can make it with my pen and will serve to give a generals idea of the fish. the rays of the fins are boney but not sharp tho' somewhat pointed. the small fin on the back next to the tail has no rays of bone being a membranous pellicle. the fins next to the gills have _____ rays each. those of the _____ eight each; those of the abdomen have each _____ 20 and 2 half formed in front that of the back of the pinnae ani has eleven rays. all the fins are of a white colour. the back is of a bluish duskey colour and that of the the lower part of the sides and belley is of a silve= =ry white. no spots on any part. the first bone of the gills next behind the eye is of a bluish cast, and the second of a light gold colour nearly white. of the eye is black and the iris of a silver white. the under jaw exceeds the uper, and the mouth opens to great extent, folding like that of the herring. it has no teeth. the abdomen is obtuse and smooth; in this differing from the herring, shad anchovey &c of the Malacapterygious Order & Class Clupea

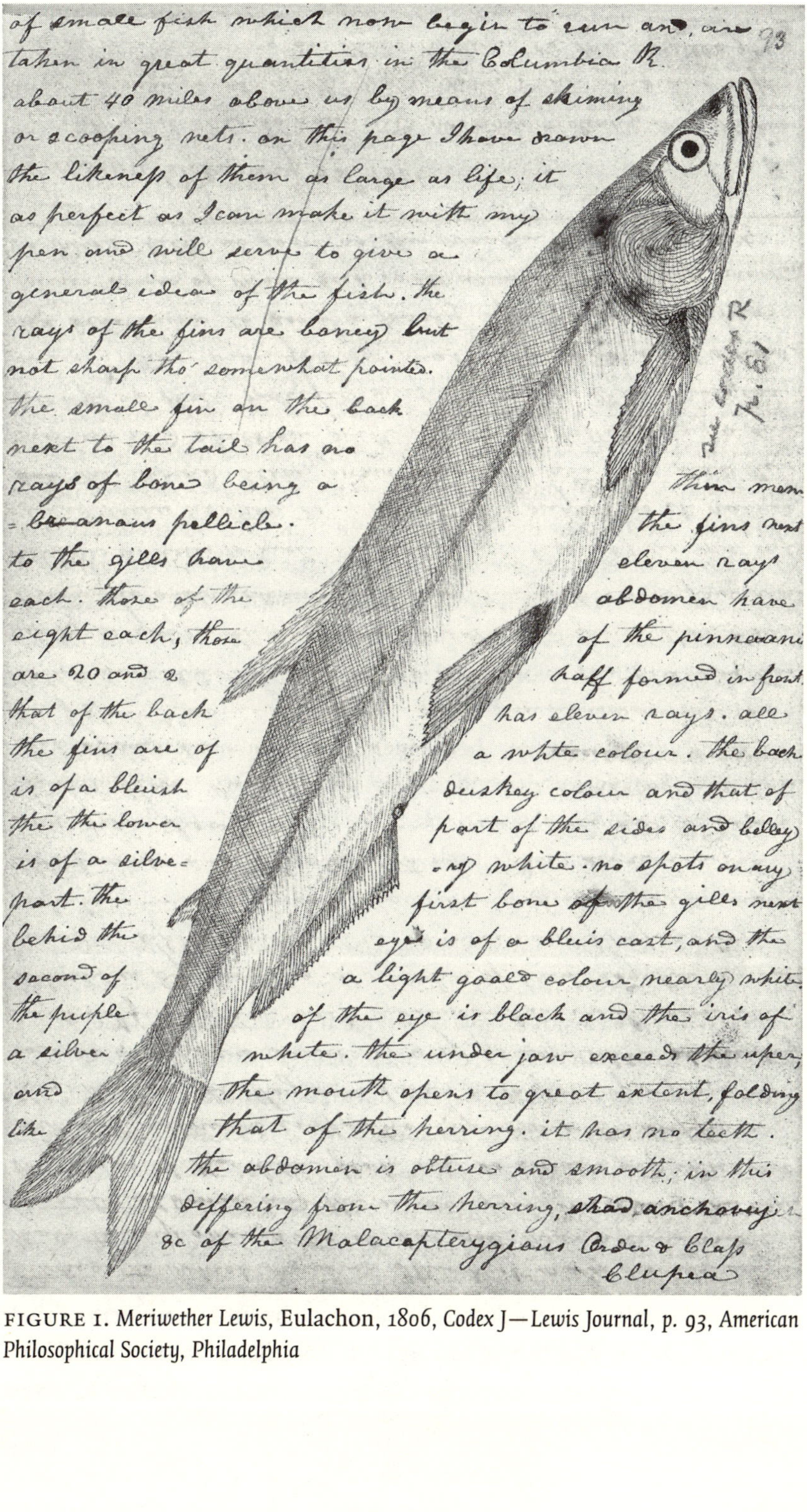

FIGURE 1. Meriwether Lewis, Eulachon, 1806, Codex J—Lewis Journal, p. 93, American Philosophical Society, Philadelphia

ing, for example) or even to estate portraits or bird's-eye views of property, which became fashionable in both Europe and America in the late eighteenth century.[5] Implicit in all these applications is the omnipotent position of the viewer as purveyor of what Albert Boime has called a "magisterial gaze," allowing a conceptual dominion over the land as well as a metaphorical or imagined glimpse into the terrain's potential or future use.[6] From this conflation with futurity, we derive the verb "to prospect," with all its allusions of mining and extractive possibilities as well as the more common associations with tangible return—"it has good prospects."[7]

Lewis and Clark's usage of "prospect" was consistent with all these meanings and was particularly appropriate to their mission. They were to seek out the prospects of the land with an eye to its future potential to the United States, and their position of viewership, at least metaphorically, was that of an omnipotent America claiming her new land and asserting her dominion over it and its inhabitants. It is clear from the journals that Lewis especially ascended rises, bluffs, hills, and buttes on a regular basis to gain a prospect on the land. Even when he did not mention the aesthetic reward of such efforts, he certainly benefited practically from such views, both as he helped guide the explorers and as he gained perspective on their larger work in the national interest.

Elsewhere in the journals, Lewis included several notable passages that indicate his familiarity with and responsiveness to other aesthetic conventions of his time. His observations at the White Cliffs of the Missouri in present-day Montana, for example, are especially significant for his effort to describe the rocky formations through architectural metaphor:

> The hills and river Clifts which we passed today exhibit a most romantic appearance.... The water ... has trickled down the soft sand clifts and woarn it into a thousand grotesque figures, which with the help of a little immagination and an oblique view at a distance, are made to represent eligant ranges of lofty freestone buildings, having their parapets well stocked with statuary; collumns of various sculpture both grooved and plain, are also seen supporting long galleries in front of those buildings; in other places on a much nearer approach and with the help of less immagination we see the remains or ruins of eligant buildings; some collumns standing and almost entire with their pedestals and capitals; others retaining their pedestals but deprived by time or accident of their capitals, some lying prostrate an[d] broken othe[r]s in the form of vast

pyramids of connic structure bearing a sereis of other pyramids on their tops becoming less as they ascend and finally terminating in a sharp point. nitches and alcoves of various forms and sizes are seen at different hights as we pass. . . . The <broken> columns did not the less remind us of some of those large stone buildings in the U' States.⁸

This sort of searching for familiar analogies had a long history in travel writing. Architectural metaphor was an especially favored device for describing unfamiliar or unusual formations, but Lewis's references to sculpture and architectural details goes beyond convention in his quite specific terminology—capitals, pedestals, niches, and alcoves—all of which reveal an awareness of art and architectural history. His allusion to ruins is also in keeping with the long-standing fascination with ancient and abandoned sites that grew in the eighteenth-century to almost cult status. In likening natural elements to the crumbling stones of ancient structures, Lewis revealed both his romantic sensibility and his rather keen familiarity with contemporary aesthetic issues.⁹

Lewis's most notable aesthetic commentary was at the Great Falls of the Missouri, where he expressly wished for an artist to capture the sight before him. After ascending to a rise overlooking the falls, he made note of the "beatifull rainbow" over the cascade, which he called a "sublimely grand specticle," and followed with a lengthy description of the scene. At last words failed, however, and he despaired, saying in frustration:

> after wrighting this imperfect discription I again viewed the falls and was so much disgusted with the imperfect idea which it conveyed of the scene that I determined to draw my pen across it and begin agin, but then reflected that I could not perhaps succeed better than pening the first impressions of the mind; I wished for the pencil of Salvator Rosa . . . or the pen of Thompson, that I might be enabled to give to the enlightened world some just idea of this truly magnifficent and sublimely grand object, which has from the commencement of time been concealed from the view of the civilized man; but this was fruitless and vain. I most sincerely regretted that I had not brought a crimee [camera] obscura with me by the assistance of which even I could have hoped to have done better but alas this was also out of my reach; I therefore with the assistance of my pen only indeavoured to trace some of the stronger features of this seen by the assistance of which and my recollection aided by some able

pencil I hope still to give to the world some faint idea of an object which at this moment fills me with such pleasure and astonishment, and which of it's kind I will venture to ascert is second to but one in the known world.[10]

In this statement, the most pointed artistic reference of the expedition, Lewis made clear his grasp of aesthetic tradition, his desire for a means of visual documentation of the sights he was encountering, and his understanding of its value for conveying the view to others far from the scene.

Salvator Rosa (1615–1673) was a seventeenth-century Italian painter famous for his dramatic landscapes filled with rocky outcroppings, windblown trees, and cataclysmic weather. Although not well-known today beyond art history circles, his work was considered paradigmatic of the visual sublime in the eighteenth and early nineteenth centuries, and his name became a standard reference to that mode of landscape depiction.[11] Equally famous at the time was James Thomson (1700–1748), a noted Scottish writer whose epic poem *The Seasons* (1726–1730; revised 1744) was the first in English to have landscape as its subject. Enormously influential on both sides of the Atlantic, this poem was a staple for anyone interested in landscape imagery until at least the mid-nineteenth century. An illustrated edition had been published in Philadelphia in 1797, and it is interesting to speculate if Lewis had seen this edition with pictures.[12]

Lewis also mentioned a camera obscura in his commentary, wishing he had brought one in order to facilitate his drawing of the falls. The term *camera obscura* (meaning "dark room") was coined by the German astronomer Johannes Kepler (1571–1630), who refined the optical device in the early seventeenth century. Essentially a lensless camera through which a scene is transferred by sunlight into a darkened space through a pinhole, the instrument was used as a drawing aid for centuries before the invention of photography. While not compact, these devices were portable (they could be as small as a manageable box) and made outline drawings as easy to produce as tracing the contours of a reflected object. Lewis's knowledge of the potential usefulness of the camera obscura, especially coupled with his mention of Salvator Rosa and Thomson, is a clear indicator of his aesthetic sophistication.[13]

After viewing the Great Falls, Lewis continued upriver where he found another equally impressive waterfall the next day. There he resumed his contemplative description in a short statement that compared the new fall to the previous one. "I now thought," he wrote, "that if a skillful painter had been asked to make a beautifull cascade that he would most probably have p[r]esented the precise immage of this one; nor could I for some time determine on which of those two great cataracts to bestoe the palm, on this or that which I had discovered yesterday; at length I determined between these two great rivals for glory that this was *pleasingly beautifull*, while the other was *sublimely grand*."[14] These complementary concepts—the beautiful and the sublime, to which the picturesque is often added—were fundamental to aesthetic theory and intellectual discourse about landscape at the turn of the nineteenth century. The definitive treatment was Edmund Burke's famous treatise *A Philosophical Enquiry into the Origin of Our Ideas of the Sublime and the Beautiful* (1757), a book Jefferson owned and recommended to others.[15] The beautiful was characterized by delicacy, smooth or soft textures, and small or human scale; most importantly, it evoked affection in the viewer. The sublime, by contrast, was identified by vastness, ruggedness or roughness, and enormity; it prompted feelings of awe. For Lewis, as with many others since, the terms were the ultimate descriptors of impressive sights, but they also revealed his familiarity with their more complex aesthetic implications.[16] Although he had neither the pencil of Salvator Rosa nor a camera obscura, his vocabulary assured that learned readers would grasp the significance of these scenes even if they could not literally visualize them.

Although it remains unclear just how much impact Lewis's statements about painters and cameras had on the planning of subsequent explorations, most major federal expeditions that followed the Corps of Discovery included some provision for visual documentation. In many cases, the artwork that resulted appeared in engraved or lithographic form in official government reports.[17] The most immediate successor, Zebulon Pike's 1806 expedition to the West, left Saint Louis before Lewis and Clark returned, and it, too, was graphically undocumented, but in 1819, the Stephen Long Expedition to the Rocky Mountains included not one but two artists, Titian Ramsay Peale (1799–1885) and Samuel Seymour (1775–1823). Their work consequently entered the history of art as the first American images of the West.[18]

Titian Peale was the youngest son of Charles Willson Peale (1741–1827), a remarkable man who served as an artistic and natural history consultant to Thomas Jefferson. The elder Peale was one of the foremost artists in the country, the founder of the first museum in the United States (Figure 2), and something of a Renaissance man, with skills in taxidermy, portraiture, natural history, paleontology, ornithology, and zoology, to name but a few. Peale had met Jefferson as early as 1774 and had painted his portrait in 1792 during the period Jefferson served in Philadelphia as secretary of state for Washington's administration.[19] Jefferson became a subscriber to the Peale museum at that time and relied upon Peale for a variety of things, including the provision of his polygraph, a device invaluable to a man of letters since it reproduced a document as it was being written.[20]

Peale and Jefferson were in nearly constant touch on issues of natural history throughout the planning period for the mission of the Corps of Discovery and throughout its journey. They discussed, among other things, the ongoing international debate about the ancient fauna of Europe and America, a topic that both engaged Jefferson intellectually and to some degree directed his hopes for the Lewis and Clark Expedition. Peale's museum housed two nearly complete mastodon skeletons that the director had excavated in 1801. Peale wrote a lengthy letter describing the bones to Jefferson only a few weeks before Lewis traveled to Philadelphia in May 1803 for instruction from several leading members of the American Philosophical Society.[21] The president naively hoped that Lewis and Clark might encounter a living mastodon in the West. If discovered, such a specimen would provide the definitive evidence the president needed for his nationalistic response to Eurocentric scientists.[22]

When Lewis traveled to Philadelphia for training, he was not expressly directed to Peale or his museum, and there is no evidence that he visited there, but it would have been an important place to gather useful information for the expedition.[23] Peale was a prominent member of the American Philosophical Society, was in close touch with the men Lewis consulted, and would have been a natural consultant for the explorer, instructing him on, among other things, the practical art of taxidermy so necessary to preserving the varied animals the explorers would send back from the field. He might also have shown Lewis his paintings, which included some of the earliest landscape views in the United States, reinforcing, perhaps, an awareness of the need for visual documentation of the terrain encountered on the expedition. Peale almost certainly would have introduced Lewis to his several sons, most of whom were not only named after artists but were respected artists in their own right.

FIGURE 2. Charles Willson Peale, The Artist in His Museum, 1822, oil on canvas, the Pennsylvania Academy of the Fine Arts, Philadelphia (gift of Mrs. Sarah Harrison, the Joseph Harrison, Jr., Collection)

The second oldest, Rembrandt Peale (1778–1860), had written to Thomas Jefferson in December of 1800 and again a few months later, asking for artistic patronage. The new president responded by sitting for his portrait and ordering a copy in the spring of 1801. In his letters, the younger Peale had appealed to Jefferson's "fondness for the fine Arts" and recalled the president's "generous conduct" to John Trumbull (1756–1843), whom Jefferson had encouraged to paint scenes from American history in the late 1780s. Peale was specifically hoping for a sponsored European sojourn on behalf of the new nation, but he also suggested that "much of my object may perhaps be answered without leaving the Country; and there may be found a situation where I may . . . persue my desired improvements."[24] The post was never granted, but if Jefferson had been inclined to suggest an artist for the Lewis and Clark Expedition in 1802–1803, Rembrandt Peale would have made a fine choice.

While in Philadelphia in May 1803, Lewis did consult with the eminent Dr. Benjamin Smith Barton, professor of botany at the University of Pennsylvania and author of the newly issued *Elements of Botany: or Outlines of the Natural History of Vegetables* (1803). This book, the first American textbook on the subject, was one of the reference works Lewis carried with him on the expedition. Significantly, the text was illustrated with thirty engraved plates, most drawn by one of the leading natural history draftsmen in the country, William Bartram (1739–1823), who himself had published a notable illustrated book, *Travels through North and South Carolina, Georgia, East and West Florida* (1791). Barton's *Elements of Botany* almost certainly served as a model for the proposed natural history section of the publication that Jefferson and Lewis envisioned after the expedition, and the president forwarded the botanist many of the specimens Lewis sent from the West for description. Although Barton did not complete this task, his influence on the expedition's attention to natural history is undisputed. Because he instructed Lewis in methods of preserving and describing plants and was so familiar with the work necessary to eventual publication, it is curious that he seems not to have emphasized the need for a draftsman who could visually portray specimens in the field.[25]

Another contact that can only be called a near miss in the history of the Lewis and Clark Expedition also serves to illuminate the congregation of minds that converged upon the project and the thinking about visual documentation of expeditions at the time. Within days of the Corps of Discovery's departure up the Missouri from Saint Louis in May 1804, the German naturalist Baron Alexander von Humboldt (1769–1859) visited Jefferson in Washington, escorted by Charles Willson Peale whom he had just visited in Philadelphia. Baron Von Humboldt was on the last leg of a long excursion through South America where he had compiled notes and observations he would later publish widely, most notably in his multi-volume opus Cosmos (1845–1870), which established him as the foremost natural historian of the mid-nineteenth century. While at the White House, Humboldt spoke to Jefferson about Peale's museum, suggesting that the government purchase the collection for the nation and move it to Washington. Over dinner, the men shared their mutual interests, not the least of which were exploration and scientific inquiry.[26]

This meeting is especially interesting since Humboldt was an accomplished artist in addition to his expertise in natural history, and he was an advocate of artists accompanying expeditions. Furthermore, his philosophy and attitudes toward the natural world were remarkably similar to Jefferson's.[27] Throughout his travels, Humboldt kept journals annotated with drawings, and he later devoted an entire chapter of Cosmos to the issue of landscape painting. "Ought any means to be left unemployed," he wrote, "by which an animated picture of a distant zone, untraversed by ourselves, may be presented to the mind with all the vividness of truth, enabling us even to enjoy some portion of the pleasure derived from the immediate contact with nature?" A few pages later, he asked optimistically, "Are we not justified in hoping that landscape painting will flourish with a new and hitherto unknown brilliancy when artists of merit shall more frequently pass the narrow limits of the Mediterranean, and when they shall be enabled, far in the interior of continents, . . . to seize, with the genuine freshness of a pure and youthful spirit, on the true image of the varied forms of nature?"[28] Although these comments were published years after his meeting with Jefferson in 1804, Humboldt's attitudes were already expressed in his own practice of combining art with exploration, and the German naturalist would undoubtedly have been fascinated with the American expedition so recently dispatched. Although his visit came too late to influence the president's plans for the Corps of Discovery, Humboldt's associations with Peale and Jefferson offer a tantalizing glimpse into the confluence of science, art, and politics that surrounded Lewis and Clark's mission.

After the party returned from the West in 1806, Meriwether Lewis assumed two major responsibilities, neither of which he successfully completed—the governorship of Louisiana Territory and the production of the published journals of the expedition. He spent several months in early 1807 in Philadelphia commissioning a publisher, John Conrad, and working with artists and naturalists to produce illustrations to accompany the text. His attention to the visual material is a clear indication that he and probably Jefferson, who took an active interest in the report, were committed to the publication's aesthetic dimension. Although Lewis did not advance the project far before his untimely death in 1809, the prospectus he and Conrad issued in April 1807 makes clear the plan for its visual imagery. Volume One was to be "embellished with a view of the great cataract of the Missouri," presumably made from Lewis's now lost sketch drawn at Great Falls. Volume Two would be "embellished with a number of plates illustrative of the dress and general appearance of such Indian nations as differ materially from each other," and Volume Three, devoted to natural history, would "be ornamented and embellished with a much greater number of plates than will be bestowed on the first part of the work."[29] It was an exceptionally ambitious plan that, had it been realized, would have been a monument in American history and exploration.

Illustrated travel and exploration accounts as well as illustrated natural history books had a long history. Jefferson, a noted bibliophile and traveler, would certainly have been familiar with such publications and anxious to have the Lewis and Clark Expedition similarly documented. In addition to numerous European examples, not to mention the centuries-old tradition of printed landscapes and city views, more immediate models for an illustrated edition of Lewis and Clark's discoveries would have been the published histories of Captain James Cook's voyages or those of George Vancouver, both of which included illustrated plates and were surely known to Jefferson.[30] Another work Lewis actually carried with him was a 1774 English edition of Antoine du Pratz's *History of Louisiana*, which was also illustrated.[31] The precedent of embellishing exploration narratives with imagery was well established, and it seems clear that the original plan for the Corps of Discovery publication was based on a carefully considered understanding of its role in continuing the tradition.

As Paul Russell Cutright discussed in his book *A History of the Lewis and Clark Journals*, Lewis spent much of his time in Philadelphia in early 1807 arranging for the images that would adorn the final volumes.[32] Most of the ethnographic and zoological artifacts from the expedition had been deposited in Peale's museum. A trained taxidermist, Peale mounted many of the specimens and drew several for the anticipated publication, writing to a friend in the spring of 1807, "The drawings for Governor Lewis's Journal I mean to draw myself to be engraved for the work."[33] We know from letters that these included a badger, an antelope, a big horn sheep, Lewis's woodpecker (named in honor of the explorer), a mountain quail (Figure 3), and a Louisiana, or western, tanager, although only the latter three drawings have survived.[34] All three are obviously intended as published specimen drawings, judging from their linearity and their vignette presentation.

Another well-known artist-naturalist, Alexander Wilson (1766–1813), also produced images of birds at Lewis's request. At the time, Wilson was hard at work on his own monumental work, American Ornithology (1808–1814), and was a logical choice to create the avian portraits, although why both he and Peale produced images of the same birds remains unclear. Four of the images appeared in Wilson's book. One, presented on a composite page with Clark's Crow, is also Lewis's Woodpecker (Figure 4), undoubtedly drawn from the same mounted specimen as Peale's image. In the printed version, the tanager was added as well. Wilson, a more accomplished ornithologist than Peale, bent the woodpecker's head toward the limb and positioned the body vertically in a posture more characteristic of the species than it appeared in Peale's drawing.[35]

Jefferson sent the botanical specimens from the expedition to the American Philosophical Society, which distributed them for study to botanists Benjamin Smith Barton, Bernard McMahon, and William Hamilton, who referred a young German-American botanical artist, Frederick Pursh (1774–1820), to Lewis when he arrived back in the East with an additional group of specimens. Lewis subsequently paid Pursh seventy dollars for drawings of plants, many of which appeared in Pursh's two-volume book Flora Americae Septentrionalis in 1814.[36] These delicately drawn and colored plates (Figure 5) are some of the most beautiful images to emerge from Lewis's ill-fated efforts toward publication. Had they appeared together in the final volume Lewis envisioned, the drawings by Peale, Wilson, and Pursh would have made a significant contribution to their respective scientific fields, as well as to art history, and would have increased the overall impact of the Lewis and Clark Expedition.

The drawing or drawings of the Great Falls of the Missouri that Lewis

FIGURE 3. *Charles Willson Peale*, Mountain Quail and Lewis's Woodpecker, ca. 1806, graphite and watercolor on paper, American Philosophical Society, Philadelphia

himself apparently drew at the site as he wished for the pen of Salvator Rosa have never been located, but they may have been the origin of two drawings of waterfalls the explorer commissioned from Philadelphia engraver John James Barralet (ca. 1747–1815) for forty dollars in 1807.[37] Barralet's drawings have since also been lost, but one of the engravings based on them, originally intended for Volume One of Lewis's planned publication, appeared in the 1817 Dublin edition of Nicholas Biddle's history of

Artistic Legacy   95

FIGURE 4. Alexander Wilson, Clark's Crow and Lewis's Woodpecker, 1808, pen and ink, graphite, and wash on paper, Academy of Natural Sciences of Philadelphia, Ewell Sale Stewart Library

the Lewis and Clark Expedition (Figure 6). Mysteriously, this edition is the only version that contains the plate, and, indeed, it seems to be the only one containing a landscape view.[38] As Stephen Dow Beckham notes, it is "the earliest known image of the Great Falls of the Missouri."[39] Even more significantly, it may be a glimpse of Lewis's drawing in which he "indeavoured

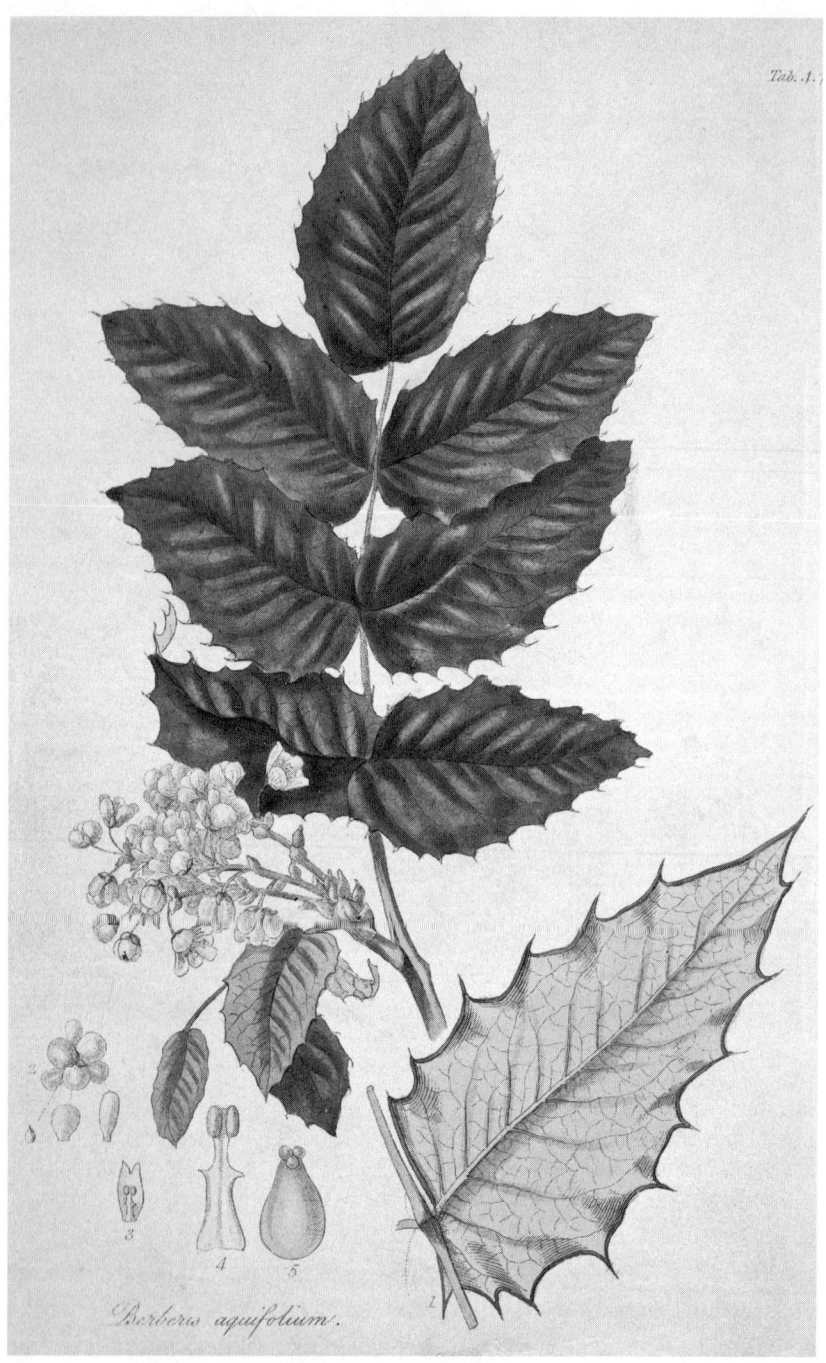

FIGURE 5. Frederick Pursh, Berberis aquifolium, Flora Americae Septentrionalis, 1814, plate 108, Academy of Natural Sciences of Philadelphia, Ewell Sale Stewart Library

Artistic Legacy 97

FIGURE 6. *John James Barralet [after Meriwether Lewis?], Principal Cascade of the Missouri, engraving, from* History of the Expedition under the Command of Captains Lewis and Clarke [sic], *Dublin: J. Christie, 1817, plate facing p. 326, Lewis and Clark College Library, Portland, Oregon*

to trace some of the stronger features of this seen." If so, Lewis indeed succeeded in giving to the world, by the assistance of Barralet's able pencil, an idea of the sight that had originally filled him with "such pleasure and astonishment."

The image is an accomplished portrayal, in keeping with the fact that the Dublin-born Barralet was a well-trained painter of landscapes and historical subjects. He had exhibited, among other places, at the Royal Academy in London before coming to the United States in 1795.[40] The falls, which fills the center of the composition, is bounded on the right by a jutting lower bank that angles in from the right. Upon the bank stand an American Indian village, several inhabitants, and a small grove of trees. Rising above them, a rocky butte further anchors the right side of the scene, directing our gaze to the center and toward a distant peak that rises above the falls. On the left, a less distinctive bank frames the opposite side of the scene, keeping our gaze contained and focused on the cascade that pours toward us in the middle ground. The cascade itself is remarkably faithful to the actual appearance of the Great Falls before the river was dammed upstream in the twentieth century, dramatically changing their appearance. This faithfulness to nature further argues for Lewis's sketch as Barralet's source because the distinctive horizontal configuration looks nothing like more famous waterfalls (such as Niagara) to which Barralet would undoubtedly have turned had he not had a direct reference. As such, the engraving, however perfected, offers an intriguing glimpse into Lewis's own attempt at artistry and assumes a greater significance than it has previously been given in both the history of art and Lewis and Clark scholarship.

For Volume Two, the ethnographic section of the planned publication, Lewis commissioned Indian portraits from Charles Balthazar Julien Fevret de Saint-Mémin (1770–1852), an artist who had fled the French Revolution in the 1790s and worked throughout the eastern United States until 1810. For Lewis, Saint-Mémin produced fourteen portraits of American Indians who visited the East from 1804 to 1807, primarily using a physiognotrace, a device that literally traced the profile of a sitter's head to create a nearly exact likeness. He had become known for these remarkable portraits and for his ingenious marketing. He provided the original portrait, an engraved plate, and twelve engravings for twenty-five dollars for male sitters and thirty-five for female, the price difference due to the greater difficulty of rendering the women's hair and clothing.[41] This modest cost and comprehensive package, as well as Saint-Mémin's reputation—his long list of eminent clients included Thomas Jefferson, Paul Revere, and Charles Willson Peale—no doubt appealed to Lewis as he planned his publication. Lewis paid Saint-Mémin $83.50 for his portraits.[42]

As Ellen Miles has ably explained, Saint-Mémin's series of American Indian portraits are among the earliest extant likenesses of Plains Indians by a non-native artist.[43] Exceptionally naturalistic, both for their unidealized and distinctive profiles and for the detailed rendering of the personal accoutrements of each sitter, these portrayals suggest both a fascination with the exoticism the figures represented and a sensitivity to their appearance as individuals. In *Mandan King*, an 1807 watercolor (Figure 7), for example, Saint-Mémin gave us a revealing glimpse of Shahaka, also known as "The Big White." This Mandan chief, along with his wife Yellow Corn (whom Saint-Mémin also portrayed in an 1807 profile), their child, and a group of Osages, had accompanied Lewis on his return east.[44] The couple was hosted by Thomas Jefferson in 1806, toured New York and Washington, and returned to their home in present-day North Dakota in 1809. Some of the Saint-Mémin portraits, including the view of Shahaka, later appeared in lithographic versions in Thomas L. McKenney and James Hall's monu-

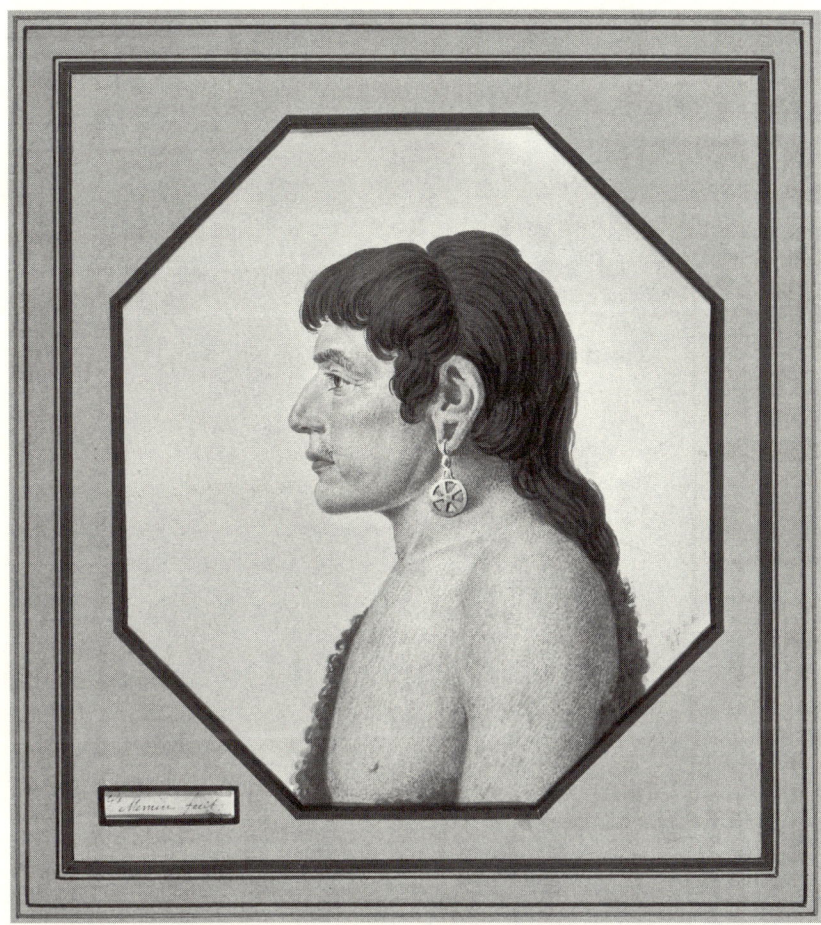

FIGURE 7. Charles Bathazar Julie Fevret de Saint-Mémin, Mandan King [Shahaka, "The Big White"], 1807, watercolor on paper, Thomas Gilcrease Institute of History and Art, Tulsa, Oklahoma

mental study, History of the Indian Tribes of North America (1837–1844). Thus, like many of Lewis's other commissions, they did eventually find a public audience in the nineteenth century, although not in connection with the Corps of Discovery expedition.

Saint-Mémin had done a profile portrait of Meriwether Lewis in 1802, which is now in the Valentine Museum in Richmond, and after the expedition, he did additional likenesses of both Lewis and Clark (1807).[45] He also did a full-figure watercolor portrait of Lewis dressed in buckskin

FIGURE 8. *Charles Bathazar Julie Fevret de Saint-Mémin, Captain Meriwether Lewis, 1807*, watercolor over graphite on paper, Collection of The New-York Historical Society (gift of the heirs of Hall Park McCullough, accession no. 1971.125)

FIGURE 9. *Charles Willson Peale, Meriwether Lewis, from life, 1807, oil on paper on canvas, Independence National Historical Park, Philadelphia*

and adorned with an ermine mantle, a gift that Lewis called a tippet from the Shoshone chief Cameahwait (Figure 8). Intriguingly, for his museum Charles Willson Peale created a full-scale wax model of Lewis, presumably from this image, dressing the figure as it appears in the portrait and including the actual ermine mantle, which was in his museum's collection. The wax Lewis, however, was not positioned with a rifle, as he is in Saint-Mémin's painting, but rather with a calumet pipe in one hand and the other hand over his breast as a symbol of peace.[46] Peale also painted his own portraits of Lewis and Clark, which he added to his museum's Gallery of Great Men (Figures 9, 10). "Mr. Lewis is richly entitled to a place amongst the Portraits of the Museum," Peale wrote, "and I hope he will do me the favor of sitting as soon as he arrives here."[47] Lewis sat for Peale in 1807,

FIGURE 10. *Charles Willson Peale, William Clark, from life, ca. 1807-1808, oil on board, Independence National Historical Park, Philadelphia*

and Clark did later. In the museum, these portraits joined the ranks of noble personages that Peale had been painting for decades, including Jefferson himself. Other artists, including American portraitist John Wesley Jarvis (1781–1839), also painted Lewis from life, and later artists Chester Harding (1792–1866), Joseph Bush (1794–1865), and George Catlin all produced images of William Clark.[48] These works did not figure into the plans for Lewis's publication, but together they provide an overall portrayal of the expedition members and their national significance.

Regrettably, Lewis's many artistic commissions were never combined into the spectacular volumes he envisioned. Even so, his effort to engage the finest aesthetic dimension for their pages indicates a strong desire to represent the expedition in its fullest visual form. In the end, however,

FIGURE 11. *Anonymous,* A Canoe Striking on a Tree, *ca. 1810, engraving, frontispiece to Patrick Gass,* A Journal of the Voyages and Travels of a Corps of Discovery, under the Command of Capt. Lewis and Capt. Clarke [sic] *(Philadelphia: Mathew Carey, 1810), Lewis and Clark College Library, Portland, Oregon*

the actual published histories and journals of the Lewis and Clark Expedition were mere shadows of what Lewis had planned. Most nineteenth-century editions lack illustrations other than maps, with the notable exception of Patrick Gass's journal. Issued first in 1807, Gass's journal was reissued by Philadelphia publisher Mathew Carey in 1810 with six amateurish wood engravings by an unknown artist (Figures 11–16). These plates have been reprinted frequently ever since, even though they were outright inventions. Cutright called them "delightfully preposterous," and Elliott Coues noted rather diplomatically that "the figures of men, trees, and animals are notable rather for the mathematical regularity of their lines than for any approach to 'curves of beauty.'"[49] These fanciful attempts aside, until modern reproduction techniques facilitated pictorial illustration at the end of the nineteenth century, most books about the Corps of Discovery's mission remained lacking in pictorial adornment.

It is easy to criticize Thomas Jefferson, a self-admitted "enthusiast on the subject of the arts," for his omission of an artist in the Corps of Discovery.[50] The president was, after all, an accomplished architect with a strong visual sense, a collector of illustrated volumes of travel and exploration, an intimate with artists and the history of art, and he should have anticipated the

FIGURE 12. Anonymous, Captains Lewis & Clark holding a Council with the Indians, ca. 1810, engraving, from Gass, Journal of the Voyages and Travels of a Corps of Discovery, facing p. 26, Lewis and Clark College Library, Portland, Oregon

FIGURE 13. Anonymous, Captain Clark & his men building a line of Huts, ca. 1810, engraving, from Gass, Journal of the Voyages and Travels of a Corps of Discovery, facing p. 60, Lewis and Clark College Library, Portland, Oregon

FIGURE 14. Anonymous, Captain Clark and his men shooting Bears, ca. 1810, engraving, from Gass, Journal of the Voyages and Travels of a Corps of Discovery, facing p. 95, Lewis and Clark College Library, Portland, Oregon

FIGURE 15. Anonymous, An American having struck a Bear but not killed him, escapes into a Tree, ca. 1810, engraving, from Gass, Journal of the Voyages and Travels of a Corps of Discovery, facing p. 239, Lewis and Clark College Library, Portland, Oregon

FIGURE 16. *Anonymous*, Captain Lewis shooting an Indian, *ca. 1810, engraving, from Gass*, Journal of the Voyages and Travels of a Corps of Discovery, *facing p. 60, Lewis and Clark College Library, Portland, Oregon*

need for and value of visual documentation of such an important expedition. At the same time, however, his sights were on other things, especially, as many have noted, the location of the long-desired Northwest Passage through North America and the diplomatic relations to be fostered with the American Indians of the Louisiana Purchase region. These issues would have more serious national consequences than even the most thorough artistic portrayal of the expedition could hope to have. In his preoccupation with such matters and with the extensive preparations he was directing (not to mention his other activities as president), he may have simply overlooked the provision of an artist for the enterprise, or he may have deemed it impractical considering the hardships the expedition would encounter on their pathbreaking journey.

In retrospect, the most immediate, and in some ways lasting, artistic impact of the Lewis and Clark Expedition may have been Titian Peale's participation in the Long Expedition in 1819, which began the long and fruitful tradition of federal exploration art. Intimately aware of the complications the lack of an artist had meant to the earlier mission, Charles Willson Peale lobbied Secretary of War John C. Calhoun for his youngest son's appointment during a portrait session in Washington late in 1818.[51] Just a few months later, after Titian had secured the position (and unaware that artist

Samuel Seymour would also accompany the party), Rembrandt Peale wrote his brother: "I suspect you will be the only Draughtsman. I therefore recommend you to practise [sic] immediately sketching from nature—I know how well you draw when you have the object placed quietly before you—but if you practice Sketching from human figures as well as animals & trees: Hills, Cataracts &c you will be able to present us with many a Curious & interesting representation. . . . Make drawings of the Indians in their warrior dresses—these will be infinitely more interesting than if made from the dresses put on white men afterwards. Give us some accurate drawings of their habitations. I have never Seen one that was decently finished."[52] If only these instructions could have been given to some eager young artist preparing to accompany the Corps of Discovery in 1803. How much more vivid our image of their achievements might have been!

NOTES

1. For more on Jefferson's artistic inclinations, see Harold E. Dickson, "'Th.J.' Art Collector," in *Jefferson and the Arts: An Extended View*, ed. William Howard Adams (Washington, D.C: National Gallery of Art, 1976), pp. 105–32. See also William Howard Adams, ed., *The Eye of Thomas Jefferson* (Washington, D.C.: National Gallery of Art, 1976). Jefferson's instructions to Lewis, dated 20 June 1803, are reprinted in *Letters of the Lewis and Clark Expedition with Related Documents, 1783–1854*, ed. Donald Jackson, 2d ed., 2 vols. (Urbana: University of Illinois, 1978), 1:61.

2. Lewis's drawing appears in Figure 1. To compare it with Clark's similar drawing of 25 February 1806, see Gary E. Moulton and Thomas W. Dunlay, eds., *The Journals of the Lewis and Clark Expedition, Vol. 6: November 2, 1805–March 22, 1806* (Lincoln: University of Nebraska Press, 1990), p. 350.

3. Such references also appear occasionally in Patrick Gass's journal. On 15 October 1805, for example, he remarks on the Snake River just before it empties into the Columbia: "This river in general is very handsome, except at the rapids, . . . [which], when the bare view of prospect is considered distinct from the advantages of navigation, may add to its beauty, by interposing variety and scenes of romantick grandeur where there is so much uniformity in the appearance of the country" (Gass, *A Journal of the Voyages and Travels of a Corps of Discovery . . . during the Years 1804, 1805, and 1806* [1807; reprint ed., Minneapolis: Ross & Haines, 1958], p. 179).

4. Lewis, 12 July 1804, *Original Journals of the Lewis and Clark Expedition, 1804–1806*, ed. Reuben Gold Thwaites, 8 vols. (New York: Dodd, Mead & Co., 1904), 1:75. Such comments are not unique to Lewis. Clark, for example, wrote on 13 June

1804, "Capt. Lewis and myself walked to the hill, from the top of which we had a butifull prospect of Serounding countrey" (ibid., p. 47).

5. For more on prospect painting, *see* James Turner, "Landscape and the 'Art Prospective' in England, 1584–1660," *Journal of the Warburg and Courtauld Institutes* 42 (1979): 290–93; Stephen Daniels, "Goodly Prospects: English Estate Portraiture, 1670–1730," in *Mapping the Landscape: Essays in Art and Cartography*, ed. Nicholas Alfrey and Stephen Daniels (Nottingham: University Art Gallery, Castle Museum, 1990), pp. 9–17; and Joni L. Kinsey, *Plain Pictures: Images of the American Prairie* (Washington, D.C.: Smithsonian Institution Press for the University of Iowa Museum, 1996), esp. pp. 17–19.

6. Boime, *The Magisterial Gaze: Manifest Destiny and American Landscape Painting, c. 1830–1865* (Washington, D.C.: Smithsonian Institution Press, 1991). A similar point is made in Angela Miller, *The Empire of the Eye: Landscape Representation and American Cultural Politics, 1825–1875* (Ithaca, N.Y.: Cornell University Press, 1993).

7. These definitions are adapted from *Oxford English Dictionary*, 1971, s.v. "prospect."

8. Lewis, 31 May 1805, *The Journals of the Lewis and Clark Expedition*, Vol. 4: *April 7–July 27, 1805*, ed. Gary E. Moulton and Thomas W. Dunlay (Lincoln: University of Nebraska Press, 1987), pp. 225–26.

9. This trope has been discussed in a number of places, but for an overview, *see* the chapter entitled "Landscape as Metaphor" in *Thomas Moran and the Surveying of the American West*, by Joni L. Kinsey (Washington, D.C.: Smithsonian Institution Press, 1992), esp. pp. 20–24. The cult of ruins is also discussed widely, but the classic text is Rose Macaulay, *Pleasure of Ruins* (1953; reprint ed., New York: Thames & Hudson, 1964).

10. Lewis, 13 June 1805, *Journals*, ed. Moulton, 4:283–85.

11. Charlotte Klonk, *Science and the Perception of Nature: British Landscape Art in the Late Eighteenth and Early Nineteenth Centuries* (New Haven and London: Yale University Press for the Paul Mellon Centre for Studies in British Art, 1996), p. 9.

12. Thomson, *The Seasons* (Philadelphia: W. W. Woodward, 1797). The four plates were by Alexander Lawson, a noted Philadelphia engraver. *See also* Douglas Grant, *James Thomson, Poet of "The Seasons"* (London: Cresset Press, 1951).

13. For the camera obscura, *see* Svetlana Alpers, *The Art of Describing: Dutch Art in the Seventeenth Century* (Chicago: University of Chicago Press, 1983), pp. 50–51.

14. Lewis, 14 June 1805, *Journals*, ed. Moulton, 4:290.

15. Burke's treatise and other texts devoted to the arts were at the top of a basic library list that Jefferson recommended to his relative Robert Skipwith in 1771. Dickson, "'Th.J.' Art Collector," p. 105.

16. The literature on this subject is vast, but *see*, for example, Mark Roskill, *The Languages of Landscape* (University Park: Pennsylvania State University Press, 1997).

17. For more on expeditionary photography, *see* Martha A. Sandweiss, *Print the Legend: Photography and the American West* (New Haven, Conn.: Yale University Press, 2002).

18. Kenneth Haltman explores the visual imagery from the Long Expedition in his Ph.D. dissertation, "Figures in a Western Landscape: Reading the Art of Titian Ramsay Peale from the Long Expedition to the Rocky Mountains, 1819–1820" (Yale University, 1992). *See also* his article, "Between Science and Art: Titian Ramsay Peale's Long Expedition Sketches, Newly Recovered at the State Historical Society of Iowa," *Palimpsest* 74 (Summer 1993): 62–81, in which he mentions that Secretary of War John C. Calhoun, President James Monroe, and Long himself included the artists as a response to the lack of visual documentation on the Lewis and Clark Expedition (p. 64).

19. Lillian B. Miller, ed., *The Selected Papers of Charles Willson Peale and His Family*, Vol. 2; pt. 1: *Charles Willson Peale: The Artist as Museum Keeper, 1791–1810* (New Haven, Conn.: Yale University Press, 1988), p. 5nn.1, 3.

20. John Isaac Hawkins invented the polygraph, but Peale worked with him on refinements. After Hawkins left Philadelphia for England in June 1803, Peale retained the American rights to the device. *See* Silvio A. Bedini, *Thomas Jefferson and His Copying Machines* (Charlottesville: University Press of Virginia, 1984).

21. Peale to Jefferson, 19 Apr. 1803, in *Selected Papers of Charles Willson Peale*, ed. Miller, 2:523–26; *see also* 11 Oct. 1801, pp. 371–75. Peale's painting The Exhumation of the Mastodon, 1806–1808, today resides in the Peale Museum in Baltimore.

22. Jefferson discussed his intense interest in the mastodon, or mammoth as he also calls it, most thoroughly in a long passage in his 1797 book, *Notes on the State of Virginia*, ed. William Peden (New York: W. W. Norton & Co., 1972). Saying that the creature reputedly "still exists in the northern parts of America," he is "certain such a one has existed in America, and that it has been the largest of all terrestrial beings" (pp. 43–47). Jefferson hoped that evidence of such a beast would soundly refute the claims of the prominent French naturalist Count de Buffon, who had asserted that European life forms were superior to those in America where, he said, species had degenerated and were smaller than comparable animals and plants in Europe.

23. Peale wrote the president again on 2 June 1803 without mentioning Lewis or his visit; whether they met or not remains unclear. *See* Miller, ed. *Selected Papers of Charles Willson Peale*, 2:532–34.

24. Rembrandt Peale to Jefferson, 17 Dec. 1800, 24 Mar. 1801, ibid., pp. 290–91, 305–6. Rembrandt Peale's 1800 portrait of Jefferson currently resides in the White House Collection in Washington, D.C. *See* Lillian B. Miller, *In Pursuit of Fame: Rembrandt Peale, 1778–1860* (Washington, D.C.: Smithsonian Institution & University of Washington Press, 1992), pp. 48–49.

25. Paul Russell Cutright, *Lewis and Clark: Pioneering Naturalists* (Urbana: University of Illinois Press, 1969), p. 25; Georgia B. Barnhill, "The Publication of Illustrated Natural Histories in Philadelphia, 1800–1850," in *The American Illustrated Book in the Nineteenth Century*, ed. Gerald W. R. Ward (Winterthur, Del.: Henry Francis du Pont Winterthur Museum, 1987), pp. 53–88, esp. 56–57. The standard practice among botanical illustrators was to work from preserved specimens, which may explain Barton's lack of emphasis on a field artist. Until the appearance of Barton's own book, American plants had been described by Europeans using dried and pressed plants sent from America.

26. Herman R. Friis, "Baron Alexander von Humboldt's Visit to Washington, D.C., June 1 through June 13, 1804," *Records of the Columbia Historical Society* 60 (1960–1962): 1–35. Humboldt's trip to the United States was arranged through the American vice-consul in Cuba, and Humboldt wrote to Jefferson upon his arrival in Philadelphia in May and was invited to Washington for dinner.

27. See Edmunds V. Bunkse, "Humboldt and an Aesthetic Tradition Geography," *Geographical Review* 71 (Apr. 1981): 127–46, and Charles A. Miller, *Jefferson and Nature: An Interpretation* (Baltimore, Md.: Johns Hopkins University Press, 1988).

28. Humboldt, *Cosmos: A Sketch of a Physical Description of the Universe*, Vol. II (New York: Harper Brothers, 1858), pp. 81, 93. Humboldt issued thirty-four volumes of his journal over a twenty-five-year period. Roughly twelve hundred copper plates illustrated his travels. Stephen Jay Gould, "Church, Humboldt, and Darwin: The Tension and Harmony of Art and Science," in *Frederic Edwin Church*, by Franklin Kelly et al. (Washington, D.C.: National Gallery of Art, 1989), pp. 94–107, esp. p. 97.

29. The Conrad Prospectus, 1 Apr. 1807, in *Letters of the Lewis and Clark Expedition*, ed. Jackson, 2:394–96. See also George Ehrlich, "The 1807 Plan for an Illustrated Edition of the Lewis and Clark Expedition," *Pennsylvania Magazine of History and Biography* 109 (Jan. 1985): 43–57. I am grateful to Gary Moulton for bringing this article to my attention.

30. Ehrlich, "The 1807 Plan," pp. 43–44. For Cook, see John Hawkesworth, ed., *An Account of the Voyages Undertaken by the Order of his Present Majesty for Making Discoveries in the Southern Hemisphere*, 3 vols. (London, 1773); James Cook, *A Voyage towards the South Pole and round the World*, 2 vols. (London, 1777); Cook and James King, *A Voyage to the Pacific Ocean*, 4 vols. (London, 1784); and George Vancouver, *Voyage of Discovery to the North Pacific Ocean and Round the World*, 3 vols. (London, 1798). For a particularly useful overview of travel literature, see Gloria Gilda Deák, *Picturing America: Prints, Maps, and Drawings Bearing on the New World Discoveries and on the Development of the Territory that is Now the United States*, 2 vols. (Princeton, N.J.: Princeton University Press, 1988). See also Barnhill, "Publication of Illustrated Natural Histories."

31. [Antoine] le Page du Pratz, *The History of Louisiana, or of the Western Parts of Virginia and Carolina: Containing a Description of the Countries that lie on Both Sides of the River Mississippi: With an Account of the Settlements, Inhabitants, Soil, Climate, and Products*, 2d ed. (London: T. Becket, 1774). This book has thirty-nine illustrations, ranging from images of native peoples to plants and animals, although the drawings are obviously by an untrained artist. Cutright notes that Benjamin Smith Barton loaned Lewis this book and that Lewis later inscribed it to Barton, saying, "it has been since conveyed by me to the Pacific Ocean through the interior of North America" (quoted in Cutright, *Lewis and Clark: Pioneering Naturalists*, p. 25). See also Cutright's "Lewis and Clark and Du Pratz," *Missouri Historical Society Bulletin* 21 (Oct. 1964): 31–35. The Barton/Lewis book is today in the Library Company collection in Philadelphia.

32. Cutright, *A History of the Lewis and Clark Journals* (Norman: University of Oklahoma Press, 1976).

33. Peale to John Hawkins, 5 May 1807, in *Letters of the Lewis and Clark Expedition*, ed. Jackson, 2:411.

34. William Clark to William D. Meriwether, ibid., p. 490. These images are in the collection of the American Philosophical Society in Philadelphia. Another image of a horned lizard has also survived, but its attribution is disputed despite the inscription in Titian Peale's hand, "Drawn by CWPeale." Some have attributed the work to Pietro Ancora who was working for Benjamin Smith Barton. See Edgar P. Richardson, Brooke Hindle, and Lillian B. Miller, *Charles Willson Peale and His World* (New York: Harry N. Abrams, 1982), p. 159.

35. *Philadelphia: Three Centuries of American Art* (Philadelphia: Philadelphia Museum of Art, 1976), pp. 207–11, and Barnhill, "Publication of Illustrated Natural Histories," pp. 60–66. The four birds in Wilson's book were Lewis's woodpecker (*Asyndesmus lewis*), Clark's nutcracker (*Nucifraga columbiana*), the western tanager (*Piranga ludoviciana*), and the black-billed magpie (*Pica pica hudsonia*). Cutright, *History of the Lewis and Clark Journals*, p. 45.

36. Cutright, *History of the Lewis and Clark Journals*, p. 42, and Cutright, *Lewis and Clark: Pioneering Naturalists*, pp. 359–60, 363.

37. Jackson, ed., *Letters of the Lewis and Clark Expedition*, 2:463n.6; Cutright, *History of the Lewis and Clark Journals*, p. 46.

38. Elliott Coues, ed., *The History of the Lewis and Clark Expedition*, 3 vols. (1893; reprint ed., New York: Dover, n.d.): 1:cxxix, was the first to note this unusual fact. Cutright in the *History of the Lewis and Clark Journals* asserted that Clark had later "stated that Barralet had made the two drawings and that they were of 'the falls of the Missouri & Columbia.' The fate of these is unknown" (p. 46).

39. Beckham et al., *The Literature of the Lewis and Clark Expedition: A Bibliography and Essays* (Portland, Oreg.: Lewis & Clark College, 2003), p. 179. Like Coues, Beck-

ham ascribes the 1817 Dublin edition print to Barralet, but he does not ultimately ascribe them to Lewis. I am grateful to Gary Moulton for bringing Beckham's new book to my attention.

40. *Philadelphia: Three Centuries of American Art*, p. 235.

41. Saint-Mémin's advertisement appeared in the Philadelphia *Aurora and General Advertiser* from 22 December 1801 through 11 March 1802 and, until recently, could be found at http://educate.si.edu/migrations/portrait/essay.html. For an excellent discussion of these portraits, *see* Ellen G. Miles, "Saint-Mémin's Portraits of American Indians, 1804–1807," *American Art Journal* 20, no. 4 (1988): 2–33. Saint-Mémin returned permanently to France in 1814. *See also* Ellen G. Miles, *Saint-Mémin and the Neoclassical Profile Portrait in America* (Washington, D.C.: National Portrait Gallery and Smithsonian Institution Press, 1994).

42. Jackson, ed., *Letters of the Lewis and Clark Expedition*, p. 411n.

43. Miles, "Saint-Mémin's Portraits of American Indians," p. 3.

44. The portraits of Big White and Yellow Corn are both in the Gilcrease Museum. They are reproduced in color in *Gilcrease Journal* 8 (Summer 2000): 59.

45. The National Portrait Gallery in Washington has engraved versions of these 1807 portraits. The Missouri Historical Society in Saint Louis has one of Saint-Mémin's originals of Lewis from 1807.

46. Richardson, Hindle, and Miller, *Charles Willson Peale and His World*, p. 158; Peale to Jefferson, 29 Jan. 1808, in *Letters of the Lewis and Clark Expedition*, ed. Jackson, 2:439–40. The wax model has long since disappeared. Wax figures were popular at the turn of the nineteenth century, but, outside of Madame Toussaud's Wax Museum in London, most have since been lost. An excellent exception is Philadelphia wax sculptor Patience Lovell Wright's full-scale figure *William Pitt, Earl of Chatham* (1779) in the collection of Westminster Abbey, London. Wright's example may have been important to Peale since her subjects included many of his own sitters, including Benjamin Franklin. See Frances K. Pohl, *Framing America: A Social History of American Art* (New York: Thames & Hudson, 2002), pp. 86–87.

47. Peale to Jefferson, 24 Dec. 1806, in *Letters of the Lewis and Clark Expedition*, ed. Jackson, 1:374n.

48. Paul R. Cutright, "Lewis & Clark: Portraits and Portraitists," *Montana, the Magazine of Western History* 19 (Apr. 1969): 37–38, 44–50. Cutright's article was an early attempt to account for the many portraits of the explorers, and although it reproduces many likenesses, it suffers from several omissions and inaccuracies. Appendix C of Cutright's *Lewis and Clark: Pioneering Naturalists*, pp. 448–56, does a better job of listing locations of portraits and other significant objects.

49. Cutright, *History of the Lewis and Clark Journals*, p. 31; Coues, *History of the Lewis and Clark Expedition*, 1:cxxi.

50. Jefferson described himself in these words to James Madison in 1785. Quoted in Dickson, "'TH.J.' Art Collector," p. 112.

51. Charles Willson Peale reported in a letter to his son Rubens, "Mr. Calhoun told me that he would write to Major Long about Titian's going on the expidition [sic] up the Missourie" (Lillian B. Miller, ed., *The Selected Papers of Charles Willson Peale and His Family*, Vol. 3: *The Belfield Farm Years, 1810–1820* [New Haven, Conn.: Yale University Press, 1988], p. 666; *see also* pp. 667n.5, 668–69).

52. Rembrandt Peale to Titian Peale, 26 Mar. 1819, ibid., pp. 706–7.

Telling Lewis and Clark Stories
Historical Novelists as Storytellers
RICHARD W. ETULAIN

"We shall henceforth know Lewis and Clark as we never knew them before," a noted editor prophesied.[1] At the same time a reviewer asked, "Are we getting too much of Lewis and Clark?"[2] Contemporary as these statements may seem, they are not part of the bicentennial. Instead, they are the prediction of historian Reuben Gold Thwaites and part of a review examining the first volumes of his *Original Journals of the Lewis and Clark Expedition* during the Lewis and Clark centennial. In the midst of the celebration of the Corps of Discovery in 1904–1906, historians, editors, and journalists would have recognized the names of Nicholas Biddle, Elliott Coues, Thwaites, and perhaps James K. Hosmer. These men had been important agents in putting the famous Lewis and Clark journals before the public and in providing historical and biographical backgrounds for the explorers' writings.[3] But in another area at the opening of the twentieth century, the Lewis and Clark Expedition had not sparked much attention. Novelists had not discovered the corps as a rich, challenging subject for their fiction. This oversight reveals a good deal about the developments of literature and regionalism in the American West and the nation as a whole.

On the eve of the Lewis and Clark centennial, American writers were in thrall to a cowboy Old West. Owen Wister's lively cowboy romance *The Virginian*, building on an earlier generation of dime novelists and other popular fictions about the cowboy, topped bestseller lists in 1902 and 1903. In that novel, Wister launched what later became known as the Western. In subsequent decades, Zane Grey, Max Brand, Ernest Haycox, Luke Short, and Louis L'Amour, among others, hardened that popular genre into familiar plot formulas, character types, and stylized, even ritual, actions. These stereotyped ingredients left little room for a Lewis and Clark story—or for any story of exploration—if not accompanied by romance, rising action, and strong conflicts between easily recognized white-and-black-hatted characters.

Another impediment to fictional treatments of the Lewis and Clark story was the slow literary development of much of the northern American West. True, by the early 1900s, Edgar Watson Howe (*The Story of a Country Town*, 1883), Joseph Kirkland (*Zury: The Meanest Man in Spring County*, 1887), and Hamlin Garland (*Main-Travelled Roads*, 1891) had begun to depict the agricultural frontier in their novels and stories. But fiction on other nineteenth-century topics was late in coming from other Northern Plains writers. Before 1900, novelists were nonexistent in the Rockies, and writers of the Pacific Northwest were addicted to romances in the vein of Nathaniel Hawthorne, as distinguished from the more realistic fiction of Stephen Crane and William Dean Howells. Northwest suffragist and writer Abigail Scott Duniway had written several novels, most of which had been serialized in her feminist newspaper/magazine *New Northwest*. But the most popular novel of the region was Frederic Homer Balch's *The Bridge of the Gods* (1890), which, gaining considerable national attention at its appearance, has been in print for more than a century.

These twin strains of the domestic and feminist fiction of Duniway and the historical romance of Balch prepared the way for Eva Emery Dye's novel *The Conquest: The True Story of Lewis and Clark* (1902), the first well-known novel about the expedition.[4] Well-educated with a master's degree in ancient studies, Dye was also an ardent suffragist. Moving to Oregon in 1890, she had become a devoted student of the area's early history, publishing in 1900 a historical romance entitled *McLoughlin and Old Oregon: A Chronicle*.[5] As Portland made plans to host the centennial of the Lewis and Clark journey, Dye's publisher encouraged her "to weave a story about that" subject.[6]

Working quickly and diligently, as her revealing papers on file at the Oregon Historical Society amply attest, Dye wrote to descendents of the Lewis and Clark families to gather unpublished stories about their ancestors. She also gained access, through the help of Thwaites, to the edited journals before his edition appeared in eight volumes in 1904–1905. From this prodigious research, Dye constructed a novel of roughly four hundred fifty pages, which she divided into three books. The first section, focusing on the valiant story of William Clark's older brother George Rogers Clark, treats the Appalachian frontier from the American Revolution to about 1800. The second and longest book deals with the expedition and events of 1803 to

1806. The final section describes Lewis's post-expedition life glancingly but traces Clark's life and his important role as a friend and negotiator with Indians through his death in 1838.

Dye's Lewis and Clark, George Rogers Clark, Daniel Boone, and Thomas Jefferson are all heroic characters. In the author's inflated prose, they are blood brothers to Achilles and Odysseus. Indeed, in an opening note, Dye writes, "A Homeric song, the epic of a nation, clusters around the names of Lewis and Clark and the border heroes of their time: their story is the Iliad of the West" (p. x). They also resemble other fictional frontier worthies in overcoming demanding, dangerous landscapes and defeating "savage" Indians.

In *The Conquest*, Dye also wobbles between the roles of historian and novelist. Trying to cover more than a century of complicated frontier history, she often steps aside — in authorial sidebars — to provide readers great globs of history that clot her narrative. To bring her protagonists into a new scene or involve them in stirring events like the Revolutionary War or the War of 1812, Dye becomes more historian than novelist. Similar problems arise in the author's other intrusions. For instance, after introducing Patrick Gass as an uneducated member of the Corps of Discovery, Dye quickly adds: "But what Pat lacked in books he made up in observation and shrewd reasoning; hence it fell out that Patrick Gass's journal was the first published account of the Lewis and Clark expedition. All honour to Patrick Gass. Of such are our heroes" (p. 168).

With one exception, Dye's Indians lack substance. They are portrayed as brutal, face-painted nonhumans. Bloody and barbarous, they are also "childlike," gullible, and fearful. If the author's Lewis and Clark figures belong in the pantheon of American heroes, their opponents are too often cardboard characters, without minds, hearts, or humanity. In this vein, Dye says of one Indian leader, "Black Partridge was a typical savage, — asking for civilisation [sic]" (p. 384).

Dye's Sacagawea, however, breaks dramatically from these portraits of Indians. This novel's "Indian princess" heroine helps one understand the myths that eventually surrounded and shaped Sacagawea. Dye, encouraged by her publisher to find a female lead for her novel, had "traced down every old book and scrap of paper, but still was without a real heroine. Finally," she adds, "I came upon the name of Sacajawea and I screamed, 'I have found my heroine.'"[7] Dye's treatment of the Indian teenage mother meshed smoothly with the contemporary interests of woman-suffrage leader Abigail Scott Duniway, an acquaintance of Dye's, and the planners of the Lewis and Clark centennial. One scholar, examining this conjunction of needs and outcomes, concludes that the "important point to the student of the Lewis and Clark expedition is that it was in Oregon that the Sacagawea myth found life and flourished."[8]

Eva Emery Dye's novel provided an influential jumping-off place for fictional treatments of the Lewis and Clark narrative. Her white male protagonists are apotheosized into godlike characters, their American Indian opponents as demons, and Sacagawea as romantic heroine. Commenting on the latter ingredient, noted editor Donald Jackson wrote: "Sacagawea was never acclaimed as a real heroine by the American public until she was, in a sense, rediscovered by Eva Emery Dye in 1902."[9] Later, University of Wyoming professor Grace Raymond Hebard did much to conflate the Sacagawea myth,[10] but Dye established important precedents in her fictional depictions. Dye's background in ancient history, her involvement in the suffragette movement, and her location in Oregon at the time of the centennial clearly influenced the shape and content of her novel. From the confluence of these backgrounds and Dye's diligent research in the pertinent original sources came an initial, widely read historical romance about Lewis and Clark. In the next few decades, novelists gave individualistic turns to these ingredients, but much of their fiction included what Eva Emery Dye pioneered early in the twentieth century.

Like Dye, Emerson Hough also wrote historical romances. He was a popular magazine writer and sometime historian emphasizing the American West in his writings during the first three decades of the twentieth century. In his novel about Lewis and Clark, *The Magnificent Adventure* (1916), Hough produced fiction similar to that in his other historical novels.[11] What one authority writes of Hough's best-known novel, *The Covered Wagon* (1922), is true of his work on Lewis and Clark: "Though the novel is allegedly factual, its real concerns are sentimentally romantic. . . . Hough cannot be credited with originating the combination of love interest with he-man adventure, which is the hallmark of his fiction, [but] he certainly was one of the most successful practitioners of this kind of western writing."[12]

Unfortunately, Hough's mishmash of romance and novelized history fails. Attempting to graft a fictional story of Meriwether Lewis's love for Aaron Burr's married daughter, Theodosia Alston, onto the expedition's history, the author is forced to distort history and falsify the characters of Thomas Jefferson, Lewis, Clark, and Sacagawea to further his sentimental and romantic goals. Lewis becomes primarily a frustrated, misanthropic lover; Clark, a carefree captain; Sacagawea, the guide of the expedition; and Jefferson, a failed president save for the success of the Lewis and Clark Expedition. Throughout his novel, Hough is also guilty of "managing" history, allowing events to serve more his contrived than his factual purposes. In the end, Hough's fiction illustrates how much the Lewis and Clark story can be manipulated.[13] In his hands, *The Magnificent Adventure* proves unsatisfactory as a historical novel because history is prostituted, sold off to the demands of popular fiction. Quite simply, Hough traveled the wrong trail; he took along a cast of distorted characters; and thus he missed his goal of producing sound historical fiction.

The best of the early fictional works about Lewis and Clark is Ethel Hueston's *Star of the West* (1935).[14] Author of several historical and domestic romances, Hueston extensively utilized firsthand accounts of the expedition and paid close attention to actual physical settings. Better than other novels on this subject, her story judiciously balances the westward and eastward legs of the journey and focuses entirely on characters known to be members of the expedition or residents in the towns, villages, or Indian encampments they visited. The author's smooth, flowing style and her clear storytelling talents also add much to her novel.

Hueston states in her novel's Foreword that she follows history exactly, save for the conversations she has created. Nearly all these dialogues are, she adds, based on the expedition's journals. The "only outright liberty taken with authentic history," Hueston writes, is in the opening chapter dealing with Charbonneau's obtaining Sacagawea (p. 8). The author is surely right in this confession since no extant evidence tells us exactly how the mixed-race interpreter secured his "squaw." Other readers demanding historical authenticity might blanch at how much Hueston elaborates on brief references in the journals. Also, the author falls victim to the Sacagawea myth, making the Indian woman a central, participating figure in nearly all of the expedition's activities and allowing her more responsibility for guiding the men than historical sources attest.

Nevertheless, the balance, persuasiveness, and other strengths of *Star of the West* outweigh these limitations. Rather than overemphasize the expedition's brief stay with Sacagawea's Shoshone people, for example, Hueston

" 'Him Ro'shones,' replied the girl"

[PAGE 219]

Drawn by Arthur I. Keller, the frontispiece of Emerson Hough's The Magnificent Adventure *(1916) shows Lewis and Clark taking directions from Sacagawea.*

places emphases where they should be: on the extended stopovers with the Mandan, Clatsop, and Nez Perce. Following the journal accounts, the author likewise makes clear, correct distinctions between the friendly Mandans, Shoshone, Nez Perce, and Clatsop and the animosities or difficulties with the Teton, Chinook and other Columbia River tribes, Crow, and

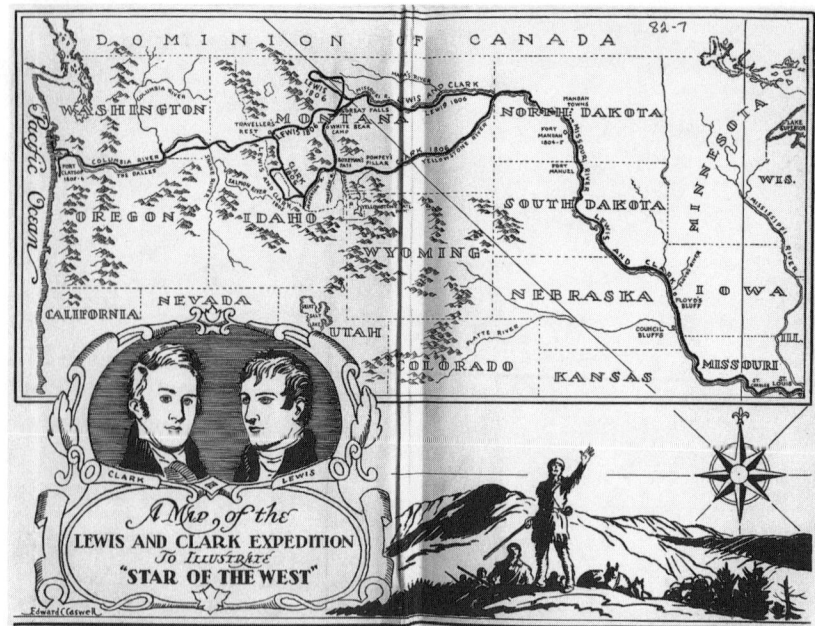

The endpapers of Ethel Hueston's Star of the West (1935), drawn by Edward C. Caswell, center on Lewis and Clark and promise a tale of heroic actions from the Corps of Discovery.

Blackfeet. The extensive sections of the novel dealing with native groups, although seen primarily through white eyes, are nonetheless more discerning than those in the other early Lewis and Clark novels.

Overall, Hueston tells an engrossing, moving story. She persuades the reader that these were the daily difficulties facing these heroic men. These were the dilemmas that the leaders Lewis and Clark faced and overcame. These were the deeds and thoughts of Sacagawea and Charbonneau. These were the reactions of Indian peoples along the trek into the wilderness. Even if later novelists such as Vardis Fisher, James Alexander Thom, and Brian Hall moved beyond Hueston in the cultural complexities their probing novels address, she produced the best of the novels about Lewis and Clark in the first half of the twentieth century.[15]

Although Donald Culross Peattie promises in the Foreword of his novel Forward the Nation (1942) "that the events . . . are all true," he embroiders considerably on those facts. He disavows the title of historian, but nowhere, he adds, has he "distorted fact." Speaking in the third person, Peattie claims, "Whatever he has recounted here that is not stated in the records he believes can be discovered there between the lines."[16] These claims notwithstanding, Peattie, a well-known naturalist and author, adds much not told in the documents, considerably dramatizes events he considers central, and elides whole months of the journey. He opens with an imagined account of Sacagawea's capture and then quickly switches to President Thomas Jefferson for two or three paragraphs. A second chapter traces the Jefferson-Meriwether Lewis friendship, and the following chapter provides nearly a dozen pages on Napoleon and his consort Josephine before recrossing the Atlantic to describe plans for the Lewis and Clark Expedition.

Peattie likewise embraces the Sacagawea myth. His brief novel plays up her role and in doing so undercuts the important contributions of several other white and Indian leaders. When Sacagawea is deathly sick near the Rockies, the author intrudes with the thought, "Do you [Lewis] understand that the whole success of your venture hangs on that girl's living through this hour" (p. 91)? A bit later the author adds that in the history of the United States, "no other woman ever served it [the country] better" (p. 109). For Peattie, Sacagawea is the guide for much of the expedition. He also distorts the journals in suggesting that Lewis is more attracted to her than Clark and that George Shannon is in love with her. When in his note on sources, Peattie "acknowledges a large debt" to Grace Hebard (pp. 280–81), one better understands his interpretation of the Indian woman. Peattie also follows Hebard in arguing that Sacagawea lived to be an old woman who died in Wyoming on 9 April 1884.

These fascinations with Sacagawea skew Peattie's story. He all but omits the expedition's earlier contact with other Indians on their way up the Missouri to visit the Mandans. We also get little after the contact with Sacagawea's people, the Shoshone. Worst of all, the return trip is telescoped into a few pages. Finally, although Peattie is a skilled, smooth stylist, his experimental plot misfires. He uses the story of the Louisiana Purchase and Napoleon's difficulties as a parallel narrative to the saga of the corps's months spent descending the Columbia and returning. Flashing quickly from the wilderness West to Washington, D.C., to speak of Jefferson and then on to Paris to depict Napoleon's failures, the author undermines his plot, making it hard to follow and more difficult to accept. Even though Peattie's story is invitingly written, he has overemphasized the importance of Sacagawea and truncated the story of Lewis and Clark in his "reading between the lines."

Of other novels written about Lewis and Clark before the mid-twentieth century, Della Gould Emmons's *Sacajawea of the Shoshones* (1943) most resembles Eva Emery Dye's *The Conquest*. Like Dye, Emmons follows closely Grace Hebard's interpretation of Sacagawea as a notable guide and interpreter for the explorers. Emmons also accepts Hebard's questionable view that the Indian woman lived until 1884. Similar to other female novelists who have written about the Shoshone woman, the author of *Sacajawea of the Shoshones* portrays the Bird Woman as romantically drawn to William Clark, and he somewhat to her.[17]

In tone, Emmons's novel reminds one of Hueston's *Star of the West*. Both works of fiction are sentimental romances, overflowing with emotional descriptions of human thoughts and actions. When the young and very pregnant Sacagawea first encounters Clark, she is immediately transformed by his helpful actions. As he lifts a heavy load of furs she is carrying, his "look of understanding and sympathy . . . turned Little Bird Woman's starved heart over and over and upset her world then and there so completely that it changed the remainder of her long life" (p. 100). Alienated from her beastly and lascivious husband Charbonneau, Emmons's Sacagawea dreams of what her life might be with a handsome, kindly, and heroic man like Clark.

Although Emmons appends a brief section of historical sources to each chapter, her book is driven more by imagination than facts. Repeatedly, she enters Sacagawea's consciousness, explaining the young Shoshone woman's inmost desires. For Emmons, Sacagawea is not only a guide and interpreter for the expedition, she virtually saves Clark's life and sometimes seems to be as important as the captains in determining the success of their journey. This novel demonstrates how strongly the myth of Sacagawea as guide had fastened on fictional interpretations of the expedition by 1950.

By mid-century, a few patterns had emerged in fiction about Lewis and Clark. Most novelists had made use of the Thwaites edition of the expedition's journals to provide a strong historical sense in their works, but they nearly always added to or subverted these sources for their fictional purposes. Some created new characters for their novels; others omitted occurrences so as to stress competing actions; and all created conversations missing from the historical sources. Even more obvious, novelists had fallen in love with Sacagawea. By the middle of the twentieth century, fiction writers had distorted her role in the expedition. They had helped create

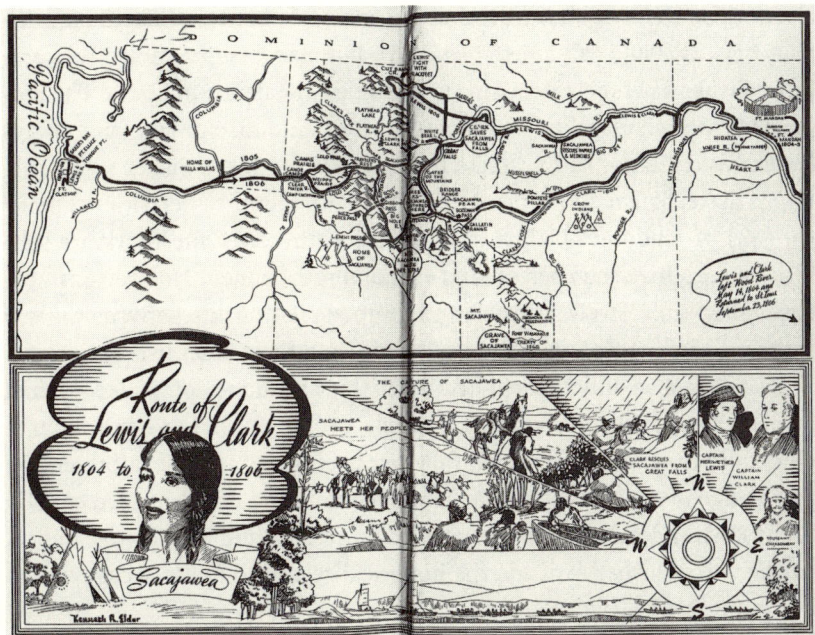

Drawn by Kenneth R. Elder, the endpapers of Della Gould Emmons's Sacajawea of the Shoshones (1943) suggest a central role for the young Indian woman on the expedition.

a Sacagawea myth that transformed her into a central figure in the journey, often making her the chief guide for the explorers. Several of these emphases continued in novels published in the next decades, but others appeared to become notable parts of the later fiction written about Lewis and Clark.

Idaho author Vardis Fisher was an American author of considerable repute by time he wrote his story of Lewis and Clark in *Tale of Valor* (1958).[18] The recipient of a Ph.D. with high honors from the University of Chicago, Fisher had already published more than twenty novels, including his Harper Prize-winning *Children of God* (1939) about the Mormons. Driven, highly individualistic, iconoclastic, and an advocate of a harsh realism in one's personal life and writings, Fisher wanted to tell his story factually—and dramatically.[19]

Fisher moves well beyond previous novelists in plumbing the characters of Lewis and Clark. Fisher's melancholy but whimsical Meriwether Lewis is witty, dry-humored, shrewd, mischievous, and a superb leader. Fisher uses a variety of terms to describe Lewis: a romantic man of "insatiable curiosity" (p. 221) and "sly mirth" (p. 349), but also "irrepressible" (p. 427). From Fisher's perspective, Clark is a wonderful balance to Lewis. The redheaded frontiersman knows Indians, is stern and disciplined, and always dependable. Clark "had no taste for . . . jests" (p. 211), Fisher writes. He might be "exhausted but [also] undaunted" (p. 290), "a determined man" (p. 344) of "indomitable" (p. 351) spirit. Both Lewis and Clark are self-disciplined, drive themselves, and care about their men. No previous novelist had so fully developed the warm, mutual relationship between the two captains, their complementary leadership, and their inner lives.

Fisher is also much intrigued with the Shoshone, or Snake, Indian woman Sacagawea. Although he avoids overemphasizing her role as a guide, he nonetheless develops fully her usefulness as an interpreter, her knowledge of roots and berries, her attachment to the red-headed captain (Clark), her indefatigable buoyancy and optimism, and her positive impact on the corps. Fisher expands the historical record to make Sacagawea an intriguing, persuasive character.

One limitation undercuts Fisher's otherwise superb novel, however. From the beginning to the end, he strains to sustain a high-pitched level of tension, stress, and threat. Opening his work with the expedition's traumatic confrontations with the Teton, or Brulé, Sioux on their way up the Missouri, Fisher then keeps his story revved up through the corps's nearly nonstop difficulties with hunger, terrain and climate, flagging morale, and their need for horses. Even though the journals reveal days of less-than-deadly strain, Fisher passes quickly over these mundane times to load up his narrative with drama. In keeping his focus on action, he devotes only fifty pages to the return trip but four hundred pages to the journey from the Sioux conflicts to the Pacific Coast in 1804–1805. Occasionally, the author makes good use of humor, including the scatological comments of the men about their sexual appetites. But this novel is deadly serious, full of the harsh realism Fisher advocated for all fiction writing.[20]

In his novel on the Lewis and Clark journey, *The Gates of the Mountains* (1963), Will Henry (Henry Wilson Allen) adopts a narrative technique he and other historical novelists often utilize.[21] Henry's fiction about Wyatt Earp, General Custer, Chief Joseph, the James brothers, and his Civil War novels employ an imaginary or tangential character through which to tell the larger story. In *Gates of the Mountains*, the shadowy character of François

("Frank") Rivet becomes a participant in and mouthpiece for the Lewis and Clark Expedition. In addition, Rivet grows up, transitioning from an idealistic, unreliable, romantic boy into a diligent, observant, and thoughtful man.

Through Rivet, Henry narrates three tales in one. First, Frank provides much of the novel's historical framework by helping Clark prepare his journal accounts and by commenting on Lewis's diary entries. Second, like so many other heroes of Lewis and Clark novels, Frank immediately and wholly falls in love with Sacagawea. Third, Frank's search for his father, who has disappeared years ago and is rumored to live among the Shoshone, provides a quest motif for the novel. On several occasions, unfortunately, Frank carries too much authorial freight, with Henry the novelist asking him to know and do things beyond his temporal ken. And his first-moment infatuation with Sacagawea is too much. At their initial meeting, Frank says: "When she raised her eyes and looked at me, my heart stopped beating. . . . I loved Sacajawea beyond time, beyond place, beyond reason. It was that way in the beginning, that way in the end; it was the *all*, the final thing" (p. 118).

Readers might dismiss, with good reason, Henry's novel as too emotional, too laden with chance and circumstance, too contrived—until they realize that the first chapters are portrayed through Frank's adolescent consciousness. Not until the idealistic boy achieves manhood in the latter sections of the novel do we see a more realistic, probing portrait of the corps, its participants, and their experiences. William Clark tries to teach Frank, but the young half-French, half-Pawnee has to learn the world's complexities through his own adventures. One of the most revealing scenes in this regard takes place when Clark takes Frank along to visit Sacagawea, the "savage" Indian, and her husband Charbonneau. When Frank sees the Indian "squaw" kill a puppy, throw it immediately, ungutted and unskinned, into a pot, and spit tobacco juice, some of which dribbles into the stew pot, he quickly realizes that he views Sacagawea through love-blinded eyes (pp. 286–87). Still, by the end of the novel, Frank chooses to remain with Charbonneau, Sacagawea, and other Indians on the Northern Plains. He has accepted his mixed-race backgrounds, grasped more of the world's complexities, and taken on growing responsibilities as a newly matured man.

Will Henry's biographer astutely argues that *Gates of the Mountain* was not intended "to introduce historical characters, but to present aesthetically pleasing historomance."[22] Indeed. By judiciously combining quotations from the Lewis and Clark journals with the imagined details of Frank Rivet's life and mind, Henry produces a hybrid historical novel, part fact and part fiction. In this juxtaposition of history and imagination, the author furnishes one of the more valuable novels about Lewis and Clark.

The lengthy historical romance *Sacajawea* (1979) by Anna Lee Waldo remains the most unusual fictional work about the expedition.[23] Selling well more than a million copies—more, perhaps, than all the other Lewis and Clark novels together—and remaining on the *New York Times* bestseller list for several months, Waldo's enormous work is two or three times longer than most other novels about the expedition. One scholar has estimated that the Lewis and Clark journals contain about one hundred ten references to Sacagawea and, if condensed, these references would fill no more than thirty to forty pages in an average-sized book.[24] But Waldo's huge novel runs to more than fourteen hundred pages. Imagination—sheer invention—dominates this fat work.

Sections of Waldo's novel suggest extensive historical research on her part. Her bibliography, extending to eighteen pages, includes citations to major manuscript collections. Even more extensive are the sixty pages of thorough endnotes. Additionally, each of the fifty-seven chapters opens with a quotation from a pertinent historical, biographical, or ethnographic source. An Epilogue augments the historical component of the novel by reviewing the controversies concerning Sacagawea's death in 1812 or in 1884. Judged from these evidences alone, the novel seems based primarily on thorough and discerning historical research. Such is not the case, unfortunately. Most of the excessively long novel comes directly from the author's fertile imagination. For example, Sacagawea's thoughts about her parents, sexual experiences, religious convictions, and her feelings about Clark, Lewis, and other members of the corps are unrecorded, yet Waldo includes chapter after chapter on these topics. Perhaps one scholar put it best in stating that the novel is "loosely based on the life of Sacagawea."[25]

Why, then, has this work attracted so many enthusiastic and devoted readers? First of all, Waldo understands apt storytelling. Her story moves; it seldom drags. Her major characters, Sacagawea, Lewis, Clark, and Charbonneau, are provocatively drawn. The author also comprehends what many general readers of fiction enjoy. After accepting Grace Hebard's case for the "long-life" version of Sacagawea's days, Waldo writes in her Acknowledgments, "I hope that my readers will be thankful for a story that begins with a child wondering about the origin of the ancient medicine circle and ends with an old woman sensing the termination of a free, nomadic culture" (p. viii). Even though historians and other academics have roundly criticized—even scorned—what they consider the inadequacies and superficialities of Waldo's romance novel, general readers have bought it by the millions—and continue to do so. It is by far the most popular of novels written about Lewis and Clark and Sacagawea.

James Alexander Thom's *From Sea to Shining Sea* (1984), a stirringly written novel, devotes the final three hundred of nearly nine hundred pages to the Lewis and Clark Expedition.[26] The long book opens with the Clark family during the American Revolution and closes with William Clark's return to his home in 1806. Throughout this expansive novel, the author keeps his attention on the personalities of his major characters. The relationships between Clark and Lewis, among the men of the corps, between the captains and their men, between the corps and native leaders, between Clark and Sacagawea, and between Clark and York—these human relationships dominate the novel. Clark, Lewis, Charbonneau, Sacagawea, York, and several of the expedition's men emerge as full, well-rounded characters in this very human story.

Thom also moves beyond other novelists in foreshadowing dramatic incidents. His descriptions of Sacagawea's entry into Shoshone country and the hours before her fortuitous meeting with her brother Cameahwait are particularly well done. Likewise, he avoids the authorial intrusions that mar so many of the other Lewis and Clark novels. On the other hand, the author's telescoping of some events is surprising considering the length of his narrative. Thom treats the nearly eleven months from the corps's arrival at Fort Clatsop until the end of 1806 in less than ten pages. That means we get almost nothing about the return trip, the difficulties with the Blackfeet, Lewis's wounding, the leave-taking of Sacagawea and Charbonneau, and the arrival in Saint Louis. The elision of all these important events and further illustrations of character development flattens out the novel's conclusion and leaves one dissatisfied with the story's ending.

Still, *From Sea to Shining Sea* remains one of the two or three most rewarding fictions about Lewis and Clark. Thom's clear literary talents, his probing depictions of personality, his adroit use of humor, his ability to suit appropriate language to individual characters greatly enlarge the literary worth of this memorable novel. Grand in conception, panoramic in organization, and probing in its treatment of character, Thom's story of the Lewis and Clark Expedition is an important contribution to the fictional treatment of this magnificent historical event.

Brian Hall's *I Should Be Extremely Happy in Your Company* (2002), a recent novel about Lewis and Clark, is, by far, the most experimental in form and content.[27] Hall's work is minimalistic in style, explicitly realistic in the treatment of sexuality, sometimes elliptical in conversations, and it frequently employs stream of consciousness in its interior monologues. But the most notable feature is the author's apt employment of several viewpoints to tell his story. We get, as expected, extensive sections from Lewis and Clark's perspectives; these sections are contrapuntally placed alongside those from Sacagawea and Charbonneau—and briefer ones from Jefferson and York. Hall takes native thoughts and actions seriously, and on most occasions, these alternating sections seem well suited to the varied narrators.

Hall's novel exudes darkness. His Meriwether Lewis, beset by his isolationist tendencies and his self doubts, leads his men but seldom befriends them. His depression and illness lead to his suicide. Even William Clark, so often treated by historians and other novelists as warm, friendly, and approachable, wonders in this novel about his achievements in his later years. Sacagawea dies in an epidemic, and York and Charbonneau wander despairingly at the end of their lives. Only Seaman's thumping tail seems to sound positive notes in Hall's novel.

Those unacquainted with the chronology and major events of the Lewis and Clark Expedition will find this novel difficult going. In fact, Hall's innovative organization and style lead to considerable confusion. Chronology, specific incidents, and sequence get lost in the conflicting perspectives. The author's tendency to overwrite—his diction and syntax often calling attention to themselves—will put off other readers. In short, Hall's novel remains a curiously mixed effort. The author's multiple viewpoints provide appealing complexity, and his innovative style reflects trends in contemporary, postmodern American literature. But his self-absorption, indeed his excessive self-reflexivity, will alienate some readers. They will also find sections of the novel, especially from Sacagawea and Charbonneau's viewpoints, irritatingly obscure. For each clear strength, the novel betrays a limiting weakness.

On more than a few occasions, historians, biographers, ethnologists, and historical editors imply that they travel the high road of discernment in studying the past while novelists, dramatists, and other creative artists traverse a lower level of understanding. Paul Russell Cutright, distinguished scholar and author of well-received books on Lewis and Clark, represents this point of view in arguing, "Generally speaking, historians look down their noses at historical novels." Fictional accounts of the expedition, he continues, reinforce this negative reaction among historians because novelists have imagined conversations and distorted actual happenings.[28] Wallace Stegner, our original Wise Man of the American West, points out some of this distaste for historical fiction from a different angle. "It is my impression," Stegner writes, "that too many trained professionals consider narrative history, history rendered as story, to be something faintly disreputable, the proper playground of lady novelists."[29]

I want to argue for another viewpoint, one that posits convergences between historians and novelists. As Stegner further points out, "Calliope and Clio are not identical twins, but they *are* sisters."[30] I believe their close family connections, their sisterhood, become clear in the concept of "story." Historians and novelists are both committed storytellers; both want readers to follow easily and well what they say about events, people, and concepts. Among those writing about Lewis and Clark, there is a long, clear line of storytelling historians from Bernard DeVoto and John Bakeless, through Donald Jackson, up to James Ronda. These historians, like novelists, create narrative peaks and valleys. Superb narrative historians like these also look for ways to hook readers with appealing characterizations, dramatic scenes, attention-catching descriptions, and poetic language.

Undoubtedly, two generations of excessive allegiances to social history, cliometrics, and cultural theory have blinded many historians to the links that connect them with novelists. But, to reiterate, narrative historians and fiction writers are tellers of tales, attempting to narrate the past through interest-whetting stories. The sooner historians re-perceive their similarities with novelists the less likely they are to scorn historical novelists, and, perhaps, the more likely to re-learn helpful storytelling techniques from those fictionists.

Conversely, novelists writing about the Lewis and Clark Expedition might attract more positive responses from historians if they re-think how they produce their fiction about the Corps of Discovery. First, novelists do not need to create fictional characters or to distort the historical record in their fiction. There is sufficient drama and human interest in the expedition's story to draw readers. The journals are replete with moments of high adventure, superb natural and human descriptions, and engrossing clashes among cultures and peoples.

Second, Brian Hall's recent novel on Lewis and Clark proves that novelists may—and should—utilize multiple voices in telling their stories. We must have the viewpoints of the white leaders—President Jefferson, Captains Lewis and Clark; but we should get the perspectives of the other officers and recruits, too, the nonelite. Mixing in the reactions of Sacagawea and other American Indians involved in the trek will also thicken fictional descriptions. Think, too, of how much the views of York, Charbonneau, and mixed-blood participants provide rich sociocultural complexities for skilled fictionists.

Third, in addition to utilizing these varied voices, novelists need to find ways to tell stories that illustrate cultural conversations and combinations as often as events of clash and conflict. Narratives that focus only on contention and controversy oversimplify and falsify the ways that Lewis and Clark found to communicate across racial, ethnic, and class barriers. Sacagawea, Cameahwait, Twisted Hair, and Coboway, for instance, hurdled racial and cultural differences to befriend and aid members of the corps. Concurrently, Lewis and Clark and their men established links of amity and alliance with native groups. Complex, even messy, fiction based on these cohering tendencies will help us to understand better the fragmented unities of our own times.

In rediscovering these large possibilities of complex storytelling, historical novelists may avoid pitfalls some have encountered in fictionalizing Lewis and Clark. They need not misrepresent or exaggerate the historical account; material aplenty for stirring fiction is available in firsthand sources about the expedition. And if novelists incorporate the varied voices and complex sociocultural relationships involved in the journey, they will produce provocative, probing narratives about one of our country's most significant stories.

NOTES

1. Reuben Gold Thwaites, quoted in *Voyages of Discovery: Essays on the Lewis and Clark Expedition*, ed. James P. Ronda (Helena: Montana Historical Society Press, 1998), p. 320.

2. Quoted in *A History of the Lewis and Clark Journals*, by Paul Russell Cutright (Norman: University of Oklahoma Press, 1976), p. 222.

3. For the most comprehensive listing of books and essays about the Lewis and Clark Expedition, see Stephen Dow Beckham et al., *The Literature of the Lewis and Clark Expedition: A Bibliography and Essays* (Portland, Oreg.: Lewis & Clark College, 2003). In this essay, I do not treat children's or young adult novels, but many are listed in the Beckham bibliography.

4. Dye, *The Conquest: The True Story of Lewis and Clark* (Chicago: A. C. McClurg & Co., 1902). Subsequent citations to this and other works discussed in this essay will be within the text.

5. The fullest account of Dye's life and writings is Sheri Bartlett-Browne, "Eva Emery Dye" (Ph.D. diss., University of Minnesota, 2002). See also Kimberly Swanson, "Eva Emery Dye and the Romance of Oregon History," *Pacific Historian* 29 (Winter 1985): 59–68.

6. Alfred Powers, *History of Oregon Literature* (Portland, Oreg.: Metropolitan Press, 1935), p. 410.

7. Ibid.

8. Ronald W. Taber, "Sacagawea and the Suffragettes: An Interpretation of a Myth," *Pacific Northwest Quarterly* 58 (Jan. 1967): 10. Paul Cutright is twice wrong in calling Dye's novel "a biography of Sacagawea" (Cutright, *History of the Lewis and Clark Journals*, p. 207n.9). It is not a biography, and the novel is not primarily about Sacagawea despite what readers have made of Dye's portrait of the young Indian woman. For a very useful study on these topics, see Donna J. Kessler, *The Making of Sacagawea: A Euro-American Legend* (Tuscaloosa: University of Alabama Press, 1996). Another, shorter study of much value is David Remley, "Sacajawea of Myth and History," in *Women and Western American Literature*, ed. Helen Winter Stauffer and Susan J. Rosowski (Troy, N.Y.: Whitston Publishing Co., 1982), pp. 70–89.

9. Jackson, ed., *Letters of the Lewis and Clark Expedition with Related Documents, 1783–1854* (Urbana: University of Illinois Press, 1962), p. 639.

10. Hebard, *Sacajawea, a Guide and Interpreter of the Lewis and Clark Expedition, with an Account of the Travels of Toussaint Charbonneau, and of Jean Baptiste, the Expedition Papoose* (Glendale, Calif.: Arthur H. Clark Co., 1932).

11. Hough, *The Magnificent Adventure: This being the Story of the World's Greatest Exploration, and the Romance of a very Gallant Gentleman* (New York: D. Appleton & Co., 1916).

12. James K. Folsom, "Hough, Emerson," in *The New Encyclopedia of the American West*, ed. Howard R. Lamar (New Haven, Conn.: Yale University Press, 1998), p. 499. The fullest treatment of Hough can be found in Delbert E. Wylder, *Emerson Hough* (Boston: Twayne Publishers, 1981).

13. Two years later, James Willard Schultz published *Bird Woman (Sacajawea)*, the

Guide of Lewis and Clark: Her Own Story Now First Given to the World (Boston: Houghton Mifflin, 1918), which juxtaposes history and fiction under the guise of history. Ostensibly a biography, *Bird Woman* fictionalizes most of Sacagawea's life. In today's terms, the work might be called a book of "creative nonfiction."

14. Hueston, *Star of the West: The Romance of the Lewis and Clark Expedition* (Indianapolis: Bobbs-Merrill Co., 1935). Hueston also authored *The Man of the Storm: A Romance of Colter Who Discovered Yellowstone* (Indianapolis: Bobbs-Merrill Co., 1936) and *Calamity Jane of Deadwood Gulch* (Indianapolis: Bobbs-Merrill Co., 1937).

15. Novels written about Lewis and Clark in the first half of the twentieth century are discussed in Larry Godfrey, "A Survey of 20th Century Novels Based on the Lewis and Clark Expedition" (Master's thesis, Washington University, St. Louis, Mo., 1962).

16. Peattie, *Forward the Nation* (New York: G. P. Putnam's Sons, 1942), p. v.

17. Emmons, *Sacajawea of the Shoshones* (Portland, Oreg.: Binfords & Mort, 1943). Emmons's novel became a primary source for the only well-known film of the Lewis and Clark Expedition, *The Far Horizon* (1955). Starring Donna Reed as Sacagawea and Charlton Heston as William Clark, the film emphasized their attractions to one another. The film's producers conveniently omitted Sacagawea's child "Pomp" with Charbonneau, evidently thinking that moviegoers of the 1950s would not accept a mother's attentions for another man. A disappointing effort, the film was widely panned.

18. Vardis Fisher, *Tale of Valor: A Novel of the Lewis and Clark Expedition* (Garden City, N.Y.: Doubleday & Co., 1958).

19. Fisher's historical research for his fiction is treated in George Frederick Day, *The Uses of History in the Novels of Vardis Fisher* (New York: Revisionist Press, 1976), and Joseph M. Flora, *Vardis Fisher* (New York: Twayne Publishers, 1965). Other useful comments on Fisher, his treatment of Indians, and Lewis and Clark appear in several essays in *Rediscovering Vardis Fisher: Centennial Essays*, ed. Joseph M. Flora (Moscow: University of Idaho Press, 2000).

20. Fisher makes a case for the harsh realism in his frontier fiction in John R. Milton, *Three West: Conversations with Vardis Fisher, Max Evans, Michael Straight* (Vermillion, S.Dak.: Dakota Press, 1970), pp. 12–14.

21. Will Henry [Henry Wilson Allen], *The Gates of the Mountains* (New York: Random House, 1963).

22. Robert L. Gale, *Will Henry/Clay Fisher (Henry W. Allen)* (Boston: Twayne Publishers, 1984), p. 36.

23. Waldo, *Sacajawea* (New York: Avon, 1979).

24. William Jeffrey Patten, "Sacagawea: The History of a Myth" (Master's thesis, Portland State University, Oreg., 1998), p. 17.

25. Beckham, *Literature of the Lewis and Clark Expedition*, p. 250.

26. Thom, *From Sea to Shining Sea* (New York: Villard Books, 1984). Thom has written another novel about an important member of the expedition: *Sign-Talker: The Adventure of George Drouillard on the Lewis and Clark Expedition* (New York: Ballantine Books, 2000).

27. Hall, *I Should Be Extremely Happy in Your Company: A Novel of Lewis and Clark* (New York: Viking, 2003). The newest novel on Lewis and Clark, more spoof and parody than traditional historical fiction, is Howard Frank Mosher's, *The True Account Concerning a Vermont Gentleman's Race to the Pacific against and Exploration of the Western American Continent Coincident to the Expedition of Captains Meriwether Lewis and William Clark* (Boston: Houghton Mifflin, 2003). Mosher's novel follows in the western tall-tale tradition stretching from Mark Twain to Larry McMurtry. I have been unable to obtain two other Lewis and Clark novels: Louis Charbonneau, *Trail: The Story of the Lewis and Clark Expedition* (New York: Doubleday, 1989), and Rita Cleary, *River Walk: A Frontier Story* (Unity, Maine: Five Star Western, 2000).

28. Cutright, *History of the Lewis and Clark Journals*, p. 210.

29. Stegner, *The Sound of Mountain Water* (Garden City, N.Y.: Doubleday & Co., 1969), p. 202.

30. Ibid., p. 205.

Photographing the Lewis and Clark Route of Discovery

GREG MAC GREGOR

Photographing the route of the Lewis and Clark Expedition came as a logical extension of a previous engagement. Between 1987 and 1994, I photographed the nineteenth-century western emigration routes, producing an in-depth photographic documentation of the Mormon, California, and Oregon trails, that culminated in publication of *Overland: The California Emigrant Trail of 1841–1870* (University of New Mexico Press, 1996). During the process, the National Park Service asked me to create a set of photographs for a new interpretive center to be located in Council Bluffs, Iowa, that would be dedicated to western exploration and emigration trails. Included in that package was to be the Lewis and Clark Trail. Initially, it seemed like a simple assignment. I was not required to be a sleuth as in the other project when, faced with a choice of three jeep tracks in the prairie, the task was to decide which one to follow (I usually resolved the problem by poring over map details or asking a local rancher). In the case of Lewis and Clark, rivers had been the route, and they would need to be included in each view. What I thought could be completed in one long season, however, stretched out over the next eight years as I found more and more to photograph as the "hook" of the Lewis and Clark story deepened in my consciousness.

What to include and what not to include had to be addressed, and my approach would be different from that in my previous endeavors. The expedition left only one trace of its passing that still remains: a signature by Clark on Pompey's Tower in central Montana. Furthermore, there are only a few places where you can stand and be certain that you are in the exact spot in which the explorers stood. Spirit Mound in South Dakota and Clark's Lookout in Dillon, Montana, are among such spots. Consequently, an "exact view" approach was not going to be easy. Clark drew meticulous maps of the entire route, marking each campsite with a small flag, but the river simply has not cooperated in staying to its course. When I finally located the site of the Iona Volcano, a steaming hill noted by Lewis near Vermillion, South Dakota, I discovered that the entire fifty-foot hill had long ago washed away into flat farm fields. The same was true for the original Sergeant Floyd burial site. Once at the top of a bluff, it is now, according to the latest research, seventy feet in the air above the Missouri, which has eroded away the bank. The Missouri River in the wide valley north of Omaha is presently about six miles from the side of the valley that Lewis and Clark experienced. Oxbow bends have been cut off; sections have been straightened by channeling; and farming interests have all dramatically altered the original river course.

These facts suggested a focus for my project. Wherever a western river flows, it becomes the center for all activities and development. Power lines, bridges, cities, cattle, recreational and commercial boats, and agriculture can all be found along its banks. Hydroelectric dams have created a huge five-hundred-mile-long lake through the Dakotas, bringing with it fisherman and fishing derbies. From the point where it joins the Mississippi at Saint Louis, the Missouri becomes channelized and is kept in that dike all the way across Missouri, Kansas, and then along the Nebraska-Iowa border for a combined four hundred upstream miles. In the Dakotas, only a couple sixty-mile stretches of river exist where the Missouri is not either the backwater of a dam or an artificial channel. One stretch is at Vermillion; the other is just north of Bismarck, North Dakota. Clearly, my project needed to comment on these changes if I was to contribute something new. Therefore, the natural wonders described by Lewis and Clark in the journals would be subjects for my photographs no matter how much change had occurred.

It is impossible to photograph the entire route of the Corps of Discovery in one season. It includes about thirty-eight hundred river miles in meandering lines, as well as a serious overland route through the rugged Bitterroot Mountains. Most roads travel north and south along sectional lines, a route that allows for on-and-off encounters with the river. In many cases, it is not possible to actually get to the river by road. Because the river easily jumps levees, which it demonstrated so adequately in the spring floods of 1992, roads in the state of Missouri are often safely distant from the river.

A similar example is encountered on the Lower Brule Sioux Indian Reservation in South Dakota, where the Missouri River travels a spectacular thirty-five-mile loop that returns back on itself to a neck of about one mile. The road cuts across the neck. Another roadless section is along the "Wild and Scenic Missouri River" of central Montana. Here only a boat can gain access. In areas such as this one, the river can at last be experienced as Lewis and Clark had experienced it, with the substitution of cattle for buffalo along its banks.

Entering middle Montana where the Fort Peck dam backwaters finally level out to streambed, the Missouri River becomes less tamed. It enters first the Missouri Breaks and then the long valleys of the eastern Rocky Mountains. Still farther west, it breaks into mountain streams that, although they have wandered from their exact original course, look basically unchanged. Next, the high country of the overland route, Lemhi Pass in the Beaverhead Mountains and the Lolo Trail over the Bitterroot Mountains, offers basically the same views and foliage as seen by Lewis and Clark. These regions continue to be popular hiking areas. While traveling in this section, I gained an appreciation for the stamina of the Corps of Discovery. Turning my canoe upstream, I found it required a three-mile-an-hour paddle speed just to stay even with the current. Somehow, the corps had managed to travel twenty miles per day upstream, my best downstream mileage.

To be interested enough in the Lewis and Clark story to retrace it, one has to be fascinated by land, by the West, its prairies, mountains, and long stretches of empty space—and to understand that fierce thunderstorms usually last only fifteen minutes. My favorite section is the rolling prairies of North and South Dakota. I was a student in Rapid City in western South Dakota but never thought about the Missouri River; instead, my weekend explorations always went west into the Black Hills. Upon "discovering" the Missouri on this project, I was captivated by it and its shoreline. The area is closest in feel to a desert (my usual photo subject) except for its abundant grass—few cities, wind, sky, so lonely, so primal.[1]

NOTE

1. This photographic essay is abstracted from Greg Mac Gregor, *Lewis and Clark Revisited: A Photographer's Trail* (Seattle: University of Washington Press, 2003). The journal entries are taken from Gary E. Moulton, ed., *The Journals of the Lewis & Clark Expedition*, 13 vols. (Lincoln: University of Nebraska Press, 1983–2001).

Saint Charles, Missouri, and Fourth Street Bridge, beginning of the voyage

21 May 1804
Set out at half passed three oClock under three Cheers from the gentlemen on the bank and proceeded on to the head of the Island (which is Situated on the Stbd Side) 3 miles
—WILLIAM CLARK

Confluence of the Kansas and Missouri rivers, Kansas City, Missouri

28 June 1804
a butifull place for a fort, good landing place, the waters of the Kansas is verry disigreeably tasted to me.
—WILLIAM CLARK

Mouth of Floyd River and abandoned stock pens, Sioux City, Iowa

20 August 1804

Sergeant Floyd much weaker and no better. . . . Serjeant Floyd as bad as he can be no pulse & nothing will Stay a moment on his Stomach or bowels. . . .

    Serj.' Floyd Died with a great deel of Composure, before his death he Said to me, "I am going away. . . . I want you to write me a letter"— We buried him on the top of the bluff 1/2 Miles below a Small river to which we Gave his name, he was buried with the Honors of War much lamented. . . . after paying all the honor to our Decesed brother we Camped in the mouth of *floyds* river about 30 yards wide, a butifull evening.

—WILLIAM CLARK

Mount Baldy, near Gross, Nebraska

7 September 1804
a verry Cold morning Set out at day light we landed after proceding 5 ½ miles, near the foot of a round mounting which I saw yesterday resembling a dome.

    Capt Lewis & my Self walked up, to the top which forms a Cone and is about 70 feet higher than . . . the high lands around it, the Bass is about 300 foot in deceding this Cupola, discovered a Village of Small animals that burrow in the grown (those animals are Called by the french Pitite Chien) Killed one & Cought one a live by poreing a great quantity of water in his hole we attempted to dig to the beds of one of thos animals, after diging 6 feet, found by running a pole down that we were not half way to his Lodges, we found 2 frogs in the hole, and killed a Dark rattle Snake near with a Ground rat . . . in him, (those rats are numerous) the Village of those animals Covs. about 4 acrs of Ground on a Gradual decent of a hill and Contains great numbers of holes on the top of which those little animals Set erect make a Whistleing noise and whin allarmed Slip into their hole— we por'd into one of the holes 5 barrels of water without filling it. . . . Camped
—WILLIAM CLARK

Plastic buffalo, Oacoma, South Dakota

17 September 1804
this senery already rich pleasing and beatiful, was still farther hightened by immence herds of Buffaloe deer Elk and Antelopes which we saw in every direction feeding on the hills and plains. I do not think I exagerate when I estimate the number of Buffaloe which could be compreed at one view to amount to 3000.

5 May 1805
we kill whatever we wish, the buffaloe furnish us with fine veal and fat beef, we also have venison and beaver tales when we wish them; the flesh of the Elk and goat are less esteemed, and certainly are inferior. . . .
    saw the carcases of many Buffaloe lying dead along the shore partially devoured by the wolves and bear.
—MERIWETHER LEWIS

Antelope Creek at Missouri River, below Pierre, South Dakota

23 September 1804

passed a Small Creek on the S. S. 16 yds wide I call *Reubens* Cr.— R. Fields was the first who found it— Came too & Camped on the S. S. in a Wood. Soon after we landed three *Soues* boys Swam across to us, those boys informed us that a Band of Sieux called the *Tetons* of 80 Lodges wer Camped near the mouth of the next River, and 60 Lodges more a Short distance above them, they had that day Set the praries on fire to let those Camps Know of our approach— we gave those boys two twists of Tobacco to carry to their Chiefs & Warriors to Smoke, with derections to tell them that we wished to Speak to them tomorrow, at the mouth of the next river.

—WILLIAM CLARK

Lily Park and Bad River, Fort Pierre, South Dakota

25 September 1804

I went with those Cheifs . . . to Shore with a view of reconseleing those men to us, as Soon as I landed the Perogue three of their young men Seased the Cable of the Perogue, . . . the Chiefs Soldr . . . Huged the mast, and the 2d Chief was verry insolent both in words & justures . . . declareing I Should not go on, Stateing he had not recved presents Suffient from us, his justures were of Such a personal nature I felt my Self compeled to Draw my Sword, . . . at this motion Capt. Lewis ordered all under arms in the boat, those with me also Showed a Disposition to Defend themselves and me, the grand Chief then took hold of the roop & ordered the young warrers away. . . .

Most of the warriers appeared to have ther Bows Strung and took out their arrows from ther quves. as I . . . was not permited . . . to return, I Sent all the men except 2 Inpt. [interpreters] to the boat, the perogu Soon returned with about 12 of our detumind men ready for any event this movement . . . caused a no: of the Indians to withdraw at a distance,— . . . Their treatment to me was verry rough & I think justified roughness on my part. . . .

we proceeded on about 1 mile & anchored out off a willow Island placed a guard on Shore to protect the Cooks & a guard in the boat, fastened the Perogues to the boat, I call this Island bad humered Island as we were in a bad humer.

—WILLIAM CARK

Northern prairie grasslands, Fort Berthold Indian Reservation, near White Shield, North Dakota

29 October 1804
The Prarie was Set on fire (or Cought by accident) by a young man of the Mandins, the fire went with Such velocity that it burnt to death a man and woman, who Could not Get to any place of Safty, one man a woman & Child much burnt and Several narrowly escaped the flame— a boy half white was Saved un hurt in the midst of the flaim, Those ignerent people Say this boy was Saved by the great Spirit medisin because he was white— The Cause of his being Saved was a Green buffalow Skin was thrown over him by his mother who perhaps had more fore Sight for the pertection of her . . . Son, and [l]ess for herself than those who escaped the flame, the Fire did not burn under the Skin leaving the grass round the boy
—WILLIAM CLARK

Ryan Dam and falls during low runoff, Great Falls, Montana

13 June 1805
I had proceded on this course about two miles with Goodrich at some distance behind me whin my ears were saluted with the agreeable sound of a fall of water and advancing a little further I saw the spray arrise above the plain like a collumn of smoke . . . which soon began to make a roaring too tremendous to be mistaken for any cause short of the great falls of the Missouri. here I arrived about 12 OClock having traveled by estimate about 15 Miles. I hurryed down the hill which was about 200 feet high . . . to gaze on this sublimely grand specticle. I took my position on the top of some rocks about 20 feet high opposite the center of the falls. . . . immediately at the cascade the river is about 300 yds. wide; about ninty or a hundred yards of this next the Lard. bluff is a smoth even sheet of water falling over a precipice of at least eighty feet, the remaining part of about 200 yards on my right formes the grandest sight I ever beheld, the hight of the fall is the same of the other but the irregular and somewhat projecting rocks below receives the water in it's passage down and brakes it into a perfect white foam which assumes a thousand forms in a moment sometimes flying up in jets of sparkling foam to the hight of fifteen or twenty feet.
—MERIWETHER LEWIS

Three Forks of the Missouri, Montana

28 July 1805

Our present camp is precisely on the spot that the Snake Indians were encamped at the time the Minnetares of the Knife R. first came in sight of them five years since. . . . the Minnetares pursued, attacked them, killed 4 men 4 women a number of boys, and mad prisoners of all the females and four boys, *Sah-cah-gar-we-ah* or Indian woman was one of the female prisoners taken at that time; tho' I cannot discover that she shews any immotion of sorrow in recollecting this event, or of joy in being again restored to her native country; if she has enough to eat and a few trinkets to wear I beleive she would be perfectly content anywhere.
—MERIWETHER LEWIS

Lewis and Clark Pass (Continental Divide, looking west),
Scapegoat Wilderness area, Montana

12 August 1805
after refreshing ourselves we proceeded on to the top of the dividing ridge from which I discovered immence ranges of high mountains still to the West of us with their tops partially covered with snow. I now decended the mountain about 3/4 of a mile . . . to a handsome bold running Creek of cold Clear water. here I first tasted the water of the great Columbia river.
—MERIWETHER LEWIS

Indian post office on Lolo Trail, Idaho

16 September 1805
began to Snow about 3 hours before Day and Continud all day the Snow in The morning 4 Inches deep on The old Snow, and by night we found it from 6 to 8 Inches deep I walked in front to keep the road and found great dificuelty in keeping it as in maney places the Snow had entirely filled up the track. . . . I have been wet and as cold in every part as I ever was in my life, indeed I was at one time fearfull my feet would freeze in the thin mockersons which I wore
—WILLIAM CLARK

Tree stump and Trojan Nuclear Power Plant, near Kalama, Washington

7 November 1805
Great joy in camp we are in View of the Ocian, . . . this great Pacific Octean which we been So long anxious to See. and the roreing or noise made by the waves brakeing on the rockey Shores (as I Suppose) may be heard disticly
—WILLIAM CLARK

Pilings and Tongue Point, Astoria, Oregon

21 November 1805
An old woman & wife to a Cheif of the Chinnooks came and made a Camp near ours She brought with her 6 young Squars . . . I believe for the purpose of gratifying the passions of the men of our party and receving for those indulgiences Such Small as She (the old woman) thought proper to accept of, Those people appear to view Sensuality as a Necessary evel, and do not appear to abhor it as a Crime in the unmarried State. . . . the womin of the Chinnook Nation have handsom faces low and badly made with large legs & thighs which are generally Swelled from a Stopage of the circulation in the feet (which are Small) by maney Strands of Beeds or curious Strings which are drawn tight around the leg above the anckle, their legs are also picked with different figures, I Saw on the left arm of a Squar the following letters J. Bowmon

27 November 1805
We proceeded on, around Point William [Tongue Point]. . . . this place the Peninsoley is about 50 yards and 3 miles around this point of Land. water Salt below not Salt above.
—WILLIAM CLARK

Wreck of the Peter Iredale on the Pacific Coast, near Fort Clatsop, Oregon

9 January 1806
The persons who usually visit the entrance of this river for the purpose of traffic or hunting I believe are either English or Americans; the Indians inform us that they speak the same language with ourselves, and give us proofs of their varacity by repeating many words of English, as musquit, powder, shot, nife, file, damned rascal, sun of a bitch &c. whether these traders are from Nootka sound, from some other late establishment on this coast, or immediately from the U' States or Great Brittain, I am at a loss to determine, nor can the Indians inform us.
—MERIWETHER LEWIS

Over, Above, and Beyond
The Lewis and Clark Expedition as Hyperhistory
JOSEPH A. MUSSULMAN

He said, "The historian, with a vast chronological account of a people, parallels it with a skip trail which stops only on the salient items, and can follow at any time contemporary trails which lead him all over civilization at a particular epoch." He said, "There is a new profession of trail blazers, those who find delight in the task of establishing useful trails through the enormous mass of the common record." He said, "The inheritance from the master becomes, not only his additions to the world's record, but for his disciples the entire scaffolding by which they were erected." The problem was, he said, that "the common record" had become so enormous as a result of specialization that research was outpacing understanding. (Senior historians today recall writing articles and books "the cowboy way"—handwriting bibliographical entries on three-by-five cards and alphabetizing them by author, cramming reading notes onto four-by-six cards and filing them by subject, shuffling the cards, and labeling them to fit into an outline—"&c. &c.," as Lewis and Clark would say.) There was a clear need, he said, to somehow surmount the limitations of alphanumeric indexing, to find a way to seek, find, sort, and select information from the skip trails of ideas that threaded themselves spontaneously through the essentially nonlinear, freely associative, curiosity-driven human mind.

His hypothetical solution, based on tools already tried and proven, including automatic telephone switching and microfilm, was "a sort of mechanized private file and library," an "enlarged intimate supplement to . . . memory," appropriately called a "memex." His name was Vannevar Bush, and he said all these things in an essay titled "As We May Think," which appeared in 1945.[1] It was a prophecy of what would eventually come to be called the World Wide Web.

Twenty years later, Theodor Holm Nelson, a graduate student at Harvard who was frustrated by the same information glut that had bothered Bush, conceived "a program intended to make possible a new unified electronic literature . . . a computer program intended to tie everything together and make it all available to everyone." His program, which he called Xanadu, has not yet materialized, but Nelson left a springboard to the Internet and the World Wide Web in the theory he termed *hypertext*, which he defined as "non-sequential writing—text that branches and allows choices to the reader."[2] Simultaneously, Douglas Englebart, motivated by the lofty goal of augmenting the human intellect, was conceiving concepts such as the mouse, hypermedia, and multiple windows.[3] The next step took place in 1989 in Geneva, Switzerland, with the creation of a digital language called HyperText Transfer Protocol (http) and the introduction in 1992 of the first text-based digital instrument to augment the meaning of the noun *browser*. In 1994, Marc Andreessen and his collaborators at the University of Illinois released Netscape Navigator, an interactive utility that opened the World Wide Web to millions of users.

In 1993, my work in writing and producing interactive audio-interpretive programs for national parks came to an abrupt close with the failure of the company that employed me. At that moment David E. Nelson, then the executive director of the Montana Arts Council and a man whose mind works somewhat like Netscape or Google, suggested a series of CD-ROMs about the Lewis and Clark Expedition, just to fill up my idle hours. He and Kevin Kirking, the former CEO of the failed company I had worked for, founded a nonprofit corporation—for which I suggested the name VIAs, from *via*, Latin for "way, trace, or trail"—to create an interactive history of the expedition and its backgrounds and to explore the connections between the journals and life in the twenty-first century. We called it *Discovering Lewis and Clark*. Encouraged by a number of individuals, including Gary Moulton, and by a few small grants, we spent three years developing the plan—or rather, watching it evolve from the five journals of the expedition. But the CD-ROM market began to dissolve just as we were gaining momentum, and by 1997, the only option left was to migrate our plan to the World Wide Web—Dave Nelson's suggestion, of course.

Though we had not yet learned the word, we were paving our own path to a hyperhistory—a collection of facts and ideas inherent in the story of the Lewis and Clark Expedition (or springing out of it), linked along a web of paths that viewers could navigate at will. There were a few models to

This image welcomes visitors to the home page of Discovering Lewis & Clark®. (VIAs, Inc., Missoula, Montana)

be studied, among which the most stimulating was James Burke's *The Pinball Effect*, a hyperhistory in print tracing twenty different journeys through "the great web of change," which can be read at least 447 different ways.[4] But Web-based models were scarce. *Encyclopaedia Britannica Online*, which opened in 1994, is a classic example—although at the present writing the entry on Lewis and Clark still contains only five hyperlinks—Meriwether Lewis, William Clark, Thomas Jefferson, Sacagawea, and Toussaint Charbonneau.[5] A Google search of "hyperhistory" in the spring of 2003 called up more than sixteen hundred "results," an apparent majority of them circling back to *HyperHistory Online*, which is a timeline containing highly compressed information about certain persons, events, and so forth—currently excluding the Lewis and Clark Expedition—plus links to hundreds of other Web sites. At midwinter 2003, a Google search on "Lewis and Clark" brought up more than three hundred eighty thousand "results"—with our trademarked *Discovering Lewis & Clark®* second on the list—"O the joy!"

Lists of facts can be prescriptions for hyperhistories, and the Lewis and Clark journals are loaded with them, compiled by the explorers themselves—Lewis's shopping list and lists of purchases, for instance, or the baling invoices written at Fort Mandan.[6] More useful as resources for hyperhistories are the growing number of online archival collections: Washington University's *St. Louis Circuit Court Historical Records Project*; James L. Reveal's *Images of the Plants Seen or Collected by Meriwether Lewis and William Clark, 1804–1806*, which is a companion to the Academy of Natural Science's *Lewis and Clark Herbarium*; the Library of Congress *American Memory Historical Collections for the National Digital Library*; the *Evans Digital Edition of Early American Imprints*; and especially the online publication of Gary Moulton's monumental *Journals of the Lewis & Clark Expedition*, recently opened by the University of Nebraska, the Center for Great Plains Studies, and the libraries of the University of Nebraska at Lincoln.

A varied workshop of tools is available to craft a hyperhistory from these resources. During the early 1990s, young explorers of the computer software industry began code-writing new paths through an ocean of ones and zeroes, those molecules of the body of http—expanding it beyond pure text. They colored it. They compressed still and moving images, as well as sound files, to slide easily through the Internet pipelines. They devised ways to draw animated images to illuminate ideas. The old separate media—print, film, audio, and video—were combined into one multimedium that engaged and involved the user interactively. Indeed, interactivity, that principle that Vannevar Bush articulated back in 1945, has almost become an end in itself, a personal exploratory journey through the "common record," enlivened by surprise, adventure, the unimaginable. With a "rollover" utility, for example, we can compare William Clark's visage as engraved by Charles de Saint-Mémin with one painted by Charles Willson Peale and judge for ourselves whether Saint-Mémin's subject was really William Clark or not. With the same device, the half-legible handwriting on one of Clark's maps or the notation on one of Lewis's plant specimens can be made clear by the highlighting of important features or with more legible underlays of text, without obscuring the beauties or details of the originals.

Panoramic photography, called QTVR, or QuickTime Virtual Reality, which the Apple Corporation developed in the mid-1990s, is a graphic tool rich with possibilities for interactivity. The viewer may move the cursor to look around, up, down, or zoom into or out of a view. Links from any number of points in a panorama can lead to pages utilizing other media. The object movie is similar to QTVR, except that an object such as a small statue remains at the center of the photograph and can be rotated by the viewer, making a hyperhistory function as a hypermuseum.

Sound can infuse life into inert words. For one thing, the voices and styles of delivery convey part of the sense and quality of some historians' scholarship. And the sounds of history are equally eloquent. The Corps of Discovery made up a community soundscape that moved back and forth across the Northwest, intersecting hour by hour with other sonic communities of people and birds and animals, and there is ample evidence in the journals that they were always aware of the sounds around them. Objects and scenes in motion, as recorded on digital video, can also be transferred to the Web. At the present time, the files must be small enough and the clips short enough—no more than two or three minutes—to be accessed quickly on the ordinary dialup Internet connection, but that limitation will continue to diminish as home computers get faster and the pipeline becomes more efficient in handling large amounts of digital information.

All these digital design tools steadily undergo improvements and innovations, and new ideas steadily evolve. In the Corps of Discovery's full range of experiences, the only qualities that cannot—not yet, that is—be digitized for hyperhistory's sake are, for instance, the flavor (sweet) and aroma (vanilla) of a well-roasted camas bulb or the feel of it in one's hand. Is there a "scratch-and-sniff" Web site in our future?

Three more things must happen before hyperhistory can become a methodology worthy of broad application. First, high standards of scholarship must be directed toward the possibilities offered by the interactive, multimedia World Wide Web. Second, if historiography is to reach any significant part of the world-wide audience this new medium provides, its practitioners must become educated in uses of the tools, for the potential audience's expectations may already be more than fifteen years ahead of our thinking. Finally, a major Web site must not only be written and designed but also continuously nourished and nursed. Also, somebody has to pay the bills.

In crafting the hyperhistory of the Lewis and Clark Expedition, we observed that the *whens* and *wheres* of the expedition comprised an epic linear timeline. Lewis himself said the journey began on 14 May 1804 at the mouth of the River Dubois, and Sergeant Ordway wrote the word "finis" at Saint Louis on 23 September 1806. But the *hows*, *whats*, and *whys* of the expedition are infinitely more interesting. The original journals themselves, those memoranda for a work in progress, more than a million words' worth, constitute a huge core script for a hyperhistory. The journals contain a universe of topics, galaxies of links, and constellations of ideas. Think of the richness of Lewis's notes on the five falls of the Missouri, written on 13 and 14 June 1805, or of his microscopic description of *Camassia quamash*, on 11 June 1806. The *explications de texte* for Clark's entry for 13 June 1804, for instance, could run to twenty-five skip trails—depending on who's counting, of course—occupying perhaps a hundred or more html[7] pages, enhanced by the full array of interactive Web tools.

Discovering Lewis & Clark® is in the process of *becoming* a hyperhistory of the expedition. It grows month by month, and its end, if it has one, is somewhere beyond the horizon. It opens with Harry W. Fritz's synopsis of the expedition's story, but that is but one of the many possible core scripts that could have been used as points of departure. It might just as well have begun, for instance, with Jefferson's instructions to Lewis and branched into an interactive hyperaccount of hits, runs, and errors.

Imagine all the books, essays, lectures, radio and television interviews, and grassroots interpretive centers—all the inquiry and understanding inspired by the expedition during the past two hundred years—linked with the original journals (including Gary Moulton's footnotes), all in html language and all word-searchable, even those resonant phonetic spellings.

Then imagine such scaffolding enhanced with all the multimedia techniques and devices native to the World Wide Web. Now *that* would truly be *hyper*—"over, above, and beyond"—history!

Improbable? Perhaps.

Impossible? Remember, as Vannevar Bush said, "The world has arrived at an age of cheap complex devices of great reliability; and something is bound to come of it."[8]

NOTES

1. Bush, "As We May Think," *The Atlantic Monthly* 176 (July 1945): 101–8.

2. Theodor Holm Nelson, *Literary Machines 93.1* (Sausalito, Calif.: Mindful Press, 1992), Preface and p. 0/2.

3. Christopher Keep, Tim McLaughlin, and Robin Parmar, *The Electronic Labyrinth*, http://www.iath.virginia.edu/elab/elab.html (accessed 21 May 2003).

4. Burke, *The Pinball Effect: How Renaissance Water Gardens Made the Carburetor Possible—and Other Journeys through Knowledge* (New York: Little, Brown & Co., 1996). Burke's www.k-web.org opened in 2004.

5. Encyclopaedia Britannica Online, http://www.eb.com, has a few accuracy problems. It states that the "group" spent the winter of 1804–1805 near the "Mandan Sioux," but although the Mandan Indians are of Siouan linguistic stock, they have never belonged to the Sioux Nation. Furthermore, the group is said to have met the Shoshone people "near present-day Armsted, Montana," although the settlement—properly spelled "Armstead"—was submerged beneath Clark Canyon Reservoir when the dam was completed back in 1964.

6. Donald Jackson, ed., *Letters of the Lewis and Clark Expedition with Related Documents, 1783–1854*, 2d ed., 2 vols. (Urbana: University of Illinois Press, 1978), 1:69–99; Gary E. Moulton, ed., *The Journals of the Lewis & Clark Expedition*, 13 vols. (Lincoln: University of Nebraska Press, 1983–2002), 3:492–505.

7. Html stands for HyperText Markup Language, a "high-level" digital language that enables Web editors and designers to use alphanumeric analogs for code in creating structure and content for a site. See "Computer Science," *Encyclopædia Britannica*, http://www.britannica.com/eb/article?eu=117723 (accessed 26 May 2003).

8. Bush, "As We May Think," p. 102.

Using Inquiry to Engage History Students
The Lewis and Clark Rediscovery Project
ROBERT J. MYERS

This book is replete with stories about the Lewis and Clark Expedition and about a country that doubled in size with the Louisiana Purchase. Historians, readers of American history, and, in particular, those who thrive on the subtleties of American history will revel in these pages. With the bicentennial of the Corps of Discovery upon us, more and more students will become acquainted with the intricacies of the westward migration and the subsequent impacts on people, places, and things. With any luck, our students will come to appreciate the lessons from the past, especially since we want them to make responsible decisions affecting our country's future.

This chapter charts the development of an online Web site about the Corps of Discovery and about the issues related to two hundred years of change subsequent to the expedition. Because there are many considerations and decisions concerning Web site development, this discussion is divided into two parts. The first section explores how history teachers can make use of this site and other resources to engage students in learning about history. The second section concerns the site itself, that is, its look and feel and its organization.

Unfortunately, as many know, our students continue to demonstrate that they do not know much about history. We have seen the statistics from the National Center for Education Statistics in which 57 percent of our twelfth graders perform below the basic standards in American history. And to think that this grade was the worst performing grade in 1994 and 2001 suggests that we are making no progress in this area. As Diane Ravitch, a member of the National Assessment Governing Board, remarked in 2002: "High school seniors registered truly abysmal scores. . . . Since the seniors are very close to voting age, or already have reached it, one can only feel alarm that they know so little about their nation's history and express so little capacity to reflect on its meaning."[1]

While many educators espouse learning history through learning hard data—dates, names, or events—I would suggest that this practice is exactly the approach that has gotten the state of knowledge about history into so much difficulty. I would go further to say that teaching history without an engaging context can lead to what Anders Henriksson, a professor of history at Shepherd College, calls "absurdities from people who (one hopes) know better." From Professor Henriksson's students, we have this memorable paragraph:

> Civilization woozed out of the Nile about 300,000 years ago.... Old Testament profits include Moses, Amy, and Confucius.... Plato invented reality.... During the Dark Ages it was mostly dark.... Machiavelli wrote The Prince to get a job with Richard Nixon.... Spinning Jenny was a young girl forced to work more than 40 hours a day.... Westward expansion ended at Custard's Last Stand.... Few were surprised when the National League failed to prevent another world war.... Hitler, who had become depressed for some reason, crawled under Berlin. Here he had his wife Evita put to sleep and then shot himself in the bonker.... It is now the age of now.[2]

Of course, we want our students to do much better than this, especially when it comes to knowledge and understanding of United States history. Yet higher order thinking on students' part is a highly elusive, yet seemingly rare, occurrence. Instead of offering maturing students opportunities to exercise independence, cultivate thinking skills, or engage in the pursuit of knowledge, teachers spend more time lecturing to them on topics that vie for air time in an already crowded curriculum.[3] The National Standards for United States history speak to the major skills we want instilled in our students: e.g., chronological thinking, historical comprehension, historical analysis and interpretation, historical research capabilities, and historical issues. And much beyond recall of historical facts is the ability to think or reason. Given a historical content, students should be able to demonstrate such skills as: differentiating between facts and interpretations, hypothesizing the influence of the past, analyzing cause-and-effect relationships, or formulating a position or course of action on an issue.

William C. and Jean K. Bruce ask these questions: "Are we lighting the way for the students who lack the ability to think logically? Are we lighting the way for those who lack philosophical or analytical skills and imagination? Are we lighting the way for those who lack the spark that sets humans so far apart from worms? Are we helping students to develop a questioning mind?" They cite poet Annie Dillard's description of being "lifted and struck," remarking: "After you're 'lifted and struck' you'll never again think that the world offers nothing new, that everything's old and jaded. Using inquiry methods to teach and to learn gives you the kind of lift Dillard wrote about; it blurs, then sharpens your eyesight. When you use inquiry methods you're struck with new strengths and abilities, to taste, to touch, to hear and to think, things you can't wait to share." They conclude, "As through the eyes of a poet, when you teach and learn through inquiry, you see ordinary things change into images that impact on you like seeing Moses part the sea."[4]

The Lewis and Clark Expedition and the changes that resulted from the Anglo migration offer an opportunity to blend the disciplines of history and geography. The expedition offers students multiple opportunities to be "lifted and struck." Like the history standards, the geography standards address the use of maps and other geographic representations. In geography standards, we look at the characteristics of human migration and how the forces of cooperation and conflict among people influence the division and control of the earth's surface. More importantly, perhaps, geography standards accent how human actions modify the physical environment and how to apply geography to interpret the present and plan for the future.

How do we reach a new level where students exhibit the content knowledge and life-long skills we espouse? Today we hear a great deal about the "No Child Left Behind" Act. One objective of this act is to have all students performing satisfactorily on standardized tests. The emphasis focused on students' test scores, however, may lead to teachers "teaching to the test," a not uncommon practice. And while test scores are certainly an indicator, Anne Lewis reports, "There is plenty of evidence around that, when teachers know their content and how to teach it at high levels to all students, 'teaching to the test' fades into the background of everyday instruction and learning." She goes on to cite research from Chicago where students from disadvantaged schools did better on standardized tests of basic skills and produced high-quality intellectual work if they had experienced high-quality instruction. Further, teachers using a variety of instructional strategies "consistently saw their students make achievement gains above the Chicago average on state tests and on nationally normed tests. Students of teachers who clung to didactic instruction made below-average scores."[5] Given the history and geography standards, the question remaining is how to engage students to think, solve problems, understand history, and apply a spatial perspective to life situations.

In designing and implementing a Web site focusing on the Corps of Discovery, the materials development team looked to inquiry as a method to engage students. Inquiry-based environments provide students opportunities to generate and revise their thinking in interdisciplinary contexts. This process takes a great deal of time, but it allows students to learn in depth. To be of use, information needs to be associated with prior knowledge and then integrated into larger knowledge structures. Such structures require students to do more than follow established sets of rules; students need to participate in the development of their own knowledge. Knowledge structures that relate previous and new knowledge with procedures used in the development of those structures evolve slowly, but they are fundamental to understanding.[6] Problem-based learning (PBL) methods, a variant of inquiry-based learning, enable students to practice connecting what they already know with what they are learning. Students can call upon and organize what they have previously learned; then, as they face new information, they can begin to reformulate their ideas—accommodating and integrating the new information with the old.

PBL facilitates inquiry-based methodology by allowing students to identify problems, conduct research into problem areas, interpret and analyze data, and demonstrate understanding through the creation of an artifact or presentation. PBL has been used in medical schools to teach students to think critically and integrate and apply knowledge in an inquiry-based approach. PBL research has suggested that these environments enhance intrinsic subject-matter knowledge, foster long-term knowledge retention, and facilitate self-directed, long-term learning skills. PBL methods emphasize "open-ended questions" that require higher-order thinking.[7] Often referred to as "ill-structured," PBL scenarios confront students with a situation that requires more information than is immediately available. Problem definitions may change as investigations continue, and there is no absolutely "right" answer.

Recent PBL research at the secondary level addressed education's emphasis in providing students with opportunities to solve problems and conduct student-directed investigations. A 1992 study suggests that teaching techniques using ill-structured problems as the center of learning may be the most appropriate way to prepare students for the kinds of challenges they will face as adults. Other research suggests that students in environments similar to PBL (group investigations) matched or exceeded progress of students in traditional classes. Additionally, students engaged in group investigations were more adept at demonstrating analysis and application of knowledge to new problems, suggesting that these environments enhanced the intrinsic motivation to learn.[8]

While PBL research suggests increased student engagement, metacognitive growth, and long-term knowledge retention, a growing body of literature points to teacher preparation as one of the keys to success. Teachers and students used to traditional instruction may be in for some surprises. It takes time, patience, and a willingness to accept risk and uncertainty to begin using inquiry-based classroom methods. It may take teachers one to two years to feel confident with these approaches to learning. Students, for example, will likely be reluctant to take risks on their own—especially if they are used to having the objectives, assignments, and problems handed to them. If they are used to standard, objective tests, then students may dwell more on what they have to do to "get their grade" than on readily adapting to the PBL format.[9] Fortunately, as countless numbers of teachers will attest, the changes they make in offering a variety of teaching methods is well worth the risk and initial uncertainties.

Using the research-based guidance discussed above, the *Lifelong Learning Online: Lewis and Clark Rediscovery Project* (http://www.l3-lewisandclark.com) began to take shape. The site contains multiple entry points to student engagement, and while it was designed primarily for K-12 students, users of any age will find interesting information. Teachers can make use of the problem scenarios for student engagement, use a variety of essential questions that can drive inquiry, or simply use the site as a resource as students learn about this period of American history.

Each module begins with a scenario, designed to put students into a context that will drive the learning process. Here is the scenario from the Pierre, South Dakota, module:

When the Corps of Discovery went up the Missouri River, they encountered a garden of plenty. Game, especially the bison, was abundant on the plains. Many Indian tribes scoffed at the white settler's goods and a chance to trade for beaver pelts because bison was so plentiful. As recently as 1800 there were an estimated 60 million bison on the plains. With the westward migration of whites, however, bison were nearly exterminated during the late 1800s. Now, many environmentalists, biologists, businesspeople, and Indian tribes are searching for ways to hasten the return of the bison.

Because you have studied the Corps of Discovery, and especially the bison, a group of businesspeople have asked your group to present a plan for increasing the numbers of bison in this country. They will need to know more about the history of the bison, the bison's near extinction, and how we can make their return economically viable. It is important to note that the businesspeople are interested in the social, cultural, and spiritual connections of the bison to American Indians.

Practitioners of problem-based learning and inquiry in general know how important it is to present a scenario to students that is relevant and authentic. Is this one? Perhaps it is; if it is not, teachers can certainly modify the scenario or create one more relevant to their students. This scenario is quite broad in its scope; it asks students to think about one of the most prominent animals in the early 1800s, its importance to Indian nations, and changes that have occurred in the past two hundred years. This scenario could find use in social studies (history and geography), science, math, business, or writing classes. Notice that there is no right or wrong answer implied. The students will demonstrate understanding, or "make their thinking visible," through their presentation or report. They could elect to say that raising bison is not economically feasible; they could also find that it is a good idea and support their recommendation with their findings.

In reference to students' thinking, reasoning, and problem-solving ability, a presenter at an inquiry symposium remarked that "students don't know what to do when they don't know what to do." In other words, when students are confronted with a problem, they flounder, waste time, immediately begin to look for solutions, or sit idly waiting for the teacher to tell them what to do. Many students will reach a high state of anxiety and begin the negotiation stage, asking, for example, "how many pages is the report?" They may also feign total incompetence, hoping the teacher will change or modify the assignment to make it more directive and easier.

The good news is that students in problem-based learning situations can generally follow these steps:

1. Read and analyze the problem scenario
2. List what is known
3. Develop a problem statement
4. List questions that need to be answered
5. Develop a plan for investigation
6. Analyze and synthesize information
7. Present findings or recommendations

This model is a standard heuristic similar to the scientific method. Students could also form hypotheses for testing (for example, that the ecosystem in western South Dakota would be supportive of large herds of bison). Students would profit from making three columns on a white board or sheet of paper with the headings: What We Know, What We Need to Know, and Plan for Action.

The What We Know column allows students to pool their preknowledge about this topic. Identifying what is known in a group will almost always result in a greater list of preknowledge than a list from any one student. Next, the What We Need to Know column generates questions that need to be answered. Many will come from reading the scenario: for example, What were the spiritual connections of the bison to American Indians? Students may also ask questions such as: What types of grasses are best for bison? Are these grasses in South Dakota? Or is there a market for bison? The list may go on for some time. If the list becomes large and unmanageable, the students can prioritize the questions and then divide them among group members to take advantage of the group's size. The process of defining the questions for investigation may be the most important step. Students gain ownership over the learning process by defining their own learning needs. What students will learn from answering these questions should, of course, have a great deal of overlap with what the teacher has identified as the desired learning outcome.

After refining the list of questions needed to be answered, students develop a plan for information gathering and investigation, or the Plan for Action. They may use the Internet, school library, or even ask experts about bison. The Corps of Discovery Web site itself will also contain information of use to students. For the Pierre module, the development team provided a list of Internet sites that deal with bison management and bison issues in general. There are also sections from biologists and wildlife managers who discuss bison-management issues. The student teams will have to practice their time-management skills in order to have the presentation ready at the appropriate time. Often, they will have to narrow the search if the scope of their investigation is too wide. Some questions of lower priority may even remain unanswered due to a time constraint.

Students familiar with the traditional "talk and chalk" classroom may be uncomfortable with the PBL format at first. It will be up to the teacher to convince students that they are researchers looking for information and solutions to problems that may not have one right answer. Here are some keys to success:

- Relevance. Look for windows into students' thinking in order to pose problems of increasing relevance.
- Challenge. The problem scenario should challenge students' original hypotheses. We have tried to make the Lifelong Learning modules engaging; do not hesitate to elaborate upon the scenario to engage students.
- Time. Students must be given time and stimulation to seek relevance and the opportunity to reveal their points of view.
- Ownership. If the teacher appears to be heading students in a particular direction, they will see that it really is not their problem. They will perceive that there is a correct solution, after all, and that it belongs to the teacher.
- Complexity. Teachers new to the PBL classroom may be tempted to give students key variables, too much information, or problem simplification. Complexity of scenarios has been shown to increase student motivation and engagement.
- Making thinking visible. Regularly asking students to elaborate sends the message that the teacher wants to know what the student thinks and why. Research indicates that "awareness of students' points of view is an instructional entry point that sits at the gateway of personalized education. . . . teachers who operate without awareness of their students' points of view often doom students to dull, irrelevant experiences, and even failure."[10]
- Questioning techniques. In a PBL classroom, teachers should act

as metacognitive coaches, serving as models, thinking aloud with students, and practicing behavior they want their students to use. Students should become used to such metacognitive questions as: What is going on here? What do we need to know more about? What did we do during the problem that was effective? Teachers coax and prompt students to use questions and take responsibility for the problem. Over a period of time, students become self-directed learners; teachers can then provide less scaffolding, fading into the background.[11]

With these principles in mind, we can turn to an exploration of the site itself. A casual Web search of the words "Lewis and Clark" turned up 1.94 million hits. Why, then, another site? This question guided the participants of the *Lifelong Learning Online: Lewis and Clark Rediscovery Project* as they began deliberations about the purpose, look, and feel of this site. The education division of the National Aeronautics and Space Administration (NASA) sponsored the site, and this consideration alone meant that, in addition to history, the site would address geography and use satellite imagery and other products brought to us by NASA. The three partners to this Rediscovery Project, the University of Idaho, the University of Montana, and the Center for Educational Technologies at Wheeling Jesuit University in West Virginia, each brought a different background and unique contributions to the project, as well. The University of Idaho was experimenting with Web sites constructed with and implemented by a database instead of the usual html programming. Both the University of Idaho and the University of Montana had anthropologists on the team who had extensive experience in working with American Indians, bringing a unique perspective to the Lewis and Clark story. And the Center for Educational Technologies had a background in design and educational-material development for the Web.

Developers often hear the refrain that Web sites are nothing more than "books online." Unfortunately, this is often the case. So what would be an advantage of a Web site over a book? Perhaps the most important is that Web sites can include interactivity in a multimedia environment. Interactivity means that users are actively engaged as participants in their own learning, a concept that works well with inquiry-based environments. The term multimedia means that more than one form of information is used in a

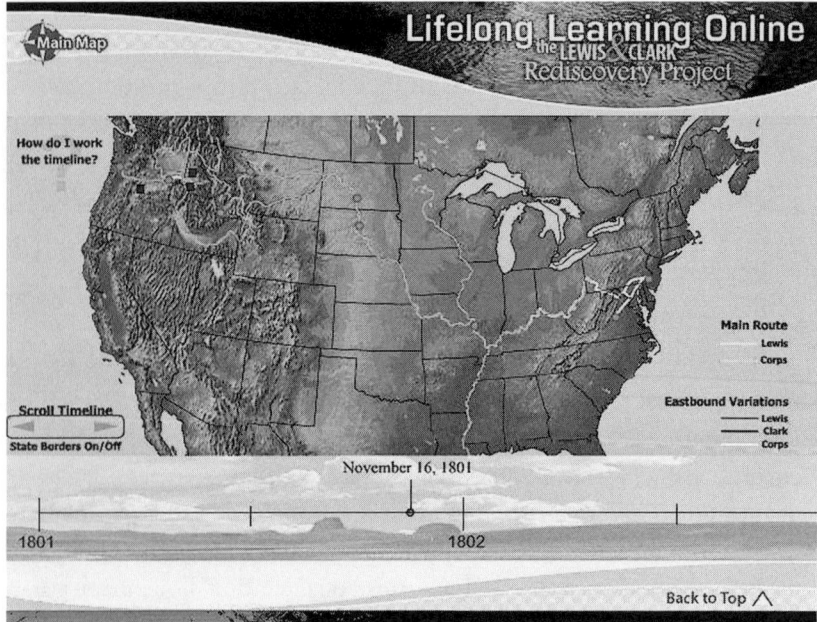

FIGURE 1. *The subject matter of The Lewis & Clark Discovery Project (http://www.l3-lewisandclark.com) is national in scope.*

site, e.g., voice, video, data, pictures, or graphics. In order to bring a unique contribution to the Lewis and Clark Web site genre, the Rediscovery production team traveled from coast to coast interviewing interesting people with stories to tell or information to share about the expedition. Typical interviewees included museum directors, historians, scientists, American Indians, and living historians. And while the video files are often large, taking some time to download, video adds an integral dimension to the site.

The site's nine modules, Philadelphia, Monticello, Saint Louis, Pierre, Knife River Villages, Great Falls, Lemhi Pass, Umatilla River, and Astoria, stretch from coast to coast, reflecting the national character of the expedition (Figure 1). Two additional modules were developed completely by Indian nations: Coeur D'Alene and Nez Perce. Another Indian-nation module, Warm Springs, is under development. The development team identified prospective interviewees at each site, contacted them, and then traveled to conduct the interviews. At the sites, we took pictures of the surrounding areas and videotaped other persons that came to our attention. Typical of this plan was a trip to Philadelphia to visit the American Philosophical

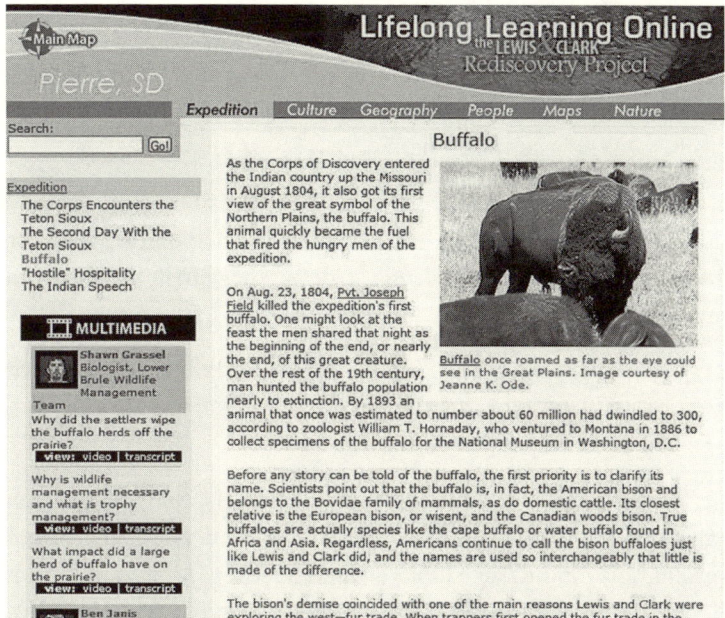

FIGURE 2. *Each module offers expedition, culture, geography, people, maps, and nature selections. The central theme for the Pierre, South Dakota, module is the bison.*

Society and the Academy of Natural Sciences, both integral to the Philadelphia module. At the same time, other team members worked on Web-page design, graphics, and maps for the geography section.

Each module consists of three major sections, Expedition, Culture, and Geography; the major sections are supported by the People, Maps, and Nature sections (Figure 2). The expedition section is designed to share with readers what happened to the Corps of Discovery during the module's segment of the journey. Many historians would argue that the most important event of the expedition in the Pierre area was the standoff between the Lakota Indians and members of the expedition. Video concerning the confrontation is included. Historian James P. Ronda speaks about the confrontation, characterizing members of the expedition as naïve travelers. He offers the view that the Anglos really did not know how to play the game. He says:

> There were real limits here. But Clark, who didn't know the game, didn't know the limits. And instead, he drew his sword and alerted Lewis and

the keelboat crew for action. The keelboat swivel gun was swung around, and perhaps, pointed at the crowd.

Soldiers with Clark made their weapons ready for action. Who knows the rules here? Who's confused here?

But as quickly as the Partisan had created the tension, Black Buffalo eased it. Fearing casualties if fighting broke out, Black Buffalo took the cable in his own hands and forcefully ordered the warriors away from the boat.

You know, the Partisan had his moment. Black Buffalo now reasserted his authority, and from now on, the story was going to be his story and his alone—or so he hoped.

Because the central theme for the Pierre module is bison, in addition to the analysis of the standoff, users can find accounts about the bison. For that reason, this module also looks at what the expedition found, what happened after the expedition, and which issues continue to get attention. For example, Shawn Grassel, wildlife biologist at the Lower Brule Wildlife Management Agency, provided an interview dealing with the impact of the bison on the prairie. Ben Jarvis, director of the Wildlife, Fish, and Recreation Department, Lower Brule Indian Reservation, spoke about the differences in impact between bison and cattle on the prairie. He also addressed the spiritual aspects of the bison and their meaning to the Lakota people.

In each module, the culture section was completed by the Indian nations from that particular location. Examples include the Lakota from South Dakota (Figure 3), the Hidatsa, Mandan, and Arikara from North Dakota, and the Blackfeet from Montana. The culture section of each module contains a broad look at the Indian nations. Users of this site will find traditional stories, information about the way of life, art, government, and the record of broken treaties. Additional information about the bison and its importance to the Lakota is a highlight of the Pierre module.

The geography section recognizes the fact that physical geography informs us about how and why people lived the way they did two hundred years ago and still do today. Students have access to what is known as geospatial data to support the geography section. In Figure 4, for example, a graphic depicts the extent of the grass prairies. A description of the soil and precipitation in the area explains a great deal about what the expedition

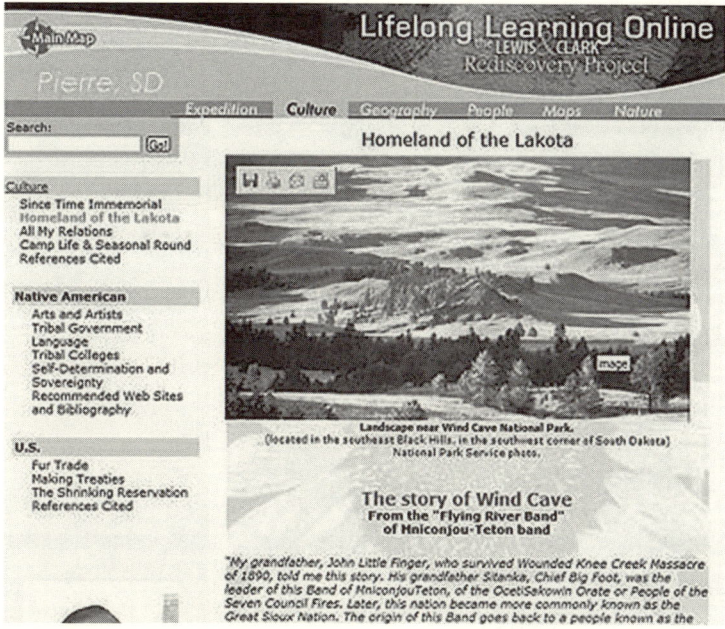

FIGURE 3. *Lakota Indians from South Dakota completed the culture section of the Pierre module.*

found. These conditions are still matters of concern today as farmers depend on the rain for crops and make decisions about what types of animals or crops will be more profitable. Here is a description of the area:

> Only about 400 miles across flat interior plains separate Council Bluffs and the Bad River. However, the Bad River gets half the rainfall (about 15 inches per year) of Council Bluffs (30 inches). Increased rainfall leaches minerals out of the ground, so soil mineral content is higher near Bad River. The average elevation of the plains increases from about 1,000 feet at Council Bluffs to about 1,800 feet at Bad River. The average temperature drops several degrees.

> These changes in climate and soil cause a dramatic change in fauna and flora. Council Bluffs is at the western edge of the tallgrass prairie that dominated the central lowland plains. Tallgrass prairie consists of a luxuriant growth of flowers and grasses that sometimes grew 10 feet high.

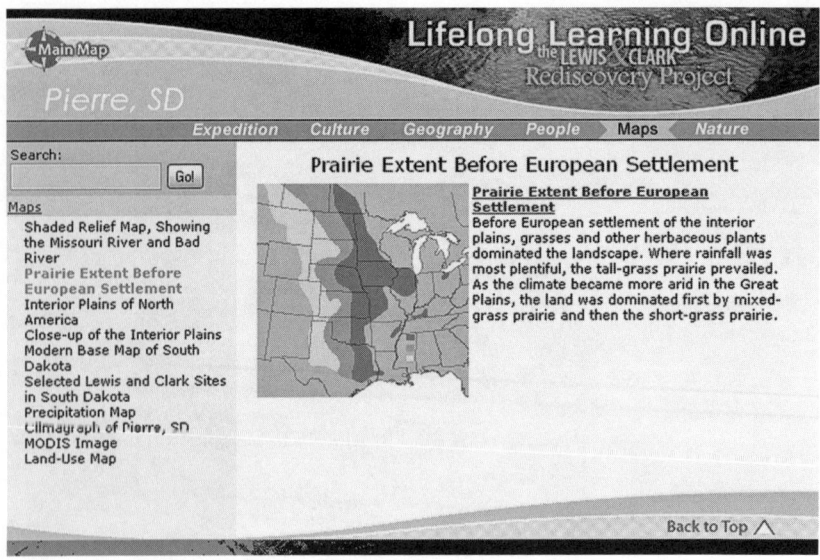

FIGURE 4. *The geography and maps sections of The Lewis & Clark Rediscovery Project explore the importance of physical geography in patterns of settlement.*

On the other hand, the Bad River is located at the western edge of the shortgrass prairies of the Great Plains. The shortgrass prairie is characterized by several species of short grasses and sage brush. Shortgrass prairie is also the land of pronghorns, prairie dogs, and bison—the Corps saw its first buffalo near Vermillion, SD.

This type of information, plus additional video from biologists, provides needed data for students working on the bison scenario. In addition, this material provides excellent reading for the casual Web user who just wants to know more about the trail and the environment found by the Corps of Discovery.

Inquiry-based, problem-based learning offers an alternative for classroom methodology, and this chapter illustrates how a Web site can be constructed to support these methods. Is our environment now complete for student engagement and the learning of history in accordance with established standards? Not quite, but these ingredients are a start. It is important to couple the use of the inquiry-based, problem-based learning methods and a site like the *Lewis and Clark Rediscovery Project* (http://www.l3-lewisandclark.com) with an attitude that suggests that history is important, that children can learn, and that they can find the subject to be rich, rewarding, and engaging. History teachers can then look for ways to hook their students and provide the spark for more than cursory learning. If we saw more of this attitude across the country, then perhaps we would no longer read about the dismal performance of our students on standard history tests.

NOTES

1. Ravitch, quoted by Kathleen K. Manzo in "U.S. History again Stumps Senior Class," *Education Week*, http://www.grade.org.pe/gtee-preal/evalua/evalo21.htm. For the statistics, *see* National Center for Education Statistics, "The Nation's Report Card: 2002 Assessment Results," *National Assessment of Education Progress*, http://nces.ed/gov/nationsreportcard/.

2. Henriksson, "Do Students Care about History?" *History News Network*, http://hnn.us/articles/594.html.

3. Yael Sharan and Shlomo Sharan, *Expanding Cooperative Learning through Group Investigation* (New York: Teachers College Press, 1992), p. 151.

4. Bruce and Bruce, *Learning Social Studies through Discrepant Event Inquiry* (Annapolis, Md.: Alpha Publishing Co., 1992), p. ii.

5. Lewis, "School Reform and Professional Development," *Phi Delta Kappan* 83 (Mar. 2002): 488–89.

6. George J. Pallrand, "The Relationship of Assessment to Knowledge Development in Science Education," *Phi Delta Kappan* 78 (Dec. 1996): 315–18.

7. *See* Howard S. Barrows, *The Tutorial Process* (Springfield: Southern Illinois University School of Medicine, 1988), and Geoffrey R. Norman and Henk G. Schmidt, "The Psychological Basis of Problem-based Learning: A Review of the Evidence," *Academic Medicine* 67 (Sept. 1992): 557–65.

8. Shelagh A. Gallagher, William J. Stepien, and Hilary Rosenthal, "The Effects of Problem-Based Learning on Problem Solving," *Gifted Child Quarterly* 36 (Fall 1992): 195–200; Sharan and Sharan, *Expanding Cooperative Learning*, p. 144.

9. Robert Myers, Steven Purcell, Jamie Little, and William Jaber, "A Middle School's Experience with Hypermedia and Problem-based Learning," paper presented at the 1993 annual conference of the International Visual Literacy Association, Rochester, N.Y.

10. Jacqueline Grennon Brooks and Martin G. Brooks, *In Search of Understanding: The Case for Constructivist Classrooms* (Alexandria, Va.: Association for Supervision & Curriculum Development, 1993), p. 60.

11. William Stepien and Shelagh Gallagher, "Problem-Based Learning: As Authentic as It Gets," *Educational Leadership* 50 (Apr. 1993): 25–28.

Finding Lewis and Clark by Stepping Away

ELLIOTT WEST

This will be a "Yeah, but . . ." essay. Such an essay can be helpful at a conference and in a volume devoted to one particular topic. When Paul Hutton tells us that the Lewis and Clark story has served as a great American myth, it is worth adding: "Yeah, but has that mythic telling of the story made the expedition seem more historically weighty than it truly was?" When Hutton, Joni Kinsey, and Dick Etulain tell us how the Corps of Discovery has inspired much art, many novels, and stores full of lunch boxes, lamps, whiskey decanters, and much more frontier *chotchke*, it can be healthy to ask: "Yeah, but what was its authentic impact and how did it fit into the broader scheme of things during its day?" The many fine sessions held in Pierre told a story of remarkable men and women, talented seat-of-their-pants scientists and geographers, fine leaders, and brave followers. That behooves us to push a bit further by wondering: "Yeah, but did these exceptional characters have advantages we tend to overlook?"

I am talking about perspective. Like many of our prime values—paying close daily attention to concerns of our loved ones, for instance—perspective is something we always agree is essential but are always in danger of neglecting. When we find an intriguing subject, we naturally are drawn into its flow of events. If its details are especially interesting and full of puzzles, we get caught up in chasing every lead into every evidentiary cranny. With that, we tend to lose sight of our subject's wider arena, which leaves us facing an annoying paradox. The more we concentrate on what we study, the less we understand. We can clarify what we know, on the other hand, as we look to our subject's broader perspective. Paradoxically, a subject's implications can expand as its influence narrows. We might see that our favored characters have not moved the world as grandly as we thought, and that can be painful, but what we now know, including the limits of our heroes' and heroines' importance, allows them to illuminate their time as they never could have if we had kept our vision more tightly focused. Stepping away, we know them and their world more fully.

All very abstract, I know, but all of us who are fascinated by Lewis and Clark and their extraordinary story can see the point if we only bring it home. Few episodes in nineteenth-century America can match that of Lewis and Clark for raw appeal. It has just about everything: intriguing personalities, high drama and dare-death escapes, fabulous landscapes and family reunions, sex and animal attacks. The story is mesmerizing, irresistible, and that is just the problem. It pulls us in, closer and closer. Our mental camera angle gets tighter and tighter, and with every step, our grasp of the larger perspective grows fuzzier. Cataloguing every stop along the way, we run the risk of missing what the journey meant. We know how many dogs the corps ate, but do we know how they (the corps and the dogs) fit into the larger scheme of things?

I will suggest a couple of ways in which we might see Lewis and Clark more clearly by stepping away. My particular approach steals shamelessly from Jim Ronda, this generation's master historian of the expedition, who has done more than anyone to encourage a broader vision of it. He entitled an essay on Jefferson's vision of the West "A Promise of Rivers: Thomas Jefferson and the Exploration of Western Waterways."[1] Rivers are crucial to understanding not only the course of the expedition but also—and this was Ronda's point—the concerns and perceptions of geographers, of statemakers, and of people like Jefferson who were both. In the case of Lewis and Clark, of course, the main rivers in question were the Missouri and the Columbia. Tracing their courses and figuring out how they fit together was the prime imperative of the captains because, in Jefferson's mind, the answers to those riverine questions were one key to how American commerce and power would manifest themselves in the Far West. I will try to pull back into a larger view of the expedition that keeps the Missouri and Columbia in the picture but, first, includes another important western river and, next, draws back far enough to see a great river on another continent. Bringing those other rivers and their promises into the picture can help put Lewis and Clark in a wider and more useful perspective.

First, we might step away far enough to see the entire Great Plains, not just its northern portion and the great course of the Missouri traveled by the corps, but also its southern expanse, including the Red River that rises

Like other unexplored rivers, the Missouri captured the attention of explorers and statemakers at the turn of the nineteenth century. This stretch of the Missouri, which lies above Pierre, South Dakota, was photographed in 1948 before dams changed the appearance of the river. (State Archives Collection, South Dakota State Historical Society, Pierre)

on the highlands of western Texas, forms part of the northern boundary of that state, and then angles through Louisiana before joining the Mississippi River. Once we step back far enough to include both the Red and the Missouri, we see that during the Jefferson years there was at least as much official concern and curiosity about that southern river, the Red, as for the ones Lewis and Clark explored to the north.

Begin with a neglected point: during Jefferson's administration there were *four* expeditions launched into the Louisiana Purchase. The other three were dedicated to solving what was, as it turned out, a far tougher puzzle than the geography of the Missouri and Columbia—the question of where the Red River originated and where it ran on its way into the more familiar country of what is today the state of Louisiana. Astonishingly, we comprehended the sources and course of the Red River only in the 1870s, nearly a decade after John Wesley Powell floated through what is usually considered the last great river mystery of the lower forty-eight states, the Colorado River's inner gorge of the Grand Canyon. But it was not for want of trying that we were slow to understand the Red River. The best-known attempt to explore it was sent out *under* but not *by* Jefferson. It was led by Zebulon M. Pike in 1805–1806 and organized by James Wilkinson, the governor of Louisiana Territory. Preceding it were two other expeditions under Jefferson's direction, those of George Hunter and William Dunbar (1804) and of Thomas Freeman and Peter Custis (1806).

What can be learned by bringing the Red River and these other expeditions into the picture? For a clue about the considerable concern over the Red, we might look back to Lewis and Clark. As Jim Ronda has pointed out, the true precipitating cause of the Corps of Discovery was not Jefferson's scientific curiosity but something more immediate—the strong suggestion in Alexander Mackenzie's *Voyages from Montreal*, his 1802 account of his Canadian journey to the Pacific (1792–1793), that England might soon make a move to control the fur trade of what we call the Oregon Country. Until then the president had merely been "playing at the imperial game," Ronda writes. Mackenzie's comments instantly provoked a sharp sense of rivalry with another nation's western ambitions and "made Jefferson a real imperialist."[2] And so it was with the southern expeditions, but with two differences. The rival was Spain, not England, and in the minds of those in power, this clash of interests was more immediately troubling. England was unquestionably the more formidable nation on the world stage, but looking around the horizon of the region that the United States had just acquired, Spain's profile was more alarming. The Spanish had settlements in eastern and southern Texas and in New Mexico along the valley of the upper Rio Grande and as far east as the Pecos River. England had economic agents in the villages of the upper Missouri River and ambitions to the Pacific, but they had nothing like Spain's settlements and military presence on what was now America's southwestern border.

For that matter, what *was* that border? Trying to answer that question raises a striking parallel to the episode of Mackenzie, his book, and Jefferson's alarm. Jefferson, it seems, was doing some writing of his own about national ambitions, in this case colliding with Spanish interests on what was now the nation's newest, fuzziest, and most contentious border. In a pamphlet he entitled "The Limits and Bounds of Louisiana," the president claimed that an earlier French presence along the Texas coast now gave the

United States title to a Louisiana reaching west and south to the "Bravo." In other words, the nation's new southwestern border was the Rio Grande.[3]

When we set Jefferson's remarkable claim alongside Mackenzie's bid for the Pacific Northwest, we begin to see, first, that not just Oregon but much of western North America was up for grabs and, second, that Jefferson was if anything more aggressive in his southwesterly ambitions than he was toward the Northwest. The picture sharpens further when we remember Spain's long-standing worry over international competitors challenging its dim power on its far-flung northern borders. Part of the reason for ceding Louisiana to France, after all, was to rely on Napoleon to blunt the potential expansion of the new American nation. Now that nation itself was on Spain's northern doorstep; its president was already making what was, to the Spanish, an outrageous and dangerous bid for position. The closer we look, the more intriguing the story gets, in both senses of the word. What was Jefferson up to in these various expeditions on the Missouri and the Red? What did Spain think he was trying and how did it respond, and how successful were these two international players?

Jefferson's bid for the Rio Grande is not quite so mind-spinning if we keep in mind that for Jefferson, as for non-Indians generally, the geography of the midcontinent was basically a speculation. He had bought Louisiana, and he knew where it started on the east (the Mississippi), but he had little understanding of where it stopped on the west, north, and south. The purchase boundaries were defined as what they had been for the French, but what was that? New France's boundary with New Spain had been long contested, and Jefferson was simply continuing the tradition of reaching as far as possible. Besides, there was a general consensus that the Rio Grande, the Missouri, and the Colorado rivers all rose from a great interior highland. Maps of the day show their headwaters bunched closely together. The impression was that from high on the Missouri it might be possible to make an easy transition to the upper Rio Grande and from there descend to that exotic interior port o' call, Santa Fe. Prevailing ignorance goes a long way toward explaining what, in retrospect, seems an outlandish territorial bid.

The larger point is that this ignorance left the geographical limits of the new republic very much in play. Lewis and Clark's mission was, in part, to sketch in our northwestern boundary, but even so they might push against the Spanish. Jefferson instructed them to discover what they could of the Missouri watershed "and especially on its southern side." They should ask about the Rio Bravo, the contemporary term for the upper Rio Grande. How far it was from the Missouri, what sort of terrain lay between, what tribes lived there—all that, the president wrote, was "worthy of particular inquiry."[4] Behind this bland comment was another promise of rivers, a bridge for American interests toward the desert Southwest as well as to the Pacific Northwest. (The Spanish recognized the threat. They sent no fewer than four military probes to find and stop the captains.) How serious Jefferson was in his claim to the Rio Grande is an interesting question, but clearly he was much aware of how fluid the situation was on the southern plains, and just as clearly he was determined to make the most of it.

An obvious first move was to explore the Red River. The promise of this river was in some ways more compelling than that of the Missouri and Columbia because staking our position there would at least establish a national base point in the push-and-shove with Spain. Jefferson was on surer ground in arguing for the Red as our southern border. By one definition (eventually confirmed), the Louisiana Purchase was defined as the western watershed of the Mississippi. If so, defining boundaries would be a matter of tracing the courses of the Mississippi's northernmost and southernmost major tributaries flowing from the west. For the northern boundary, that meant the Missouri. By following it to its headwaters, Lewis and Clark were roughing out the northwest border of the republic. The corresponding river to the south was the Red. Mapping its course was a high priority, regardless of what came of the Rio Grande claim. Besides, in contrast to the Rio Grande, at least we were on the Red; the United States occupied the river's final run through lower Louisiana. By sending agents to trace the river from there to its source, Jefferson might fill in a geographical blank spot while pushing his claim at least that far against Spain.

Thus the Hunter-Dunbar expedition was originally meant to explore the Red, but, given troubles with the Osages and probable resistance from Spain, it was diverted up the Ouachita River into Arkansas.[5] Later what was formally dubbed the Exploring Expedition of the Red River, but what Jefferson tellingly called "the Grand Expedition," that of Thomas Freeman and Peter Custis, was sent up that crucial southern river, around the famous "great raft" (the hundred-mile logjam blocking all navigation), up to a point in present Bowie County, Texas. There, at a spot that came to be called Spanish Bluff, a large Spanish command intercepted the party and sent them home.[6]

Zebulon Pike's better-known expedition is an even more vivid reminder of American southwestward interests. He was sent by General James Wilkinson, the spectacularly corrupt governor of Louisiana Territory who was entangled with Aaron Burr in some scheme, never precisely revealed but clearly intending to play on the bubbling ambitions in the lower Mississippi valley toward Texas and beyond. Rather than ascending the Red, Pike's ostensible strategy was to approach it higher up its course, beyond the great raft and Spanish patrols, pursue it to its source, and then trace it downstream. After returning some Osages to their village on the central plains, Pike's men dropped down to the Arkansas River, followed it to the Rockies, passed over the Front Range, and in the San Luis Valley came upon the Rio Grande, which Pike claimed to have mistaken for the Red. Another Spanish command (possibly on its way to block Lewis and Clark) arrested Pike's men there and escorted them to Santa Fe and Chihuahua before sending them back to Louisiana.[7]

Stepping far enough away from Lewis and Clark to include the southern plains, we see that expansionist tensions were highest with Spain, not with England, and that the zone of greatest abrasion was not the Missouri and Columbia but along the Red and Rio Grande. Tension was so high there that in early 1806, as the corps journeyed home, the United States faced a genuine threat of war with Spain over our new disputed border.[8] The point is worth stressing because the popular fascination with Lewis and Clark tempts us toward a flawed syllogism. Its major premise: In less than fifty years after 1804, the United States expanded to the Pacific Ocean (true). Its minor premise: The Lewis and Clark Expedition was an early contributor to that expansion (true). Its conclusion: The expedition was a prime event in propelling the United States to the far edge of the continent (false).

The flaw in the logic will be familiar to all magicians and dealers of three-card monte. What people think is happening depends on where people look. Our fascination with Lewis and Clark points our attention to the west and north, and because we know that in less than fifty years the nation was on the Pacific, we assume that northwestward was the direction expansion took and that the corps was the force behind it. "Yeah, but," we can now add, "the government's much greater concern was to the west and *south*." And when we follow up on that reminder, we see that in fact it was southwestward that expansion mostly took its course. True, Lewis and Clark would be an immediate stimulus to the fur trade, which, in turn, would help flesh out our knowledge of the West and its passways and would stimulate interest in the region. But even here the most important explorations by mountain men were south of a parallel running through the Great Salt Lake. Meanwhile, Missouri merchants were opening trade with Santa Fe, and thousands of southerners were settling in Mexican Texas, which lit the fuse of the Texas Revolution of 1836. At that point, the Pacific Northwest was feeling only the first faint American presence, the tentative Protestant missions to the country's native peoples. Farmers migrating to Oregon in the 1840s added something to our westward momentum, but the prime stimuli were our souring relations with Mexico, our desire for Santa Fe, California, and the port of San Francisco, and our annexation of Texas in 1845. The thrust of national growth after 1804 was indisputably toward the Southwest, the country probed by Freeman, Custis, and Pike. By comparison, whatever Lewis and Clark began was tenuous and feeble.

We can certainly all agree, on the other hand, that the nation expanded, and did so vigorously. Accounts of westward expansion, whichever route an author emphasizes, typically exude a feeling of raw, unstoppable power. Traditionalists write that the republic's superior virtues gave it natural advantages as it pressed against lesser adversaries. Critics write more darkly of a domineering young nation muscling its way westward. Both sides have this in common: They assume that America's rapid advance to the Pacific is explained primarily by the nation's unique properties, its economic, cultural, even spiritual dispositions. Predictably, both have trotted out Lewis and Clark to make their points. To one, the captains were worthy precursors of American destiny. To the other, they were early agents of imperialist bullies.

Which calls for another "Yeah, but . . ." The emphasis on our peculiarly national puissance is a bit overdone. For good or ill, we hear, the United States wielded power explained by our unique institutions. "Yeah, but," we should ask, "didn't we have plenty going for us—and didn't Lewis and Clark have plenty going for their enterprise—that had nothing to do with our values, our economy, our national power?" As an example of what we might learn from that question, we can look at what we now know played a crucial role in global conquest during the modern age—disease.

Historians have looked mostly at European contact diseases that became devastating "virgin soil epidemics" when suddenly introduced among New World native populations with no evolved resistance to them.[9] A grim biological and virological frontier moved along with or ahead of advancing Europeans and Euro-Americans. Indian peoples, their numbers thinned, their economies assaulted, and their psyches shaken, were far less an obstacle than they would have been otherwise. Contact diseases such as smallpox, measles, and influenza were highly effective weapons—albeit ones that were wielded unintentionally—in the conquest of the New World and of the American West in particular.

There was much more to the role of diseases than that, however. In the case of Lewis and Clark, for instance, we might ask about diseases that were *not* there. I realize this sounds odd on the face of it. If we start listing the threats that pioneers did not face—samurai warriors, for instance, and king cobras—we will need a lot of paper. But let me argue that some diseases absent in far western expansion are pertinent for a couple of reasons. First, those absent diseases could influence indirectly key events in westward expansion, including one of great importance to the Corps of Discovery. And second, such diseases can show us how factors that had nothing to do with national character and institutions helped determine the patterns of global empires, including the one Lewis and Clark helped bring into being in North America. Regarding this second reason, a coincidence of timing makes their expedition a pretty dramatic example of what we can learn.

Diseases were transmitted to the New World out of several "pools" or "reservoirs" in the old.[10] Out of reservoirs in Europe and the Mediterranean basin came the contact, or "crowd," diseases, those transmitted person-to-person, usually by human fluids—airborne droplets or feces—that sent New World populations plummeting. But those were not the only ones in play. The Old World held another disease pool, older and deeper than Europe's. Africa south of the Sahara Desert is home to afflictions apparently part of the human condition for many thousands of years. Many are not contact but vector diseases. They spread, that is, not person-to-person but by means of mediators, typically insects, that work a terrible messenger service, bearing a virus, bacterium, or parasite from one human or animal host to another. Tripanosomiasis, or sleeping sickness, is spread through the tsetse fly, for instance. The two diseases that have played the greatest role in patterning New World conquest are malaria and yellow fever. They are transmitted among people via mosquitoes, several species of *Anopheles* in the case of malaria, *Aedes aegypti* for yellow fever. In frost-free tropical regions where those insects live year round, these two diseases can be endemic — that is, always around and flaring now and again into epidemics, usually when a number of heretofore unexposed persons arrive. Outside those areas, malaria and yellow fever occur in warm-weather epidemics. Generally speaking, the farther north of the endemic regions, the shorter the season of danger, the less frequent the epidemics, and the less troublesome the diseases.[11]

In the Americas, malaria and yellow fever have been endemic in the Caribbean, Central America, and northern South America. Except for the Gulf coast and the southernmost Mississippi valley, however, the United States lies north of the diseases' deepest entrenchment. In summer, malaria would flare up throughout the Mississippi and Ohio river valleys, in much of the South, and well up the Atlantic coast. Yellow fever epidemics were most frequent along the Gulf coast — New Orleans had twelve in thirty-five years — and they flashed intermittently in ports of the Atlantic and the Mississippi. An infamous outbreak in Philadelphia in 1793 carried away 10 percent of the city's population, and in the summer of 1878, one out of ten residents of Memphis died. Still, compared to tropical America, the virulence and relative threat was considerably weaker in the United States, and above about the fortieth parallel the incidence dwindled rapidly.[12]

What, you are probably asking, does this have to do with Lewis and Clark? In terms of a direct connection, the answer is "nothing." In a sense, that is just the point. A little later, I will suggest why it is noteworthy that the captains of discovery did not have to worry about such afflictions. First, however, we should recall that if we look for indirect connections, diseases from the African pool turn out to be important indeed to the Lewis and Clark story.

To see this fact, we need to step away again, farther this time, so our view includes not just all the Great Plains but all of North and Central America and the West Indies. Now consider how and when yellow fever arrived in the New World. European crowd diseases so ravaged the densely settled islands of the West Indies that native populations had essentially collapsed by the mid-seventeenth century. To work the lucrative sugar plantations, the Spanish began importing African slaves. Almost certainly yellow fever arrived on some slave ship with mosquito eggs and larvae in its water casks and the virus in the blood of suffering crewmen. When the crewmen debarked and the mosquitoes hatched, yellow fever had jumped from one hemisphere to another. The first epidemic occurred in 1647 in Barbados, the Caribbean's busiest port. During the next half-century, others raged ferociously through the islands of the American tropics—raged, that is, especially against Europeans. African slaves had mostly been infected as children, when the effects of "yellow jack" are minimal, and had survived into immunity; those infected as adults apparently enjoyed a resistance, just as Europeans had to their own crowd diseases.[13]

In the grim story of diseases and empire, Europeans in tropical America suddenly found themselves not on the giving but the receiving end. Such had long been the case on the other side of the Atlantic, where the terrible toll of fevers had given Africa's west coast the nickname of the "white man's grave."[14] European soldiers and mercantile agents there were confined to a few Atlantic outposts, and even so they died at a stunning rate. Those ports were entrepots of the slave trade, and the traffic between them and the Indies, in effect, recreated the West African situation in the Caribbean. The historian Alfred Crosby, Jr., coined the term "Neo-Europes" for areas where plants, animals, and diseases have been transplanted from that continent. The West Indies became a "Neo-Africa," first in terms of these diseases and then, because whites avoided this region for the same reasons they shunned West Africa, in terms of its population. As the slave population of the sugar islands stabilized and grew, that of whites remained static and small. By the end of the eighteenth century, the Caribbean was overwhelmingly African American.

This situation set the stage for a remarkable chain of events ending with our purchase of Louisiana. In 1800, Napoleon acquired Louisiana with plans to make it the granary feeding the sugar island of Santo Domingo, the cash cow of France's New World empire. A rebellion among African Americans fearing a reimposition of slavery, however, threatened French control of this colonial jewel. To suppress it, Napoleon dispatched an army of nearly thirty thousand troops under his brother-in-law Leclerc.[15] Within weeks the French seemed to gain the upper hand. Then yellow fever struck. In this Neo-Africa, soldiers died by the thousands, four thousand alone in September 1802. An officer wrote that his men "die by the hundreds daily, like dogs, like flies, they disappear unaccountably."[16] Soon the insurrectionists rebounded and used their overwhelming black-to-white numerical advantage to batter the French while suffering enormous losses of their own. Eventually Leclerc, two thirds of his staff, and 80 percent of his troops perished. A despairing Napoleon, facing the loss of thousands more troops and realizing he would soon be back at war with England, trimmed his American ambitions just as Jefferson's agents arrived with an offer to buy New Orleans. Suffering from both low spirits and poor cash flow, Napoleon unloaded the entire territory at a bargain price.

Timing, they say, is everything, but behind the lucky alignment of events was a more fundamental shaping force. Just as the immigration of European contact diseases made the New World generally a killing ground for American Indians, so the colonization of African vector diseases, especially yellow fever, made tropical America nearly as much a "white man's grave" as the steamy posts on the Bight of Benin. The result was what we might call the Yellow Zone, a region on either side of the Atlantic from just south of the equator to roughly the thirtieth parallel where African fevers kept European populations down and weakened the European colonial grip. England's Atlantic colonies and the young American republic certainly had their nasty moments with tropical diseases, but sitting where the Yellow Zone faded out, in the latitudes of saving frosts, they never became anything like the killing ground extending west and east from Sierra Leone and the Ivory Coast to the Antilles and Yucatan.

Stepping away, the first and most obvious thing we see is that Lewis and Clark were vanguards of an expanding society whose gross outline was determined by factors having nothing to do with human will. Climate, insects, and invisible animals helped set the outer limits of what this nation could and could not be. Looking southward into the Indies, we see how another alignment of those same factors set very different limits. The circumstances in time turned harshly against Europe's superpower, giving the United States a matchless chance at growth and security and instantly elevating the purpose of Lewis and Clark's journey from exploration to national definition. The name of the fine city of "Pierre," South Dakota, should remind us that every step of national development has been partly a product of intricate connections among seemingly unrelated events, patterns, and forces far beyond the most prominent actors' awareness and understanding, much less their influence. Today we are speaking English in Pierre, not French, in part because of the Atlantic slave trade and African mosquitoes.

It is a healthy reminder of how little Lewis and Clark had to do with the fundamental course of events—in this case, with whose empire they were exploring and what its social character would be. This perspective should never lessen our admiration for what they did as individuals. It merely emphasizes how much of what happens is beyond any individual's sway. In this spirit, we might ask what other advantages the captains unwittingly carried with them. We have seen how global patterns of disease had their way in national demography and imperial diplomacy, allowing European domination in North America and helping shift territories from one empire to another. But what about the actual processes of exploration and expansion? European contact diseases mowed away native peoples as Euro-Americans advanced into the continent. But what about diseases *not* there, the vector diseases of the Yellow Zone? Did they have a role?

As it happens, a provocative coincidence gives us a chance to pursue that question. To see it, we have to step back yet again, farther still, enough to see not only North America and the Indies but also the far side of the Atlantic and the western coast of Africa. Here, as Lewis and Clark were ascending the Missouri to its head, crossing the continental divide, and descending the Clearwater and Columbia, another crew of explorers were seeking out another great watercourse. The river was the Niger. The expedition was headed by a tall, powerful, long-armed, and large-handed Scotsman, Mungo Park.

A veteran of other West African forays, Park had been hired by the Africa Association, a group of wealthy Englishmen.[17] His assignment, like that of the Corps of Discovery, was to solve an enduring river riddle, but in his case the question was not where the Niger began but, strangely, where it ended. Because it bled off into several channels through a marshy delta, no outsider knew whether it flowed to the Atlantic or into some other stream. It was Park's job to find out while also securing "local knowledge" of the region's peoples and probing the possibilities of "commercial intercourse." With these instructions, so strikingly similar to Lewis and Clark's, Park left from England at the end of January 1805, arriving in Africa two months later. He assembled a crew of forty-five. Besides himself, his brother-in-law, and another English friend, there were an army lieutenant named John Martyn, thirty-five soldiers, two sailors, and four carpenters. On 4 May, this African corps of discovery set off to strike the Niger on its upper reaches. The plan was to float it from there to its mouth.[18]

Here, then, were two expeditions parallel in time and in general purpose, both ably commanded and adequately supplied, each in its way drawn by the promise of rivers. But when we plot them on that wide map of the trans-

Atlantic world, when we lay over that map the Yellow Zone, the realm of those bug-borne diseases that helped give Louisiana to the United States, and when we shade in where the threat of infection was strongest and weakest, immediately we see a striking difference. Lewis and Clark were departing from the zone's outermost rim, breaking free of its grip. Park and his men were walking right into its fevered heart. Both expeditions, furthermore, left journals documenting their respective journeys. This fact allows us to set the documents side-by-side and chart experiences in these coincident probings of two continents. The results are revealing.

Lewis and Clark were wintering in the Mandan villages, forging war axes in return for corn, when Park left for Africa, and the Scotsman reached his jumping off place for the Niger, behind schedule, the day Lewis had his famous frantic race with the corps's first grizzly.[19] The Americans were on the Marias River when the African rainy season began with a dumping on 10 June. Immediately Park's men sickened. Private Shaddy Walter died of fever on 28 June, the day after Clark reported Sergeant Nathaniel Pryor's stomach problems much improved.[20] More on the Niger expedition soon were dying outright or falling away, not to be seen again. On 19 August, the day Clark wrote of pausing by a "butifull Stream" in what is now Idaho, Park reached the Niger. His command had shrunk from forty-five to nineteen.[21]

For the Corps of Discovery, the weeks that followed were difficult. They complained of cold and hunger during their crossing of the northern Rockies. Meanwhile their counterparts in Africa continued to sicken and die, the corpses occasionally stolen from camp by packs of jackals. Park paused at the village of Sansanding to build a flat-bottomed boat, and after writing a chipper letter to his wife and a more solemn one to his patron ("I shall set sail . . . with the fixed resolution to discover the termination of the Niger or perish in the attempt"), he cast off on 19 November as Clark enjoyed a hearty venison breakfast and explored the Washington coast.[22] Survivors now were down to Park, Martyn, and three soldiers, one deranged. Fifteen hundred miles downriver, probably during the late January of the Americans' soggy stay at Fort Clatsop, the boat was attacked while passing through rapids. All those aboard, apparently now down to two or three, drowned.[23]

Lewis and Clark lost one man to an illness unrelated to the time and place of their travels. Park's expedition was annihilated, directly or indirectly, by African-based diseases that to Europeans stood as a nearly impenetrable wall around the tropical Atlantic world. The twin expeditions give us a grimly arresting illustration of the relative advantages of empire-making outside the Yellow Zone. In particular, it adds to our perspective of the extraordinarily rapid conquest of the Far West, the national expansion that Lewis and Clark helped set in motion. Behind that expansion were indeed the engines of national power—an exploding population, a vigorous economy and an inventive technology, a steely confidence and sense of superiority, and, most certainly, the skills and courage of individuals like the captains of discovery. But we should also toss into the balance the barriers that these forces did not encounter. Microscopic agents helped set the patterns of imperial power. What is striking about our westward expansion is that it was aided both actively, by European-based epidemics accompanying the invaders, and passively, by African diseases that stepped aside to allow conquest here while blocking it elsewhere—and indirectly contributed nearly a million square miles to the republic.

Stepping away gives us perspective, and while perspective can take away some of the gloss of a favorite topic, in return it always gives us a truer appreciation. Putting Lewis and Clark in the larger context of Jeffersonian concerns, of the thrust of expansion, and of global patterns of empires can pare back the significance and meaning sometimes given to them. But not to worry. There remains plenty to admire and learn from the Corps of Discovery. Who those thirty-two men and one woman were, how they thought and what they believed, how they related to one another and to the Indians they met and how the Indians related to them, and their descriptions of the western country during a time of rapid and wrenching changes—all this and more provide a wide window into Jeffersonian America, East and West. The extraordinary writings of the expedition invite us into our own explorations into those documents. If the historical impact of the expedition was limited, the insights and pleasures of its journals are, as far as I can tell, limitless. Finally there is the narrative itself, compelling and irresistible. Lewis and Clark did not have the long-term consequences we too often assume, and their mythic glare threatens to blind us to far larger forces at work. But to that I say: "Yeah, but their story is as revealing and captivating as any in American history."

NOTES

1. James P. Ronda, *Finding the West: Explorations with Lewis and Clark* (Albuquerque: University of New Mexico Press, 2001), chap. 1, pp. 1–16.

2. Ibid., p. 64.

3. Thomas Jefferson, "The Limits and Bounds of Louisiana," in *Documents Relating to the Purchase and Exploration of Louisiana* (Boston: Houghton Mifflin & Co., 1904), pp. 7–45.

4. Saul K. Padover, ed., *The Complete Jefferson, Containing His Major Writings, Published and Unpublished, Except His Letters* (New York: Taylor Publishing Co., 1943), p. 913.

5. Remarkably, there is no scholarly work on this expedition. For its journal, see Mrs. Dunbar Rowland, comp., *Life, Letters and Papers of William Dunbar . . . Pioneer Scientist of the Southern United States* (Jackson: Press of the Mississippi Historical Society, 1930).

6. A fine short history of this expedition can be found in Dan L. Flores's lengthy introduction to *Jefferson and Southwestern Exploration: The Freeman & Custis Accounts of the Red River Expedition of 1806* (Norman: University of Oklahoma Press, 1984), pp. 3–90.

7. Like the other southern expeditions, Pike's journey begs for new scholarship. The only book-length study is more than half a century old: W. Eugene Hollon, *The Lost Pathfinder, Zebulon Montgomery Pike* (Norman: University of Oklahoma Press, 1949).

8. The United States seized a Spanish garrison in eastern Texas, and in retaliation the region's commandant sent more than nine hundred troops to confront the Americans. Wilkinson arranged a detente and established a neutral zone between the contending forces, but the basic confrontation was unresolved. Both sides understood that America's momentum and Spain's defensiveness would keep relations close to a flash point.

9. The seminal article and book that began this vigorous line of research were Henry F. Dobyns, "Estimating Aboriginal American Population: An Appraisal of Techniques with a New Hemisphere Estimate," *Current Anthropology* 7 (Oct. 1966): 395–416, 425–49, and Alfred W. Crosby, Jr., *The Columbian Exchange: Biological and Cultural Consequences of 1492* (Westport, Conn.: Greenwood Press, 1972).

10. Of the many books on the various aspects of this topic, the most satisfying overview remains William H. McNeill, *Plagues and Peoples* (Garden City, N.Y.: Anchor Press, 1976).

11. The literature on malaria and yellow fever is considerable. For the basics, readers might consult Philip H. Manson-Bahr, *Manson's Tropical Diseases: A Manual of the Diseases of Warm Climates* (Baltimore, Md.: Williams & Wilkins Co., 1966), pp. 36–77, 282–98; Stanley C. Oaks, Jr., et al., eds. *Malaria: Obstacles and Opportunities* (Washington, D.C.: National Academy Press, 1991); Paul F. Russell, *Man's Mastery of Malaria* (London: Oxford University Press, 1955); George Augustin, *History of Yellow Fever* (New Orleans: Searcy & Pfaff, 1909); George K. Strode, ed., *Yellow Fever*

(New York: McGraw-Hill Book Co., 1951). For a highly readable recent work on mosquito-borne diseases by an international authority, see Andrew Spielman and Michael D'Antonio, *Mosquito: A Natural History of Our Most Persistent and Deadly Foe* (New York: Hyperion, 2001).

12. J. H. Powell, *Bring Out Your Dead: The Great Plague of Yellow Fever in Philadelphia in 1793* (Philadelphia: University of Pennsylvania Press, 1949); Jo Ann Carrigan, *The Saffron Scourge: A History of Yellow Fever in Louisiana, 1796-1905* (Lafayette: Center for Louisiana Studies, University of Southwestern Louisiana, 1994); Khaled J. Bloom, *The Mississippi Valley's Great Yellow Fever Epidemic of 1878* (Baton Rouge: Louisiana State University Press, 1993).

13. Kenneth F. Kiple and Virginia H. Kiple, "Black Yellow Fever Immunities, Innate and Acquired, as Revealed in the American South," *Social Science History* 1 (Summer 1977): 419–36.

14. Philip D. Curtin, *Death by Migration: Europe's Encounter with the Tropical World in the Nineteenth Century* (Cambridge: Cambridge University Press, 1989), p. 160.

15. For more on the insurrection, see Thomas O. Ott, *The Haitian Revolution, 1789-1804* (Knoxville: University of Tennessee Press, 1973), and T. Lothrop Stoddard, *The French Revolution in San Domingo* (Boston: Houghton Mifflin Co., 1914).

16. Quoted in Ott, *Haitian Revolution*, p. 179.

17. There are three standard works on Park: Kenneth Lupton, *Mungo Park, the African Traveler* (Oxford: Oxford University Press, 1979); Stephen Gwynn, *Mungo Park and the Quest of the Niger* (New York: G. P. Putnam's Sons, 1935); and Ronald Miller, ed., *Mungo Park's Travels in Africa* (1907; reprint ed., London: J. M. Dent & Sons, 1969).

18. Lupton, *Mungo Park*, pp. 150, 152-55.

19. Gary E. Moulton and Thomas W. Dunlay, eds., *The Journals of the Lewis & Clark Expedition*, Vol. 3: *August 25, 1804-April 6, 1805* (Lincoln: University of Nebraska Press, 1987), pp. 280-81, and Vol. 4: *April 7, 1805-July 27, 1805*, pp. 84-85.

20. Ibid., 4:274-76, 337; Miller, ed., *Mungo Park's Travels in Africa*, pp. 308, 321-22.

21. Moulton and Dunlay, eds., *Journals of the Lewis & Clark Expedition*, Vol. 5: *July 28, 1805-November 1, 1805* (Lincoln: University of Nebraska Press, 1988), p. 124; Miller, ed., *Mungo Park's Travels in Africa*, pp. 351-52.

22. Moulton and Dunlay, eds., *Journals of the Lewis & Clark Expedition*, Vol. 6: *November 2, 1805-March 22, 1806* (Lincoln: University of Nebraska Press, 1990), pp. 68-69; Miller, ed., *Mungo Park's Travels in Africa*, pp. 365-66.

23. Lupton, *Mungo Park*, pp. 204-10.

CONTRIBUTORS

RICHARD W. ETULAIN is professor emeritus of history at the University of New Mexico. He specializes in the history and literature of the American West and has authored or edited more than forty books. Among his recent volumes are *Telling Western Stories: From Buffalo Bill to Larry McMurtry* (1999), *Women of the Wild West* (2003, with Glenda Riley), *New Mexican Lives* (2002), and *Western Lives: A Biographical History of the American West* (2004). He is at work on a biography of Calamity Jane and a general history of the American West.

WILLIAM E. FOLEY, professor emeritus of history at Central Missouri State University, is the general editor of the Missouri Biography Series. He is author or editor of numerous books, including *The First Chouteaus: River Barons of Early St. Louis* and *Genesis of Missouri: From Outpost to Statehood*. His recently published biography *Wilderness Journey: The Life of William Clark* is available from the University of Missouri Press.

PETER KASTOR is assistant professor of history and assistant director of American Culture Studies at Washington University in Saint Louis. He received his B.A. from Franklin & Marshall College and his Ph.D. in history from the University of Virginia. He is the author or editor of three books and numerous articles and essays. His most recent book, *The Nation's Crucible: The Louisiana Purchase and the Creation of America*, was published in 2004 by Yale University Press.

JONI L. KINSEY is associate professor in the School of Art and Art History at the University of Iowa, specializing in American art. She earned her M.A. and Ph.D. from Washington University in Saint Louis. Her article here draws on her longstanding interest in landscape imagery and art relating to American exploration, which she first examined in *Thomas Moran and the Surveying of the American West* (1992) and again in *Plain Pictures: Images of the American Prairie* (1996).

NANCY TYSTAD KOUPAL is director of the Research and Publishing Program of the South Dakota State Historical Society. Her books include *Baum's Road to Oz* (2000) and *Our Landlady* (1996), and she is northern plains editor of *The Encyclopedia of the Great Plains*, published in 2004 by the University of Nebraska Press.

GREG MAC GREGOR is professor emeritus of art and photography at California State University, Hayward. He received an M.A. in photography from San Francisco State University in 1970 and an M.S. in physics from South Dakota School of Mines and Technology in 1964. He has been photographing the Great Basin between Colorado and California for the past twenty years. Two exhibitions, *The California Emigrant Trail of 1841* and *Lewis and Clark Revisited*, are on national tour into 2006. Both projects are also available as books.

JOSEPH A. MUSSULMAN is the producer and principal writer of *Discovering Lewis & Clark®*, a hyperhistory-in-progress at http://www.lewis-clark.org, which focuses on issues, values and visions relating to the expedition. A teacher, author, lecturer, cartographer, and former faculty member in the School of Fine Arts at the University of Montana, he holds two degrees from Northwestern University and a Ph.D. in humanities from Syracuse University.

ROBERT J. MYERS is a senior instructional designer and program manager at the Center for Educational Tecnologies, Wheeling Jesuit University. He specializes in problem-based and online learning and is the team leader responsible for developing content for the Lewis and Clark Rediscovery Project (http://www.l3-lewisandclark.com). He is also the principal investigator for the Tri-State History Consortium, a Teaching American History Grant Program sponsored by the United States Department of Education.

ROBERT MCCRACKEN PECK is a naturalist, writer, and historian with a special interest in the history of science, art, exploration, and travel. As senior fellow and librarian of the Academy of Natural Sciences in Philadelphia, he has chronicled scientific research expeditions on five continents, written six books on the history of natural history, and guest-curated art and science exhibitions for museums and libraries throughout the United States.

JAMES P. RONDA holds the H. G. Barnard Chair in Western American History at the University of Tulsa and is a past president of the Western History Association. A specialist in the history of the exploration of North America, he is the author of many books, articles, and essays. Among his best-known books are *Lewis and Clark among the Indians* (1984); *Astoria and Empire* (1990); *Voyages of Discovery: Essays on the Lewis and Clark Expedition* (1994); *Jefferson's West: A Journey with Lewis and Clark* (2002); and *Finding the West: Explorations with Lewis and Clark* (2003).

ELLIOTT WEST, Alumni Distinguished Professor of History at the University of Arkansas, Fayetteville, teaches and writes on the social and environmental history of the American West. He is the author of six books on topics ranging from western saloons to children on the frontier. *The Contested Plains: Indians, Goldseekers, and the Rush to Colorado* (1998) won several awards, including the Francis Parkman Prize. He has twice received his university's award as teacher of the year.

W. RAYMOND WOOD was trained at the University of Nebraska (B.A., M.A.) and at the University of Oregon (Ph.D.) and has taught anthropology at the University of Missouri since 1963. His work has been largely historical for the past two decades, during which time he has specialized in Lewis and Clark and their predecessors, the early cartography of the Missouri River, and the American Indians that lived along the Missouri.

INDEX

abolition movement, 39. *See also* slavery
Academy of Natural Sciences, 60, 64, 67, 71, 73, 155, 168
Adams, John, 65
adventure: American experience of, 7–8
Africa exploration, 186–88
African Americans: McDowell, Mississippi Fred, 7; Scipio (slave of Clark), 55; Waters, Muddy (formerly McKinley Morganfield), 1; York (slave of Clark), 45
alcoholism, 37, 48–49
Alston, Theodosia, 117–18
American Indians: in art, 98–106; disease and depopulation of, 15–17, 181–83, 185; expansionism of, 15–16; in fiction, 116–20, 124–25; hyperhistory and, 167–70; intertribal politics of, 10–13; land cessions, 51; national sovereignty and, 34–35, 39–41; white settlement and, 48–49. *See also* specific tribes by name
American Philosophical Society, 58, 64–65, 71, 73, 77n.16, 79n.38, 88, 168–69
American West: importance of rivers in, 175–77; journey of exploration in, 1–2; in literature, 114–15, 128–29; photographic documentation of, 134–49; role of disease in, 181–88
animal collections, 66–72, 78n.28, 92–95
Arapaho Indians, 15
Arikara Indians, 13–20, 170–71
Arkansas River exploration, 35, 180
art and illustrations, 60–61, 67, 80–88, 91–107, 156
Ashley, William H., 21
Ashley Island, 19, 21
Assiniboine Indians, 15–19
Audubon, John James, 68–70, 78n.28

Bad River, 10, 20, 143, 170–72
Barralet, John James, 94–98
Barton, Benjamin Smith, 58–64, 75, 90, 93
Bartram, William, 75, 76n.2, 90
Battle of Fallen Timbers, 49
Biddle, Nicholas, 58, 67, 94–95, 114
Bird Woman, 131n.13. *See also* Sacagawea
bison: importance of, 141, 163–64, 170–71
Blackfeet Indians, 118–20, 127, 170–71
Black Hills, Indian migration, 19
Bodmer, Karl, 81
Bonaparte, Napoleon, 30, 32, 178, 184–85
botanical collections, 58–66, 74–75, 76n.2, 77n.16, 93
Bourgmont, Etienne Véniard de, 13

Brulé Sioux Indians, 10, 20, 136
Bry, Henry, 34
Burr, Aaron, 35, 117–18, 180
Bush, Joseph, 102
Butterfield, John, 4

Calhoun, John C., 106–07, 109n.19
California, 4, 21, 181
Cameahwait, 70, 127
Canadian North West Company, 19–20
Catlin, George, 81, 102
Cedar Island, 21
Chaplin, Charlie, 1
Charbonneau, Toussaint, 45, 118–22, 155
Cheyenne Indians, 15, 18
chiefs, tribal, 12–13
Chinook Indians, 118–20, 150
Chisholm, Jesse, 4
Choctaw Indians, 34
Chouteau, Pierre, 52
Clairborne, William C. C., 33
Clark, Ann Rogers, 46–47
Clark, Edmund, 49
Clark, George Rogers, 47–50, 115
Clark, John, 46–47
Clark, Jonathan, 49
Clark, William: as American myth, 174–75; children of, 51–52, 54; education of, 47–48; family background of, 46–47; in fiction, 115–21; in film, 132n.17; financial background of, 38, 50, 55–56; health of, 49; hyperhistory and, 153–56; as Indian agent, 38, 40, 50–53, 55; Louisiana Purchase and, 25–28; Madison and, 38–39; marriage of, 50–51, 53–54; military service of, 49; portraiture, 47, 99–102, 119; on slavery, 55–56; as territorial governor, 35, 38–41, 52
Coeur D'Alene Indians, 168
collections. *See* animal collections; botanical collections; fossil collections; mineral collections
Colorado, 3–4
Colorado River, 176–77, 178–79
Colter, John, 1
Columbia River, 147, 175–77, 180
community: American experience of, 8
Conrad, John, 92
Corps of Discovery: animal collections of, 66–72, 78n.28, 92–93; bicentennial celebration of, 25; botanical collections of, 60–66, 74–75, 76n.2, 77n.16, 93; centennial celebration of, 114; in fiction, 129–30; fossil collections of, 74–75, 79n.41; goals of, 25–28; hyperhistory and, 152–56, 161–73, 163–73; illustrations and art of, 80–84, 106–07; journals of, 52; legacy of, 188; mineral collections of, 72–73, 79n.38–40; photographic documentation of, 134–49; published reports of, 58, 60–61, 67–68, 71–72, 91–92, 102–03, 114; scientific activities of, 60, 75–76; topographic reporting of, 71–72. *See also* Voyage of Discovery
Coues, Elliott, 114
Council Bluffs, 134, 171
Crow Indians, 15, 118–20
cultural revolution, 1
culture, American Indian, 15–16, 170–71, 181
Cumberland Road, 2

Custis, Peter. *See* Freeman-Custis Expedition
Cutright, Paul Russell, 92–93, 129

Dakota Territory, 4. *See also* North Dakota; South Dakota
D'Eglise, Jacques, 21
depopulation: 15, 181–88
Des Moines River, 20
diplomacy, government: by Clark, William, 55; foreign relations and, 31–32; Indian alliances and, 20, 34–35; Mississippi Crisis and, 28–30, 32. *See also* foreign relations
Discovering Lewis & Clark®, 153–58
disease, 15–17, 181–88
District of Louisiana, 36. *See also* Louisiana Purchase
Drewyer, George, 71
Drouillard, George, 133n.26
Dunbar, William, 177
Duniway, Abigail Scott, 115
Dye, Eva Emery, 115–17, 131n.8

education, history, 159–63
Ellicott, Andrew, 72
Embargo of 1807–1809, 32
Emmons, Della Gould, 122
Enlightenment thought, 26, 48–49
epidemics, 15–17, 181–83
expansion, American: Indian migration and, 15–16; Indian rights and, 55; intertribal rivalries and, 10–13; Louisiana Purchase and, 25–28, 178–79; photographic documentation of, 134–49; role of disease in, 181–88; western, 180–81. *See also* settlement, white
exploration: American journey of, 1–2; American myth in, 174–75; Corps of Discovery, 25–28, 31–32; federal western surveys, 81–82; Freeman-Custis Expedition, 35, 177, 179–80; Hunter-Dunbar Expedition, 166, 179; importance of rivers in, 175–77; Long Expedition, 71–72, 87, 106–07, 109n.19; Michaux, Andre, and, 65; photographic documentation of, 134–49; Pike Expedition, 35, 71, 87, 177, 180; published reports of, 58–59; role of disease in, 181–88

fiction: Lewis and Clark Expedition in, 114–29
Fisher, Vardis, 123–24
Florida cessation, 29–30, 42n.9
Floyd, Sergeant, 135, 139
forced removal, Indian, 40–41, 55
foreign relations: American expansionism and, 180; exploration and, 177; trade and boundary disputes, 31–32. *See also* France; Great Britain; Spain
Fort Clatsop, 82, 118–20, 127, 151
Fort Osage, 51
Fort Peck, 136
Fort Pierre, S.Dak., 143
fossil collections, 74, 79n.41
France: French Revolution, 32; Louisiana Purchase and, 28–31, 177–79; Santo Domingo slave rebellion, 33–34, 184–85. *See also* foreign relations
Freeman-Custis Expedition, 35, 176–77, 179–80
French traders, Missouri River, 13–14, 21

Gass, Patrick, 21, 71, 74, 79n.41, 103, 107n.3, 116
gazetteer of American journeys, 5
geography, 72, 161–62, 170–72. *See also* maps
Goodnight, Charles M., 4
governance, American Indian, 39–41. *See also* territorial government
Great Britain: Africa exploration, 186–88; Embargo of 1807–1809, 32; imperial rivalry and, 177; Missouri River trading of, 19–20, 51–52. *See also* foreign relations
Great Trading Path, 3
Gregg, Josiah, 4
Guthrie, Woody, 1, 6

Haiti, Republic of, 30
Hall, Brian, 128–30
Hall, James, 98–99
Hamilton, Alexander, 65
Hamilton, William, 75, 76n.2, 93
Hancock, Judith, 50–51, 54
Harding, Chester, 102
Harrison, William Henry, 39–40
Hebard, Grace Raymond, 117–18, 121, 126
Heney, Hugh, 21
Henry, Will (Henry Wilson Allen), 124–26
herbarium. *See* botanical collections
Hidatsa Indians, 14–19, 170–71
history: American myth in, 174; fiction merging with, 114, 128–30; hyperhistory (digital interactivity with), 153–58; teaching and understanding of, 152, 159–73
home: in American journeys, 5–6, 8–9
Hopi Indians, 16

Hosmer, James K., 114
Hueston, Ethel, 118–20
Humboldt, Alexander von, 91–92, 110n.26, 110n.28
Hunter, George, 177
Hunter-Dunbar Expedition, 179
hyperhistory: Internet and, 152–58

Idaho, 148
illustrations and art, 60–61, 67, 80–88, 91–107, 156
Indiana Territory, 36, 38–39
Internet. *See* hyperhistory; World Wide Web

Jackson, Andrew, 40–41, 43n.20
Jarvis, John Wesley, 47, 102
Jefferson, Thomas, 27; American expansionism and, 178–79; American Indian sovereignty and, 39–41; exploration of the West and, 35, 64–65, 87–88, 174–77; in fiction, 116, 118, 121; Florida cessation and, 42n.9; foreign relations of, 32–33; hyperhistory and, 153–56; portraiture, 102; Voyage of Discovery and, 25–28, 103–06, 109n.22
Joplin, Janis, 8
journals: Clark, William, 54–55; Corps of Discovery, 52, 71, 75–76, 78n.28; Gass, Patrick, 103, 107n.3; Humboldt, Alexander von, 91; hyperhistory and, 157–58; illustrations and art in, 80–84; legacy of, 187–88; photographic documentation from, 135–36; published reports of, 58–59, 60–61, 91–92, 102–03, 114; as source for fiction, 115–16, 118; topographic reporting in, 72, 80–87

journey: American history as, 1–7
Jusseaume, René, 20

Kansas River, 138
Kentucky, 47–49, 74
Kerouac, Jack, 2–5
Knox, Henry, 65

Lakota Sioux Indians, 20, 169–70
Lambert, Alymer, 61–64
Lawson, Alexander, 67, 69
learning and understanding history, 159–73
Leclerc, Charles Victor Emmanuel, 184
Lewis, Meriwether: American myth of, 174–75; as cartographer and surveyor, 72; in fiction, 115–21; hyperhistory and, 153–56; Louisiana Purchase and, 25–28; Madison and, 37–38; military service of, 49; as naturalist, 58–60, 66; portraiture, 99–102, 112n.45, 119; as presidential secretary, 49–50; as territorial governor, 36–41, 50, 91–92; as writer, 84–87
Lewis and Clark Rediscovery Project, 163–73
Library Company of Philadelphia, 59
Library of Congress, 155
Lisa, Manuel, 52
literature: Lewis and Clark in, 114–15, 128–29
Livingston, Robert R., 29
Loisel, Réne, 21
Long Expedition, 71–72, 87, 106, 109n.18
Long Walk, 4
Louisiana. *See* Territory of Orleans
Louisiana Purchase: American expansionism and, 25–28; bicentennial of, 25; boundary disputes and, 35, 177–78; defining the, 28–32, 178–80; expeditions in, 176–77, 179–81; negotiations for, 184–85; territorial government for, 31–32; Territory of Orleans, 32–33. *See also* District of Louisiana; Louisiana Territory
Louisiana Territory: Clark as governor of, 38–39; Clark as Indian agent of, 50–53; creation of, 36; Lewis as governor of, 50–52; Michaux, Andre, and, 77n.19; statehood for, 44n.24; Wilkinson as governor of, 180. *See also* Missouri Territory
Loving-Goodnight Trail, 2
Ludlow, Noah, 53

McDowell, Mississippi Fred, 5
McKenney, Thomas L., 98–99
Mackenzie, Alexander, 177
McKenzie, Charles, 53
McMahon, Bernard, 61, 93
Madison, James: Clark and, 38–39; expedition financial support and, 65; Florida cessation and, 42n.9; Lewis and, 37–38; Mississippi Crisis and, 29; presidency of, 36–37; as secretary of state, 36, 43n.20
Mandan Indians: Big White (Shahaka), 98–99, 112n.44; culture of, 14, 158n.5, 170–71; depopulation of, 15–19; in fiction, 121; White Coyote (Shehekeshote), 4, 52; Yellow Corn, 1, 4, 98
maps, 5, 15, 72, 120, 123. *See also* geography
medical care, 59
Meehan, Thomas, 64

Mexico, 24–35, 180–81
Michaux, Andre, 65, 77n.19
migration, western: 1804 tribal distribution, 19–20; Indian expansionism, 15–17, 17–18; photographic documentation of, 134–36; white exploration and settlement, 21–22
military service: of Lewis and Clark, 49
mineral collections, 72–74, 79n.39–40
Minnesota, 17
Minnesota River, 20
Mississippi Crisis, 28–30, 32
Mississippi River, 20, 179
Mississippi Territory, 38–39
Missouri River: American expansionism and, 175–76, 180; early exploration of, 13–14; Great Falls, 85–86, 93–98, 145; importance of, 175–79; Indian migration to, 31–33; photographic documentation of, 134–39, 142–46, 176; as trade route, 10–11, 20–21
Missouri Territory, 38–39, 44n.24. *See also* Louisiana Territory
Mobridge, S.Dak., 19
Monroe, James: foreign relations of, 32; Mississippi Crisis and, 29; as president, 109n.19; as secretary of state, 36, 43n.20
Montana, 134–36, 145–47
Mormon Trail, 2
Morris, Robert, 65
Mullen, John, 4
Mullen Road, 2

names: importance of in history, 2–5
Natchez Trace, 2, 52

National Aeronautics and Space Administration (NASA), 167
National Road, 3
Nelson, Willie, 1, 5
Neutral Ground, 35
New Mexico, 4, 16, 177, 180–81
Nez Perce Indians, 118–20, 168
Niger River exploration, 186–88
North Dakota, 135, 144

Omaha Indians, 17, 20–21
Ord, George, 71–72
Ordway, Sergeant, 157
Oregon, 4, 21, 150–51, 177–78, 180–81
Oregon Historical Society, 115
Osage Indians, 21, 51, 98, 179–80
Oto Indians, 21

Pacific Northwest, 178, 180–81
Park, Mungo, 186–88
Patterson, Robert, 72
Pawnee Indians, 21
Peabody Museum, 70
Peale, Charles Willson, 67–71, 78n.33, 80–81, 87–89, 94, 101–02
Peale, Rembrandt, 90
Peale, Titian Ramsay, 87, 106–07, 109n.19
Peattie, Donald Culross, 120–21
photography: *camera obscura*, 85–86; digital interactive, 156; visual documentation and, 87; of route of Voyage of Discovery, 134–36
Pierre, S.Dak., 10, 176
Pike, Zebulon M., 35, 71, 87, 177, 180
Plains Cree Indians, 15
politics, tribal, 12–13
Pomp (son of Sacagawea), 45, 132n.17
Pompey's Tower, 134

Ponca Indians, 20
Powell, John Wesley, 176–77
Prairie du Chien, 20, 52
Pratz, Antoine le Page du, 59, 92, 111n.31
prejudice: American experience of, 7
Pursh, Frederick, 60–64, 75, 93, 96

racial prejudice, 7
Radford, Harriet Kennerly, 54
Red River exploration, 175–78, 178–80
religious prejudice, 7
reservation system, Indian, 21–22, 40–41, 55
retrocession, 28–29
Revolutionary War: Clark family and, 46
Rio Grande exploration, 35, 177–79, 180
rivalry, 10–13, 175–77, 181–88
rivers: in western exploration, 175–77
roads: in American journeys, 5–8. See also trails
Rosa, Salvator, 80, 85–86
Route 66, 2, 5, 9

Sacagawea: in art, 81; Clark and, 45; in fiction, 116–21, 124, 126–27, 131n.8; in film, 132n.17; hyperhistory and, 153–56; Lewis on, 146; myth of, 121–23, 174–75
Sac Indians, 51
Saint Charles, Mo., 137
Saint Louis Missouri Fur Company, 52
Saint-Mémin, Charles Balthazar Julien Fevret de, 81, 98–101, 112n.45, 156
Santa Fe. See New Mexico
Sargent, Charles Sprague, 64

Say, Thomas, 71–72
Scipio (Clark's slave), 55
Seaman (Lewis's dog), 128
Sergeant Floyd burial site, 135, 139
settlement, white: and bison extermination, 163–64; exploration and, 20–22; Indian rights and American, 55; Kentucky, 48–49; photographic documentation of, 134–49; territorial government and, 38–39, 40–41; Texas, 180–81. See also expansion, American
Seybert, Adam, 73, 79n.38
Seymour, Samuel, 87, 106–07
Shannon, George, 121
Shawnee Indians, 51
Sheyenne River, 18
Shoshone Indians, 19, 70, 118–21, 158n.5
Sibley, John, 34
slavery: Clark, William, and, 55–56; Clark family and, 46–47; French colonial, 30, 33–34, 184–85; New World introduction of, 183–84; statehood and, 39; in Territory of Orleans, 33
smallpox, 16–17. See also disease
Smith, Robert, 36
social prejudice, 7
South Dakota, 134–35, 141–43
Spain: American expansionism and, 178–81; boundary disputes of, 34–35, 189n.8; Florida cessation and, 29–30, 32, 42n.9; imperial rivalry and, 177–78; Indian alliances with, 34; Louisiana cessation and, 178; Louisiana Purchase and, 28; slavery and, 183–84. See also foreign relations

Spanish Missouri Company, 20
specimens. *See* animal collections; botanical collections; fossil collections; mineral collections
Spirit Mound, S.Dak., 134
statehood, 38–39, 44n.24. *See also* territorial government
Sully, Thomas, 27
Sutaio Indians, 15, 19

Tabeau, Pierre-Antoine, 21
teaching and understanding history, 159–73
territorial government: boundary disputes, 35–36; Clark and, 36, 38–41, 50–52; creation of, 31–33; District of Louisiana, 35; financing and expansion of, 34–35; Lewis and, 36–41, 50–52; Louisiana Territory, 36; Territory of Orleans, 33. *See also* statehood
Territory of Orleans, 33, 36, 38–39
Teton Sioux Indians, 12–13, 118–20, 142
Texas, 34–35, 175–78, 180–81, 189n.8
Thom, James Alexander, 127–28, 133n.26
Thoreau, Henry David, 4
Thwaites, Reuben Gold, 114–15, 122–23
trade goods: European, 13–14, 19–22; importance of, 163–64; intertribal politics and, 10–13, 15; Sioux dominance in, 19–20
trading posts, Missouri River, 20–21, 51
trading rights, retrocession and American, 28–29

tradition and culture, Indian: depopulation and, 15–16
Trail of Tears, 2
trails: significance of, 2–3. *See also* roads
treaties, 28, 51
tribal organization, 12–13
Trumbull, John, 90
Truteau, Jean Baptiste, 20
Tuckerman, Edward, 64
Twain, Mark, 4

University, Wheeling Jesuit, 167
University of Idaho, 167
University of Montana, 167
University of Nebraska, 155
University of Pennsylvania, 58, 90
University of Washington, 155
University of Wyoming, 117

Van Buren, Martin, 43n.20
Vérendrye, Sieur de la, 14
Virginia, 46–49
visual documentation, 80–88, 91–98
Voyage of Discovery: defining the goals of, 31–32; legacy of, 188; Louisiana Purchase and, 25–28; perspective on, 174–75; photographic documentation of, 134–49. *See also* Corps of Discovery

Waldo, Anna Lee, 126–27
warfare, 12–13, 17–18
War of 1812, 38, 52
Warrior's Path, 2–3
Washington, 149
Washington, George, 65
Waters, Muddy (formerly McKinley Morganfield), 1

Wayne, Anthony, 49
western migration, Indian, 15. See also American Indians; expansion, American
Wheeling Jesuit University, 167
Whitman, Walt, 5
Whoop-Up Trail, 4
Wilderness Road, 2–4

Wilkinson, James, 177, 180, 189n.8
Wilson, Alexander, 67–69, 93, 95
Wolfe, Thomas, 2
World Wide Web: Lewis and Clark on the, 153–56, 159, 161–73

Yankton Sioux territory, 19–20
York (Clark's slave), 45, 55–56, 128–30